CRITICAL INSIGHTS

Coming of Age

CRITICAL INSIGHTS

Coming of Age

Editor
Kent Baxter
California State University, Northridge

SALEM PRESS
A Division of EBSCO Publishing
Ipswich, Massachusetts

Cover Photo: © Chris Whitehead/cultura/Corbis

Editor's text © 2013 by Kent Baxter

∞ The paper used in these volumes conforms to the American National Standard
for Permanence of Paper for Printed Library Materials, Z39.48-1992 (R1997).

Library of Congress Cataloging-in-Publication Data
Coming of age / editor, Kent Baxter.
 p. cm. -- (Criticial insights)
 Includes bibliographical references and index.
 ISBN 978-1-4298-3731-6 (hardcover) -- ISBN 978-1-4298-3779-8 (ebook) 1.
Bildungsromans--History and criticism. 2. Teenagers in literature. 3. Adoles-
cence in literature. 4. Coming of age. I. Baxter, Kent.
 PN3448.B54C64 2012
 809'.39353--dc23
                          2012019658

PRINTED IN THE UNITED STATES OF AMERICA

Contents_____

Resources

About This Volume

Kent Baxter

Without a doubt, the biggest challenge in compiling this collection of essays on "coming of age" was deciding where to begin and where to end. Arguably, every literary period has visited this theme, in one form or another, and in contemporary Western society, coming of age has become the foundation of entire literary/filmic genres and entertainment conglomerates. Clearly, the theme of coming of age is so omnipresent in literature that any attempt at a comprehensive overview would be doomed from the start. However, two approaches to this topic presented themselves: This could be a collection of essays on a specific conception of coming of age that materialized in a particular cultural/historical moment, or this could be a collection that provided a number of snapshots of coming of age from various time periods and cultures, with no pretensions of giving the whole picture. Ultimately, the second approach prevailed.

Reaching from Homer to Sherman Alexie, *Critical Insights: Coming of Age* features two overview essays and thirteen detailed case studies of coming-of-age stories, explicated by some of the most knowledgeable and insightful scholars in their respective fields of study. The overview essays provide a broad view of the history of the depiction of coming of age in literature and its reception/interpretation by theorists and critics. Each case study provides a singular glimpse into how the coming-of-age paradigm was articulated and dramatized by a particular author, how this construction reflects value systems and beliefs of a unique period/culture, and how this theme resonated—and continues to resonate—with a specific reading audience. Spanning a wide variety of historical periods, geographical locations, and cultures, these essays are expansive in their breadth of coverage, and each is quite detailed in its depth of analysis.

As I discuss in my overview, "Critical Reception," and as Steven Mintz discusses in his "Coming of Age in History," the parameters of coming of age differ greatly depending upon a social group's historical footing, mainly because beliefs about what constitutes adulthood, and, concomitantly, pre-adulthood, have changed over time. Additionally, as Rachelle D. Washington and Michelle H. Martin demonstrate in their essay, and as Beth A. Wightman demonstrates in hers, the coming-of-age story is very much a product of the cultural value systems of a society and often becomes a blank slate upon which are projected anxieties about many related, and seemingly unrelated, issues. For example, in Martin and Washington's explication of Mildred Taylor's Logan Family Novels ("In Search of Mildred Taylor's Womanists: Feminist Agency in the Logan Family Novels"), the authors demonstrate how Cassie Logan's coming-of-age journey entails a negotiation with the intricacies of the racist South. Wightman's comparison of Charlotte Brontë's *Jane Eyre* (1847) and Jean Rhys's *Wide Sargasso Sea* (1966), entitled "'Not now. . . . Not yet': Developmental Difficulties in *Jane Eyre* and *Wide Sargasso Sea*," argues that although these novels were written many years apart, they are both framed by Britain's imperial coming of age.

Thus, what all four of the essays in the "Critical Contexts" section of this collection show, by way of introduction, is how differently coming of age has been conceived by different cultures and time periods and how these stories have been used to objectify issues relevant to specific cultural/historical moments. Such is the case with the eleven essays in the "Critical Readings" section of this book as well. Starting with what is possibly the oldest manifestation of coming of age in literature, William G. Thalmann argues in his essay "Coming of Age in Homer's Ithaca" that in the *Odyssey*, Telemachus and Nausicaa come of age by manipulating the quite stringent social codes and gender/age roles in Homeric society to serve their own interests. Moving forward 2,400 years or so, we see another set of social codes traversed by the characters coming of age in Shakespeare's works. In "Coming of Age in Shakespeare," Heather James explains the ways in which Shakespeare adapted the conventions of Greek and Roman comedy to construct a new, and still quite influential, coming-of-age paradigm, in which the protagonist must learn what it means to be true to oneself. Moving forward in time a couple more centuries and transitioning from drama to poetry, we see a quite different paradigm of coming of age, which is not even bound by chronological age. In "A Romantic Poet Comes of Age Over and Over Again," Richard Matlak examines three poems by William Wordsworth, which, he asserts, represent three different concepts of coming of age that can tell us much about the poet's own journey from a higher innocence through Nature to a fortitudinous acceptance of God's will.

Given the temporal, geographical, and cultural distance between these first three authors, it is perhaps no surprise that their depictions of coming of age would be so different. But even within the same time period and geographical location, we can find distinctly different coming-of-age experiences. Consider, for example, Louisa May Alcott's *Little Women* (1868) and Mark Twain's *Adventures of Huckleberry Finn* (1885)—both written by American authors, published only two decades apart. Anne K. Phillips and Greg Eiselein argue in their essay "The Varieties of Adolescent Experience: Coming of Age in Alcott's *Little Women*" that even though the March sisters and Laurie Laurence must negotiate changing familial and social relationships, they all come of age in a slightly different manner. And these are quite different from Huck Finn's experience, who, according to Roberta Seelinger Trites in her essay "Irony and Moral Development in *Adventures of Huckleberry Finn*," grows up surrounded by a racist culture that he must reject in order to come of age as an independent moral agent.

In keeping, perhaps, with the high modernist tradition in literature, the early twentieth-century author James Joyce depicts a coming-of-age moment that is largely internalized and markedly different from the processes of socialization seen in Alcott and Twain. In his essay "Stephen Dedalus and the Other: Interiority, Language, and Gender in *A Portrait of the Artist as a Young Man*," Vincent J. Cheng argues that Stephen Dedalus's "development," if such a term even applies, is intimately related to language, which results in a solipsistic resistance to the socialization often associated with coming of age.

The intricate and problematic relationship between identity and language forayed by Joyce is the mainstay of many twentieth-century depictions of coming of age, including one of the most iconic: J. D. Salinger's novel *The Catcher in the Rye*. As Annette Wannamaker argues in "'Missing Everybody': Language and Identity in *The Catcher in the Rye*," Salinger's work is more of a coming-to-terms novel than a coming-of-age novel: Holden Caulfield has to come to terms with the fact that language is an imperfect system—"phony," as he might describe it—and a system over which he has little influence.

The last four essays in this collection reference many of the themes, traditions, paradigms, and problems discussed in the wide variety of coming-of-age stories introduced above, but they do so while paying particular attention to gender and ethnicity. As Jane Hedley explains in her essay, "Coming of Age in Bronzeville: Gwendolyn Brooks's *Annie Allen*," the "*Anniad*" of Brooks's work circles back in interesting ways to the epic tradition of Homer, but it does so to challenge a poetic tradition that takes little interest in lives like Annie Allen's, and it requires a new paradigm for Annie's African American voice to be heard. Racism and poverty lead to some of the conflicts, stress, confusion, and danger that individuals like Antonio Márez y Luna must come to terms with while coming of age. In "Ready or Not: Antonio Márez y Luna Is Thrown into the World of Rudolfo Anaya's *Bless Me, Ultima*," Phillip Serrato aligns this coming to terms with the Heideggerian notion of "Being-in-the-world." In "Song for a Murdered Cousin: Violence in *The Woman Warrior*," Tomo Hattori shows how, in Maxine Hong Kingston's influential work, the narrator's realization of the scale of violence that the women in her family have mastered to become full human subjects is the basis of her own experience of coming of age.

And, finally, bridging the beginning and end of the twentieth century, Amelia V. Katanski examines Zitkala-Ša's autobiographical essays (published between 1900 and 1902) and Sherman Alexie's young adult novel *The Absolutely True Diary of a Part-Time Indian* (2007) in her essay "School Stories: Education, Coming of Age, and the American Indian Literary Tradition," in order to show how school is a potentially devastating site where American Indian students have been forced to address complex questions of identity. However, in both of these works, the authors demonstrate that they can be active agents who resolve these identity questions through their spirited, generative, narrative creativity.

Such is this collection's overview of the theme of coming of age in literature, an overview that, if it proves anything, proves that each culture has adapted this theme to its own ends. Each protagonist comes of age in his or her own way or does not come of age at all. Indeed, one of the biggest surprises of this project was how many of the characters analyzed in these essays do not really come of age, at least not in any conventional sense. For example, although Telemachus displays maturity in a number of scenes, in the end he must become subordinate to his famous father, which adds a great deal of ambiguity to his passage into adulthood. Matlak identifies not just one but three different coming-of-age concepts in the poetry of William Wordsworth. Huck Finn's decision to "light out to the territory" at the end of Twain's novel could be read as a type of rejection of society that is at odds with coming of age. Wannamaker argues that *The Catcher in the Rye* questions whether coming of age is even possible because language itself is ultimately incapable of expressing such an arrival. The closest thing we get to closure comes with Alcott's novel *Little Women*, but as Phillips and Eiselein demonstrate, Alcott's reluctance to allow any of her characters to realize their "fairy tale lives" is reflective of the cultural restrictions of the time and of the novel's realism.

It is as if, for many of these protagonists, the coming-of-age moment occurs sometime later, outside the text, or, maybe even more interestingly, it does not occur at all but is rather just a theoretical endpoint toward which these protagonists develop. On some level this makes sense, since it is, after all, the journey of coming of age that interests us most as readers—a journey, as this collection attests, that has been the preoccupation of authors and readers from the earliest literary texts and continues unabated to this day.

On "Coming of Age" _____

Kent Baxter

"I don't want ever to be a man," protests one of the most well-known figures in children's, and maybe all Western, literature. Peter Pan's protestation instigates a fantastic flight into the "Neverland" of perpetual childhood, filled with adventure, excitement, and, perhaps most important, no adult supervision. But, by the end of the play (and J. M. Barrie's novelization of it), Peter's refusal turns him into a monstrous renegade, dangerously outside the norms of society. As the Darling children and the lost boys return to the security of home, family, and society, Peter hovers outside the window, a tragic symbol of what must be sacrificed to stay forever young. "He had ecstasies innumerable," Barrie tells us, "but he was looking through the window at the one joy from which he must be for ever barred" (225).

But what if Peter Pan had grown up? Awaiting him in Barrie's text are either the hollow education and career paths pursued by the Darling brothers or the ridiculous and petty life of Mr. Darling himself, pathetically trying to restore a sense of order to the unbridled chaos of his life. At first glance, Wendy appears to offer a type of middle ground, as she serves as a conduit between Peter and the generations of children who come after, but even she, in many ways, ends up a sad figure of domestic servitude, a sellout to the Edwardian status quo. Barrie's play leaves us little hope really, which may be why he tells us right off that "[Age] two is the beginning of the end" (7). Ultimately, the most beloved depiction of childhood in Western literature is about how it must end.

In an interesting and telling way, the dilemma that is Peter Pan, and possibly the force behind Barrie's text about him, is charged by our fascination with and anxieties about coming of age. The bittersweet tragedy surrounding the boy who never grew up and the children who did shows the far reach of this literary and cultural paradigm and also reveals its complexity. As Barrie's text evidences, in addition to its most recognizable contemporary incarnation in the "young adult" or "young reader" novel, coming of age echoes quite loudly in many books for children and adults, and in many time periods before our own. Additionally, as *Peter Pan* so poignantly shows us, coming of age is a literary and cultural construct that is fraught with powerful and often quite contradictory emotions. To come of age is a characteristically difficult process, as all the characters in Barrie's text attest. To put a very fine point on it, you must come of age *correctly*. Any attempt to avoid or circumvent the process or cheat is quite simply unnatural and leaves one outside the window of society.

Why is this so? Why has coming of age been such a central preoccupation of literary texts and a perpetual source of fascination for the readers who consume them? And what exactly does this expression mean? The *Oxford English Dictionary* (O.E.D.) defines "coming of age" as "such duration of life as ordinarily brings body and mind to full development; years of maturity or discretion, or what by law or custom are fixed as such," and it cites occurrences of the expression "come of age" as early as the eighteenth century, with various incarnations of this phrase appearing as far back as the twelfth century. But these are just articulations of a concept that, arguably, has been with us in one form or another since the time of Homer.

A quick glance at the table of contents of this volume and the "Additional Works on Coming of Age" list at the end illustrates the fact that the notion of "coming of age" is omnipresent in both Western and non-Western texts from many time periods and can mean many different things to many different cultures. Clearly, as a literary topic—perhaps like all omnipresent topics in literature—it is singularly coherent, but still open enough to resonate with many (quite different) cultures/historical periods and to sustain unique human stories. We do not want to oversimplify such a richly complex and adaptable topic, but all of these stories have some similar qualities, and an examination of these qualities might help identify some common trends, and, subsequently, unique deviations from these trends.

The "of age" portion of the term "coming of age" typically signifies adulthood. At some point in these literary works, quite often at the end, the protagonist joins the community associated with adulthood; the transition is typically marked by an event that signifies it. The individual may not always "become an adult," but he/she quite often engages in an activity or exhibits a quality that is associated with adulthood. The "coming" part of "coming of age" implies some sort of movement. So, in its most basic sense, a coming-of-age narrative often depicts the movement from the pre-adult stage (defined rather differently in these texts) to adulthood (also defined rather differently in these texts). The developmental arc of the protagonist is motivated by the desire to become an adult, and this journey toward adulthood quite often entails struggle. To put a fine point on it, "coming of age" signifies an arrival at a destination (consistent with the *O.E.D.*'s specification that body and mind have reached "full development"), but the story happens before this arrival, and the story is what interests us.

One could, of course, define this developmental arc in a number of different ways. From the standpoint of individual development, characters often come of age by overcoming an external circumstance or an internal character flaw; moving into adulthood in this sense means finding one's place in the world or overcoming a flaw that is holding one back from living a fully effective life. From a narrative standpoint, the coming of age of an individual character or a number of characters often provides closure to a source of tension or conflict; it is not uncommon for the protagonist to encounter a "blocking character" who demands evidence that the protagonist has grown up. From a cultural/ historical standpoint, these coming-of-age moments are often signified by rites of passage that resonate with the readership of the text. "Rites of passage" is an expression used by anthropologists to describe ceremonies or events that mark important transitions in the developmental process. Marriage, graduation, home ownership, and getting a full-time job are all events that mark a movement into adulthood in contemporary culture, as does attaining various legal rights, such as the right to vote or to serve in the military. As the O.E.D. definition tells us, "maturity" is designated by law and custom. Such rites of passage are often material, but they have great psychological power. Getting a full-time job, for example, enables financial independence, which in turn can inspire independence from parents and a certain ownership of one's thoughts and behaviors.

Such is the basic structure of the coming-of-age story, but, once again, it would be possible to name as many pieces of literature that deviate from this structure as adhere to it. Perhaps it is this very adaptability, and, paradoxically, society's insistence on its essential functionality—i.e., everyone must come of age—that make coming-of-age stories so versatile and so appealing. But, clearly, there are other reasons for this appeal as well. From the viewpoint of narration, one of the reasons coming-of-age stories make such good reading is because the journey from pre-adulthood to adulthood is fraught with dramatic tensions that resonate with all readers. In his book *S/Z*, literary theorist Roland Barthes observes that, fundamentally, narration works by making "expectation . . . the basic condition for truth: truth, these narratives tell us, is what is at the end of expectation. This design," Barthes goes on to say, "brings narrative very close to the rite of initiation (a long path marked with pitfalls, obscurities, stops, that suddenly comes out into the light)" (76). Couched in these terms, the "truth" at the end of coming of age might be the adult that the character ultimately becomes. This adulthood might be signified by a cultural event (the rites of passage mentioned earlier) or by the solution to the developmental problem initiated by the protagonist at the beginning of the narration ("Who am I?" "Where do I belong?" "How do I fit in?"). However it is framed, the "rite of initiation," the movement from immaturity to maturity, dissolution to coherence, question to answer incites readerly desire and propels the narrative forward. The "truth" at the end of these coming-of-age stories is the complete, cohesive, stable sense of self that the protagonist achieves, or simply the notion that we do in fact develop in some systematic, meaningful manner. In most of these stories, the development of the character from pre-adulthood to adulthood shapes and drives the plot. Because there is such a logical sequence of events in this process, these texts essentialize this development as human truth, or at least some very believable approximation. To put it another way, coming-of-age stories self-substantiate the development of self by establishing the horizon of development and then initiating narrative desire—the motivating force that makes the reader turn the page—toward that goal/truth/ending. Narrative desire in this case is motivated by the desire for the completion of development, or at least its progress.

Perhaps what makes these stories so compelling is that the story—the plot, the developmental arc, the theme—is predicated upon human development, which essentializes coming of age as a unique human truth and personalizes it as something shared by every person. Such fictions may very well fly in the face of what we, as readers, experience in our own lives. After all, how many of us really feel like we have a stable sense of self or, for that matter, have actually arrived at adulthood? Still, the basic plot structure of the individual searching for his/her place in the world and arriving at a stable sense of self, an ending, is a highly compelling and recognizable form for literary art. Perhaps it is the fact that these portrayals are so different from our own experiences that makes it so.

Storytellers and writers have found limitless ways to spin this basic story structure. Even though the basic paradigm of coming of age outlined here functions in a linear manner and is based upon an understanding of identity as a unified, singular construct, plenty of coming-of-age stories are not linear, or even cumulative, and many end with a much more fluid concept of adult identity. Often, the development of the individual might be a return to some essential sense of self that was lost. "Development," in this case, might be loosening the shackles that society has forced upon the individual. Or, to situate this counter-narrative in a slightly different space, becoming an adult might mean realizing that identity is contextual or that there is no place for the subject in a world that chooses not to acknowledge individuals because of their ethnicity or gender. One does not think of Stephen Dedalus from James Joyce's *A Portrait of the Artist As a Young Man*, for example, as someone who "joins the adult community" exactly, but he does define himself against the context of this community, which offers him some insight into who he is. He comes of age in his realization that he is alienated from those around him and that his adulthood lies somewhere else. "When the soul of a man is born in this country there are nets flung at it to hold it back from flight," Stephen tells his friend Davin. "You talk to me of nationality, language, religion. I shall try to fly by those nets" (203). In other words, Stephen will try to fly into adulthood as it has been constructed within Joyce's text.

What is essential to all of these stories, whether it is realized or not, is the gesture toward individuation and, for good or ill, some sort of self-knowledge about one's status in society. Individuation and self-knowledge are essential to stories about coming of age, even if these processes, as is the case with Stephen Dedalus, result in a clearer understanding of the status quo one defines one's self against. But, once again, the omnipresence of the coming-of-age story in literature is a result of the many ways that this "truth" can be told. Consider, for example, the many generic incarnations of the coming-of-age story. The three most prevalent modern incarnations have been the bildungsroman, the novel of adolescence, and the young adult novel. In *Season of Youth*, Jerome Buckley defines the typical bildungsroman, which he situates largely in nineteenth-century British society, as follows:

> A child of some sensibility grows up in the country or in a provincial town, where he finds constraints, social and intellectual, placed upon the free imagination. His family, especially his father, proves doggedly hostile to his creative instincts or flights of fancy, antagonistic to his ambitions, and quite impervious to the new ideas he has gained from unprescribed reading. . . . He therefore, sometimes at a quite early age, leaves the repressive atmosphere of home (and also the relative innocence), to make his way

independently in the city. . . . There his real "education" begins, not only his preparation for a career but also—and often more importantly—his direct experience of urban life. . . . By the time he has decided, after painful soul-searching, the sort of accommodation to the modern world he can honestly make, he has left his adolescence behind and entered upon his maturity. (18)

In her book *Growing Up Female: Adolescent Girlhood in American Fiction*, Barbara White distinguishes between the bildungsroman and the novel of adolescence, which, she argues, is largely a creation of the twentieth century. In addition to noting that Buckley largely discusses male protagonists in his overview, White points to some distinct differences between the two genres. These include the age of the protagonist, who is typically a teenager in the novel of adolescence; the focus on conflict with adult society in the novel of adolescence; and, perhaps most important, the fact that, unlike the bildungsroman, the novel of adolescence does not always end with a positive and seamless initiation of the protagonist into existing adult society. "Not all novels of adolescence include initiation," she explains. "In fact, the protagonist may actively avoid or refuse it. If the hero is initiated at all, the initiation often occurs suddenly at the end of the novel and is ambiguous in nature" (14).

The young adult novel is a fairly recent marketing creation and largely a genre defined by its intended teen readership. In her book *Disturbing the Universe*, Roberta Seelinger Trites has this to say about the thematic differences between the bildungsroman and the young adult novel:

The postmodern awareness of the subject's inevitable construction as a product of language renders the construct of self-determination virtually obsolete. As a result, the popularity of the traditional *Bildungsroman* with its emphasis on self-determination gives way to the market dominance of the Young Adult novel, which is less concerned with depicting growth reverently than it is with investigating how the individual exists within society. Growth is possible . . . if growth is defined as an increasing awareness of the institutions constructing the individual. But following World War II, maturity, adulthood, being harder to define, ceased to be privileged as the narrative goal in literature written for youth. The Young Adult novel, then, came into being as a genre precisely because it is a genre predicated on demonstrating characters' ability to grow into an acceptance of their environment. (19)

In this case, "maturity" is an understanding of how one's identity is contextual and may vary depending upon the particular context.

Each of these modern generic incarnations of the coming-of-age story have very distinct characteristics that reflect the cultural/historical context within which they were created, but they all, in one way or another, reference the fundamental transition from pre-adulthood to adulthood. Even if the conclusion of the novel is that there is no adulthood for the character to inhabit, that state of marginalization or invisibility is based upon a construction of adulthood—sometimes located outside the text itself—from which the protagonist is forever barred. Even if the protagonist realizes that such a state is contextual, fluid, and transitory, this realization marks the ending of a developmental process.

These generic incarnations of the coming-of-age story, and the many others that have come before, are diversified even more by the fact that the components of this story structure have been defined quite differently, based upon the cultural/historical context of the literary text. Take, for example, the basic categories of the "pre-adult" and the "adult" that I used earlier in my description of the basic coming-of-age paradigm. Common parlance for "pre-adult" in contemporary Western culture is "teen," but, arguably, this word has only been with us for a half a century or so. Before there were "teens," there were "adolescents," but the term was a demographic designation and developmental category that was not really used with any frequency and specificity until the end of the nineteenth century. Before there were adolescents there were "youth," but this term seems to have designated a much broader age spectrum, in some cases from as young as eight to as old as the mid- to late twenties. Concomitantly, of course, the different specifications of "pre-adult," whether they are youth, adolescent, or teen, shape how adulthood is conceived. The diverse ages of the various protagonists in coming-of-age stories from different time periods are indicative of the slipperiness of these categorical definitions. But, also, the unique problems facing these various protagonists are shaped by the respective culture's attitudes toward these age categories, whether it be child, youth/adolescent/teen, adult, or elderly. A good example of this might be the character of Telemachus in Homer's *Odyssey*. Telemachus battles, literally and figuratively, to make a name for himself in adult society. Part of what he battles against is the influence of his father. Both of these challenges are shared by many adolescents in contemporary coming-of-age texts, but to categorize Telemachus as such would be to miss out on the unique status of the pre-adult in Homer's time and subsequently the unique definition of adulthood that so eludes him.

These designations have been shaped by socioeconomic forces, religion, education, the legal system, and the media, to name just a few, and as they have been shaped, so has the context within which these coming-of-age stories have been created. Coming-of-age stories both reflect and shape our beliefs about age categories and, of course, what is entailed in the very process of aging itself. Always, though, the pre-adult stage, whatever name and form it takes, is characterized by its shapeability; this adds narrative tension because the individual can go in either a good or bad direction; "good" and "bad," of course, are defined in many different ways according to the parameters of the texts at hand. The human drama cannot unfold unless the protagonist has freedom and subjectivity, or at least an implied right to these qualities that has been blocked by some individual, institution, or belief system.

At the root of these age categories and the transition between them are all sorts of questions about the nature of identity. Thus, coming of age is without a doubt the most philosophical of literary topics. The quest to assimilate, which is often tempered by the careful guarding of one's individuality, is a drama that is ripe for reflection on the true nature of identity. Where ultimately does identity come from? Occupation? Marriage? Religion? The body? Does one find one's identity by identifying with external objects and people in the world or by renouncing such objects and people in pursuit of a kind of pure singularity? Is there such a thing as a "pure singularity"? Furthermore, invoking one of the most powerful voices in the modern conception of coming of age, Sigmund Freud, what if these external factors are just manifestations of some psychological crisis? The answers to these questions have varied widely depending upon culture and time period.

And what about ethnicity, socioeconomic class, and gender? Do these categories always define how one is perceived (or not perceived) by others? Do they limit or enhance how one may be defined as an "adult"? Coming-of-age stories have lent themselves to an intense examination of race, class, and gender because their protagonists are often forced to negotiate these pre-existing categories of identity as they transition into, resist, or are excluded from adulthood. One of the lessons that Cassie Logan must learn in Mildred Taylor's novel *Roll of Thunder, Hear My Cry*, for example, is how to negotiate a pre-existing, racist stereotype of her as "black girl" in a way that offers her some subjectivity and power over her own life. "White ain't nothin'," she immaturely tells her mother after experiencing one of her first encounters with racism. "It is something," her mother teaches her. "White is something just like black is something" (127).

Additionally, the in-between stage of adolescence has been commonly used as a metaphor for second-generation immigrants—caught between the "old country" culture of their parents and the "new country" culture of the new civilization that surrounds them—or the colonized other, situated between the colonial and the subaltern culture.

Consider the identity crisis of Kim, the title character of Rudyard Kipling's 1901 novel, who is born of an Irish father, raised by an aunt in India, and then, upon learning his father's nationality, schooled as a British intelligence officer. "Who is Kim?" he asks himself repeatedly throughout the novel, foraying the complexity of a developmental process that is not only split between age categories, but nationality and race as well.

However it is framed, this transition into adulthood is often predicated upon a delicate balance between one of the most prevalent binaries in Western thought: individual and community. How do I become an adult without losing my individual sense of self? How do I maintain an individuality without becoming invisible to those who must recognize me and affirm my existence? Indeed, "finding one's place in society" (arguably one of the most common endings to a coming-of-age narrative) is in itself a telling contradiction. Does one cease to be "one" (a singular entity) when one becomes a member of society?

The paradoxical tension of many coming-of-age stories is how to maintain the individuality one has sought throughout the pre-adult stage (leaving home, disobeying authority figures, questing for independence) and still assimilate into society (finding a place in the world, making a name for yourself). To put a finer point on it, how can the protagonist's coming-of-age process end with an individuation within society? This is a question, of course, with a limitless number of answers, which may be part of the reason coming-of-age narratives have persisted; without a doubt, the most interesting aspect of these coming-of-age stories is how the author comes up with an ending that works. As readers, we can hardly wait to get there. Conventional wisdom would tell us that an unadulterated individuality awaits us at the end of the process, but it is rarely that simple.

Individuality is meaningless, of course, if one is not a member of a community that can define one as an individual. In Mark Twain's *Adventures of Huckleberry Finn*, Huck's escape to the river is a type of pursuit of individuality and a rejection of society, but, when he is by himself, away from Jim, his intense fear of being alone becomes apparent. "When it was dark I set by my camp fire smoking, and feeling pretty satisfied," he tells us about one of those times. "But by and by it got sort of lonesome, and so I went and set on the bank and listened to the currents washing along, and counted the stars and drift-logs and rafts that come down, and then went to bed; there ain't no better way to put in time when you are lonesome; you can't stay so, you soon get over it" (51).

Equally as menacing for these characters' coming of age is the threat of the complete assimilation into society—"selling out," as it is called in popular parlance. How disgusted we would be as readers of Salinger's *The Catcher in the Rye* if Holden Caulfield decided to take the advice of his teacher, "old Spencer," and "play the game." Instead, we get this: "Game, my ass. Some game. If you get on the side where all the hot-shots are, then it's a game, all right—I'll admit that. But if you get on the other side, where there aren't any hot-shots, then what's a game about it? Nothing. No game" (8). This response is far more satisfying, perhaps because it allows us the illusion that Holden's coming-of-age battle—even if it is a fiction—is an authentic one, a search for his "true" self.

Often, the (literal or implied) ending of the coming-of-age story is the ability to find one's place in the world without sacrificing some unique sense of self. The most memorable coming-of-age stories, one might argue, are the ones that manage to achieve this ending in a way that is both compelling and believable or the ones that use this expected ending as a way to expose societies that do not allow for such freedom. In addition to, or perhaps as a consequence of, providing a space to contemplate the nature of identity, these coming-of-age texts also reflect back our own values and belief systems. The liminal space of youth/adolescence/teen can provide unique insight into what the status quo defines as a legitimate adulthood in society. Thus, these coming-of-age narratives lend themselves quite well to social critique. Becoming an adult in some cases means loosening one's "pure," "childlike" conception of the world and seeing the reality of social injustice and corruption. For some, that lesson is enough; others find that they must battle against a corrupt adult society and pave a new road to righteousness. The metaphor of the new generation overthrowing the old has not been lost on many authors of coming-of-age texts, many of whom see their own work (with its various aesthetic innovations) as part of a new wave in artistic expression that is overthrowing the old guard. This is perhaps why so many of the heroes of these coming-of-age stories are artists themselves: they are symbols, as it were, of broader cultural trends and innovations. If you cannot find your place in society, the next best thing is to create a new society or a work of art that exposes the injustice of your alienation.

On the other hand, in the same way that these depictions of the youth/adolescent/teen can serve as a form of social critique, they can also be constructed in such a way that reflects broader anxieties about the next generation or certain characterizations of pre-adulthood that serve to empower the adult. It is clear that in most of the coming-of-age stories, adulthood is privileged, in that it is the stable endpoint of conflict. And, taking this argument one step further, one might say that the more severe the conflict during the pre-adult stage, the more stable the resultant adult identity. The "crisis" of the pre-adult stage is often characterized in ways that are particularly threatening to adult society, such as the rebellion against authority that is so prevalent in these texts. As mentioned earlier, the liminal space of the pre-adult often serves as a critique of the status quo, but if such a critique is taken a few steps further it could take the shape of a full-fledged revolution. Perhaps this is part of the appeal of the coming-of-age story, at least to an adult reading audience; it enables adults to conceptualize their own fears of social instability and loss of power.

Some have surmised that these coming-of-age texts could function as scripts or instructional manuals for pre-adults that enforce a certain proper path toward becoming an adult. Such a reading is without a doubt supported by the fact that so few coming-of-age stories are actually written by pre-adults. One might argue that, by definition, the coming-of-age story must be filtered through the adult perspective. But the argument for coming-of-age stories as scripts for proper behavior becomes more problematic when we consider readership. Without a doubt, in contemporary society, the coming-of-age story is most often marketed as a young adult novel and cordoned off to a specific section of the bookstore or library, and, largely because of this, these stories are most often read by teens. But such distinct publishing categories, and in particular the clear distinction between adult and young adult literature, have only been with us, arguably, since the end of the nine-teenth century. Additionally, however hard we try to contain these sto-ries within their own section and readership, clearly many young adult texts and coming-of-age stories are marketed to and read by adults. An excellent example of this ability to defy categories is the Harry Potter series, a coming-of-age story so prevalent in our society that categoriz-ing its genre and readership in terms of age is highly problematic.

Coming of age is a rich and complex cultural phenomenon that can tell us a great deal about who we are or, in many cases, who we imagine ourselves to be. Ultimately, the categories, the journey, and the truth therein are situated within the text at hand and resonate in cer-tain ways depending upon the cultural/historical moment of the reader. However, we are still left with the preponderance of it all. Why has coming of age as a literary topic persisted and thrived? One reason is that these stories assure us that we have some freedom in choos-ing the paths we take to adulthood and thus we have ownership of the people we become. Although I am clearly overlaying a contemporary frame on many of these texts, one might argue that coming of age is a uniquely democratic concept, even if it exposes the inequalities that exist in democratic societies.

Still removed from this enormous cultural enterprise called com-ing of age is Peter Pan. But he is by no means alone in his exile. Our society has always had a place for those who resist making the transi-tion, so much so that we have a psychological theory to explain them, known as "Peter Pan syndrome." Such a "malady" is clearly indicative of the centrality of the coming-of-age story in our society and the cultural need for the coming-of-age process. After all, we adults know that there is no pixie dust or magic island for those who do not make the transition; only dirty looks and stiff reminders to "act your age," even if it is only acting. "Don't want ever to be a man?" I'm sorry, you have no choice.

Works Cited

Barrie, J. M. *Peter Pan*. New York: Penguin, 2002.

Barthes, Roland. *S/Z*. New York: Hill & Wang, 1974.

Buckley, Jerome Hamilton. *Season of Youth: The Bildungsroman from Dickens to Golding*. Cambridge, MA: Harvard UP, 1974.

Joyce, James. *A Portrait of the Artist as a Young Man*. New York: Penguin, 1985.

Kipling, Rudyard. *Kim*. New York: Bantam, 1983.

Salinger, J. D. *The Catcher in the Rye*. Boston: Little, 1991.

Taylor, Mildred. *Roll of Thunder, Hear My Cry*. New York: Puffin, 2004.

Trites, Roberta Seelinger. *Disturbing the Universe: Power and Repression in Adolescent Literature*. Iowa City: U of Iowa P, 2000.

Twain, Mark. *Adventures of Huckleberry Finn*. New York: Norton, 1999.

White, Barbara A. *Growing Up Female: Adolescent Girlhood in American Fiction*. Westport, CT: Greenwood, 1985.

CRITICAL
CONTEXTS

Critical Reception_____

Kent Baxter

The critical approaches to coming of age in literature have been as diverse as the novels, stories, poems, and plays that depict this theme. In many ways, an overview of the critical reception of the coming-of-age theme could be an overview of literature itself, since the transition from pre-adulthood to adulthood has been a preoccupation of so many authors from Homer to the present.

Even within the critical landscape of a particular literary text, one can find a wide variety of approaches taken to the central theme of coming of age. Consider, for example, the critical history of one of the most iconic (and, arguably, most controversial) figures in modern coming of age texts: Holden Caulfield, from J. D. Salinger's 1951 novel *The Catcher in the Rye*. In a 1974 discussion of Holden's "neurosis," James Bryan explains that the "the urgency of Holden's compulsions, his messianic desire to guard innocence against adult corruption . . . comes of a frantic need to save his sister from himself" (Salzberg 107). Attempting to place the novel more succinctly in a social context, Carol and Richard Ohmann have this to say about Holden's conflict with society: "When a situation or act seems phony to Holden, it evidences bad class relationships, or public ritual, or both. . . . Holden rounds on mores and conventions that are a badge of class. He also revolts against convention itself" (Salzberg 130). And in a 1990 essay, Mary Suzanne Schriber argues that "the popularity and the ascription of broad significance and exceptional literary importance to *The Catcher in the Rye* can be traced to . . . assumptions that the male is the normative, and to androcentric theories of American literature in which American fiction is routinely framed and taught" (Salzberg 235). These three excerpts from analyses of Holden—representing a psychological, a Marxist, and a feminist view, respectively—are just a few of the almost limitless approaches critics have taken to Salinger's novel, some even arguing that *The Catcher in the Rye* is not a coming-of-age text at all.

Thus, the wide array of approaches to coming of age are not only a result of the many literary works from many different periods and cultures that engage with this topic; they also spring from the marked breadth of the topic itself. Perhaps because the transition from pre-adulthood to adulthood has been so central to the ways we understand ourselves, it reverberates on many different levels and in many different modes of discourse, leaving it open to quite varied interpretations.

Still, without a doubt, a survey of the critical heritage of coming-of-age texts reveals some clear trends and important paradigm shifts. As is the case with the three excerpts above, many of the approaches to *The Catcher in the Rye*, for example, focus on the central issue of character development (or lack of development). Perhaps such a focus on character is often central to analyses of coming-of-age texts because many aspects of the text (plot, structure, symbolism, theme) revolve around, and evolve from, the protagonist's journey from pre-adulthood to adulthood. Although, once again, the analysis of character is often guided by the unique structure and meaning of the text at hand, there are three common ways that critics have approached this issue. It is perhaps no surprise that the predominant approaches to analyzing character development in many coming-of-age texts are oriented around the three most influential theoretical approaches to coming of age in Western society: Arnold Van Gennep's notion of "rites of passage," Sigmund Freud's notion of the "unconscious," and Erik Erikson's notion of the "ego identity."

The expression "rites of passage" was coined by Arnold van Gennep in his 1909 book by that name. In his pioneering work, Van Gennep described three phases (separation, transition, and reincorporation) that marked the socialization process of the individual. But, often, the expression "rites of passage" has been associated with symbolic events or processes in literature that mark the ending of the coming-of-age process. For example, in her book, *Coming of Age in Shakespeare* (1981), Marjorie Garber argues that "[rites of passage] mark a turning point in the life of the individual, and it is of such turning points—

crises and peripeties—that drama is made" (17). Garber notes that, at least in Shakespeare's plays, these theatrical rites of passage signal the growth of the individual. As Garber points out, a typical Shakespearean protagonist comes of age in the following manner: "As he grows to maturity—as he comes of age—the novice is separated from the former identity, and integrated into a new social role" (19). So, for example, in *Romeo and Juliet*, "When Romeo doffs his name, declaring in the balcony scene, 'Henceforth I never will be Romeo,' he transforms himself. The doffing of the name is a rite of passage, which symbolizes his transition from the clan of the Montagues and the bands of joking youths to the role of Juliet's lover, soon to be her husband" (25–26). In this case, Romeo's coming of age—or, at least, a portion of this coming-of-age process—is marked by a theatrical event, characterized by a linguistic and social change.

Christopher LaLonde takes a similar approach to the fiction of William Faulkner in his book *William Faulkner and the Rites of Passage* (1996). LaLonde explains that the rites-of-passage paradigm provides a particularly rich frame for Faulkner's work because, in his coming-of-age novels and stories, "rites of passage and identity are bound together, as they are in life, for rites of passage are fundamental social constructs with which a culture attempts to confer identity. They are essential for the transformation of a physical, corporeal being into a person" (5). An example of this transformation can be found, according to LaLonde, in the protagonists of Faulkner's novel *Light in August*:

> The lives of Joe Christmas and Lena Grove are governed by their attempts to achieve ritual passage into the stage of marriage. Christmas's life becomes a pattern of ritualized actions culminating in his death as a result of his failure to achieve the passage he had desired; Lena's attempt to achieve the social change of state from woman to wife in order to sanction her impending natural change of state from childless woman to mother dictates both her actions and the actions of those she meets. (97–98)

Both Garber and LaLonde demonstrate that rites of passage in literature are particularly rich because these rites are indicative of changes in character. Such changes might be entirely psychological in nature. Although Sigmund Freud, for all intents and purposes, devoted much of his life's work to understanding the individual's transition from pre-adulthood to adulthood and the ways in which this process shapes the psyche of the individual, his discussion of the parent-child relationship, in particular the tension between the essential psychological need for parent and the force for separation from this parent, has been particularly influential in critical discussions of coming of age. Jerry Griswold, a specialist in children's literature, explains in his book *Audacious Kids: Coming of Age in America's Classic Children's Books* (1992) that the recurring story structure in many American coming-of-age texts published in the second half of the twentieth century is largely an effect of a recurring psychological conflict within the protagonists themselves: "The journey in these children's books is an extravagant symbol of separation from the parents. It is the apex of the traumas of exposure. But it also marks a second birth, or a transition to a second life . . ." (11). In this case, Dorothy's journey in L. Frank Baum's novel *The Wonderful Wizard of Oz* is representative of her own psychological maturation: "The Land of Oz is the Kingdom Without: an imaginative and extravagant version of America. But it is also and simultaneously the Kingdom Within: Dorothy's own circumstances reimagined at large, an extrapolation of her own oedipal or family problems" (41). In regard to Mark Twain's *Adventures of Huckleberry Finn*, Griswold argues that Huck's trip down the river is a process whereby he separates himself from various father figures, a key aspect of a Freudian approach to coming of age:

As Huck glides down the river, the novel moves from one episode to another in which father figures are discredited.

The first of these occurs when, with Jim apparently out of the novel forever, Colonel Grangerford is introduced. . . . Despite what is admirable about him . . . the High-born Father is discredited. Not surprisingly, Jim is now resurrected and brought back into the story. But his presence constitutes only a temporary solution, as the next episode makes clear. (62)

Although many critics such as Griswold have used Freud's notion of the Oedipus complex as a frame to understand coming-of-age texts, a more prominent psychological approach to character has been Erik Erikson's theory of socialization. Erikson spent most of his career developing a life-span theory of human development, composed of eight stages, but he is most well known for the fifth stage of this paradigm: puberty and adolescence. Adolescence is at the center of Erikson's theory because it is the stage, in Erikson's mind, in which the development of a social identity (a sense of "I") is most crucial. This "search for identity"—and the looming threat of "identity confusion" that is a part of this search—is an effective critical approach to the traditional character arc of the coming-of-age story, which, reaching back to the earliest literary texts, has often involved both individuation and a search for one's place in broader society. In his book *Rebels: Youth and the Cold War Origins of Identity* (2005), Leerom Medovoi argues that, for various cultural reasons, Erikson's work was particularly influential in mid-twentieth-century American society, and his notions of the development of a social identity, either directly or indirectly, found their way into many critically acclaimed coming-of-age novels, including Ralph Ellison's *Invisible Man*, Saul Bellow's *The Adventures of Augie March*, and J. D. Salinger's *The Catcher in the Rye*. Medovoi notes:

Written by the three most celebrated authors of the immediate postwar years, these novels shared certain noteworthy characteristics. . . . In each the narrator takes us along on his picaresque journey through a social environment bent on controlling or manipulating his sense of self. In each, the protagonist's resistance to these forces of manipulation may be read as a defense of personal identity. (65)

More specifically, in his analysis of Ellison's *Invisible Man*, Medovoi observes:

> It is in the scene that makes the Invisible Man's psychopolitical domination most explicit, at the factory hospital when he is strapped to an electroshock device bent on 'entirely changing the personality,' that the word 'identity' makes its first major appearance. . . . It is at this point that the Invisible Man actively begins his efforts to rebel against the Bledsoes, Nortons, and others whom he has heretofore faithfully obeyed. . . . In the end, however, though attracted to Rinehart's technique of manipulating what Erik Erikson would have called the 'role expectations' of others, the Invisible Man embraces a more robust concept of identity, one that stems from both self-discovery and a self-assertive refusal to submit blindly to the equally blind demands of those who embody social authority. (67)

In this case, the completion of the character arc is a stable sense of self ("ego identity," in Eriksonian terms), even if this ending is marked by a realization that there is no place for this self in mainstream society.

Whether the character's movement (or lack of movement) from pre-adulthood to adulthood is framed by rites of passage, psychological conflict, or a search for his or her place in the world, the parameters used to understand and discuss this movement vary significantly, based upon the historical and cultural context of the literary text at hand. One important and influential area of discussion in the critical reception of coming-of-age texts has been an analysis of this change; more specifically, how the various developmental categories that are so central to coming of age (childhood, youth, adolescence, the teen, the adult) have been defined in different ways in different time periods and cultures. The shape of the coming-of-age moment is greatly influenced by the various age categories of those who experience it. The transition between the developmental categories of the child, adolescent, and adult, is, of course, a result of how these various categories are defined. As many critics have noted, the varying definitions of each of these categories affects the relative age at which transition between categories occurs. But, also, the ways in which each of these categories is defined shape the conflicts and resolutions that each character must face in the process.

In his often-cited *Centuries of Childhood: A Social History of Family Life* (1962), Philippe Ariès argues that the most familiar term of our contemporary discussions of coming of age—the term "adolescence"—was actually not used with any precision or frequency until the nineteenth century. In a detailed study of the European school system, for example, Ariès concludes that "in the twelfth and thirteenth centuries, children of ten and boys of fifteen were mixed up with adults; in the fourteenth and fifteenth centuries, children and adolescents continued to study together but were separated from adults" (164). Furthermore, in such schools, the "the word *puer* and the word *adolescens* were used indiscriminately. Preserved in the Bibliothèque Nationale are the catalogues of the Jesuit College at Caen, a list of the pupils' names accompanied by comments. A boy of fifteen is described in these catalogues as *bonus puer*, while his young schoolmate of thirteen is called *optimus adolescens*" (25). According to Ariès, the lack of distinction between the *puer* and the *adolescens* is indicative of a society that made no distinction between the two as demographic entities and a culture in which individuals passed from childhood to adulthood with no pronounced or extended transition period. Such insights into how human development was discussed and conceived have significant implications for the way we approach texts about coming of age from these periods.

Building on, and sometimes taking issue with, Ariès's work, many critics have analyzed how the term "youth" was often used in texts before the nineteenth century to designate the pre-adult. John Gillis, for example, has pointed out in his book *Youth and History: Tradition and Change in European Age Relations, 1770-Present* (1974), that the parameters of the term "youth," as it was used in texts from the seventeenth and eighteenth centuries, were much less precise than is the case with our contemporary conception of adolescence: "What they commonly called 'youth' was a very long transition period, lasting from the point that the very young child first became somewhat independent of its family, usually about seven or eight, to the point of complete independence at marriage, ordinarily in the mid- or late twenties" (182).

In contrast to "youth," "adolescence," a term that began to be used with more frequency at the end of the nineteenth century, designates a specific period between thirteen and eighteen that is markedly distinct from childhood and adulthood. This period is also characterized in large part as a time of conflict. As I have noted in my own study, *The Modern Age: Turn-of-the-Century American Culture and the Invention of Adolescence* (2008):

> The development of the public high school and the juvenile court system are material effects of a new space opening between childhood and adulthood, and these changes made teens a more conspicuous presence in American society. But, also, such rehabilitative measures were predicated upon largely negative assumptions about this new demographic. These attitudes were articulated and justified in the earliest full-length theoretical treatments of what would become popularly known as 'adolescence.' (4)

Such a new conception of this pre-adult phase can, of course, be seen in the coming-of-age literature of the time as well, from the "bad boy" books at the end of the nineteenth century to the "problem novels" that were so popular in the middle of the twentieth century.

This connotation of conflict and rebellion has been inherited by the contemporary incarnation of this developmental stage: the teen. In *Huck's Raft: A History of American Childhood* (2004), Steven Mintz observes that the word "teenager" did not really enter the popular lexicon until it was first used in a 1941 article in *Popular Science Monthly*; emerging from this decade, according to Mintz, was "the bored, restless, volatile teenager who combined a child's emotions with an adult's passions and was estranged from parents and other authority figures"

(253). Taking issue with this dating of the invention of the category of the teenager, in his book *Teenage: The Creation of Youth Culture* (2007), Jon Savage identifies the symbolic beginning of the teenager in 1945 when the *New York Times Magazine* published "A Teen-Age Bill of Rights," but he argues that the phenomenon represented by this term had been a part of Western society for many decades. "From the last quarter of the nineteenth century," he observes, "there were many conflicting attempts to envisage and define the status of youth—whether they were concerted efforts to regiment adolescents using national policies, or through artistic, prophetic visions that reflected the wish of the young to live by their own rules" (xv).

However we date the categories of "youth," "adolescent," and "teen," it is clear that they are culturally defined. These cultural/historical analyses of the developmental stage of youth/adolescence/teen have greatly shaped our understanding of the topic of coming of age, because they enable us to better understand how this transition, and the different stages of which it is composed, has been conceptualized by the different societies that produced these literary texts. We may be tempted to align Homer's *The Odyssey* and J. D. Salinger's *The Catcher in the Rye* as two coming-of-age texts, but they are coming from two very distinct societies that defined this process in different ways. Part of the critical history of coming of age has been an attempt to better understand this difference.

I've been discussing coming of age thus far as a cohesive and identifiable literary motif that dates back at least to the time of Homer, but one interesting aspect of the critical reception of coming-of-age texts is that it is not really until the nineteenth century that any recognizable coming-of-age genre takes shape. The parameters of this genre, and the terms critics have used to discuss it, have been far from stable. The bildungsroman, which, translated, means "education novel," was a popular genre in German literature in the early decades of the nineteenth century and became a recognizable novel form in English, and later American, literature in the middle of the nineteenth century. Although there are exceptions to any broad generalization, novels such as Jane Austen's *Mansfield Park*, Charlotte Brontë's *Jane Eyre*, and Charles Dickens's *David Copperfield* do follow a similar pattern that was clearly popular in the nineteenth century and has remained with us, in various forms, to this day. Critics have often used this term as a correlate for coming of age. In his book *Season of Youth: The Bildungsroman from Dickens to Golding* (1974), Jerome Buckley describes the genre this way:

> A child of some sensibility grows up in the country or in a provincial town, where he finds constraints, social and intellectual, placed upon the free imagination. His family, especially his father, proves doggedly hostile to his creative instincts or flights of fancy, antagonistic to his ambitions, and quite impervious to the new ideas he has gained from unprescribed reading. . . . He therefore, sometimes at a quite early age, leaves the repressive atmosphere of home (and also the relative innocence), to make his way independently in the city. . . . There his real "education" begins, not only his preparation for a career but also—and often more importantly—his direct experience of urban life. . . . By the time he has decided, after painful soul-searching, the sort of accommodation to the modern world he can honestly make, he has left his adolescence behind and entered upon his maturity. (18)

This definition works well with the various nineteenth- and early twentieth-century novels Buckley examines—such as Dickens's *David Copperfield*, George Eliot's *The Mill on the Floss*, Thomas Hardy's *Jude the Obscure*, and D. H. Lawrence's *Sons and Lovers*—and, clearly, there is a popular interest in and prolific production of this form of the coming-of-age story that is unique to this time period. But, as mentioned earlier, the age when an individual moves from pre-adulthood to adulthood and the rites of passage through which one passes are quite different, depending on time period and culture. Some have argued that the distinct developmental stages of the adolescent and the teen have shaped the bildungsroman genre, to the point where, after the turn of the twentieth century, it has developed into something almost entirely different. In her book *Growing Up Female: Adolescent Girlhood in American Fiction* (1985), for example, Barbara White distinguishes between the bildungsroman and the novel of adolescence, which, she argues, is largely a creation of the twentieth century. Differences between these two generic manifestations of the coming-of-age story include the age of the protagonist (who is typically a teenager in the novel of adolescence), the focus on conflict with adult society in the novel of adolescence, and, perhaps most important, the fact that, unlike the bildungsroman, the novel of adolescence does not always end with a positive and seamless initiation of the protagonist into existing adult society. "Not all novels of adolescence include initiation," White explains; "in fact, the protagonist may actively avoid or refuse it. If the hero is initiated at all, the initiation often occurs suddenly at the end of the novel and is ambiguous in nature" (14).

Although authors still create coming-of-age stories that could be identified as a bildungsroman or novel of adolescence—as defined by Buckley and White, respectively—the most common contemporary generic incarnation of this story is arguably the young adult novel, or, even more recently, the novel for young readers. In her book *Disturbing the Universe: Power and Repression in Adolescent Literature* (2000), Roberta Seelinger Trites makes the argument that this more recent genre is predicated upon a new way of conceptualizing adulthood, the traditional endpoint of the protagonist's movement through the coming-of-age character arc. "Following World War II," she points out, "maturity, adulthood, being harder to define, ceased to be privileged as the narrative goal in literature written for youth. The Young Adult novel, then, came into being as a genre precisely because it is a genre predicated on demonstrating characters' ability to grow into an acceptance of their environment" (19). Such an "acceptance of environment" is predicated upon the protagonist's understanding that identity is contextual and not as essential or stable as it was portrayed in the bildungsroman of an earlier time period.

As can been seen in these discussions of character, age categories, and genre, two clear trends emerge in the historical critical reception of the coming-of-age theme. By learning more about the cultures that produced these stories and calling into question some of the unfounded assumptions that readers have made about the characters that inhabit these texts, these trends have achieved a greater understanding of the intricacies of this literary motif. Nowhere have these trends become more apparent than in the discussions that focus on how gender and ethnicity function in these literary works. In her book, *The Myth of the Heroine: The Female Bildungsroman in the Twentieth Century* (1987), Esther Kleinbord Labovitz makes the point that the quest for self-identity that has been presented by Buckley and others as being a basic component of the nineteenth-century bildungsroman does not really reflect the reality of female pre-adults, since their lives were almost totally devoted to the service of others. "Insofar as the nineteenth-century woman in Europe was concerned," Labovitz explains, "her 'apprenticeship' as an unmarried, single woman was assumed to be spent in serving the family group and, if middle class, in entertaining or being entertained; an apprenticeship she could end by accomplishing her masterpiece, making a 'good marriage'" (4). Thus, according to Labovitz, it is not until at least the early decades of the twentieth century, when society better supported the rights of women and provided venues for women to pursue some search for their place in the world, that the female bildungsroman came into existence, as evidenced by such novels as Dorothy Richardson's *Pilgrimage*, Simone de Beauvoir's *Memoirs of a Dutiful Daughter*, Doris Lessing's *Children of Violence*, and Christa Wolf's *The Quest for Christa T.*

An interesting and thoughtful reconsideration of the psychological approach to coming of age is offered by Katherine Dalsimer in her book *Female Adolescence: Psychoanalytic Reflections on Works of Literature* (1986). Taking issue with a critical (and psychological) tradition that, she argues, favors the male adolescent experience, Dalsimer observes:

> At every phase of adolescence, not only at its ending, but from its beginning, it is necessary to consider how the distinctive nature of the girl's experience may shape developmental processes. . . . Adolescence is set in motion by a biological event, the advent of puberty. But this is a different event for the girl than for the boy—and its psychological ramifications different, I believe, in ways that have not been fully articulated. (10)

Dalsimer offers psychological interpretations of the characters in five literary works from different periods: *The Member of the Wedding*, *The Prime of Miss Jean Brodie*, *The Diary of Anne Frank*, *Romeo and Juliet*, and *Persuasion*. Thus, Dalsimer argues, in Muriel Spark's novel *The Prime of Miss Jean Brodie*, since the language to discuss adolescent sexuality is often articulated in male terms, the main characters, Sandy and Jenny, are initiated into sexuality by observing an older role model, Miss Brodie. A similar projection occurs between Juliet and her nurse. Indeed, Dalsimer concludes that unique to the female adolescent coming-of-age experience—at least in the literary works she analyzes—is the importance of the mother figure:

> These works of literature suggest that at every phase of female adolescence, and in every aspect—from the beginning changes in the contours of the body, in the awakening of sexual feeling, in the forming of new friendships and in love, in the making of those choices that will define, for that individual, her womanhood—all of these developments take place in the context of this continuing relationship. (140)

In her study of African American and West Indian coming-of-age novels, *Ten Is the Age of Darkness: The Black Bildungsroman* (1995), Geta LeSeur argues:

Black novels of childhood, although having some of the characteristics of the European or White bildungsroman, cannot be grouped with any of these novels. They are distinct in their content and presentation because of the facts of Black history alone, the trappings of class and color, and the general circumstances of home, family, and community. (21)

Thus, in her study of Richard Wright's *Black Boy,* James Baldwin's *Go Tell It on the Mountain,* Toni Morrison's *The Bluest Eye,* George Lamming's *In the Castle of My Skin*, and Austin Clark's *Amongst Thistles and Thorns*, LeSeur notes similarities with the bildungsroman described by Buckley earlier—particularly in the lack of a father figure, restrictive setting, pursuit of education, and rites of passage—but she also notes that the African American bildungsroman has a strong theme of exile, and that the protagonists often have to negotiate a racist culture that severely impedes the journey toward adulthood and independence.

In *Negotiating Identities in Women's Lives: English Postcolonial and Contemporary British Novels* (2002), Christine Wick Sizemore provides an interesting reevaluation of the popular coming-of-age theories of Erik Erikson, which, she argues, have been interpreted too narrowly by other critics. Sizemore uses Erikson as a frame to discuss coming-of-age stories about "hybrid" experiences, such as those of individuals between cultures or on the margins of society. She writes:

Erikson's name is most often associated with the concept of 'identity crisis,' which freezes 'identity' as a label for Western adolescents' search for adult roles and implies the ability to achieve the very 'fixed, stable' identity. . . . The concepts I find most useful in Erikson's thought present the adult personality as continually developing in an effort to comply with the various 'tasks' or 'tensions' of adult life. This aspect of Erikson's thought fits well with the structure of novels in which protagonists often change and develop throughout the course of their lives. (9–10)

Some coming-of-age novels Sizemore includes as examples of this are Tsitsi Dangarembga's *Nervous Conditions*, Margaret Atwood's *Cat's Eye*, Keri Hulme's *The Bone People*, Anita Desai's *Clear Light of Day*, and Margaret Drabble's *The Radiant Way*.

Labovitz, Dalsimer, LeSeur, and Sizemore are just four examples of many critics who have attempted to unravel how gender and ethnicity factor into the coming-of-age experience, and who have challenged critics to reevaluate the canon of coming-of-age texts with these factors in mind. Without a doubt, one of the most powerful influences on the formation of this canon has been the educational system, and, subsequently, one of the most popular forums for the consumption of coming-of-age texts has been the secondary school and college classroom. While this is a result of the cultural significance of many of these texts and their rich complexity, it is also a result of a tacit belief that students will be more interested in coming-of-age stories because they involve the stage of life being experienced by high school students or college undergraduates. Such an argument has formed the basis of many defenses of the use of young adult literature, and, more generally, coming-of-age stories, in the curriculum.

For example, in a 2001 book, *Teaching Reading in High School Classes*, Lois Stover argues that "young adult literature is, by definition, about the problems and issues of adolescence; therefore such literature can motivate many adolescent readers more readily than those works so often presented in surveys of British, American, and world literature" (qtd. in Ericson 118). Stover asserts that not only are such texts going to be more interesting to students but they can, for all intents and purposes, aid them with their own coming-of-age process: "reading such books helps young adults begin to understand how we define ourselves in relationship to the norms of our particular culture. Discussing such books can then facilitate consideration and redefinition of those boundaries against which a sense of self is formed and tested" (qtd. in Ericson 128).

In a 2001 article in the *English Journal*, entitled "How Classics Create an Aliterate Society," Donald Gallo makes a similar argument for the inclusion of young adult literature in the secondary school classroom, writing that "the most appealing characteristic of young adult novels, of course, is their high interest level. In short, we can teach high school students literary skills with YA books while everyone enjoys the reading activity" (37). In his 1989 book *Novels of Initiation: A Guidebook for Teaching Literature to Adolescents*, which contains chapters on coming-of-age texts such as *The Catcher in the Rye*, *Adventures of Huckleberry Finn*, *To Kill a Mockingbird*, and *The Member of the Wedding*, David Peck has this to say about the importance of "novels of initiation" in the secondary school curriculum:

> Why have I stressed the initiation process in selecting novels for this book? The obvious answer is that so many of the books popular in high school happen to have that central focus: American writers are obsessed with the idea of adolescence, and young people quite naturally enjoy reading about themselves, or characters of their own age. (xix)

Similarly, the assumption that texts about coming of age will be more appealing to teen readers is at the heart of Joan Kaywell's popular four-volume resource, *Adolescent Literature as a Complement to the Classics* (1992–1997), which suggests various curricular connections that teachers can make between "classic" literary texts and young adult literature. Many of these connections are based upon coming-of-age themes, and many of the classics that are referenced in her collection of essays are about coming of age, including *Adventures of Huckleberry Finn*, *To Kill a Mockingbird*, *Jane Eyre*, *The Odyssey*, *My Antonia*, *Oliver Twist*, *Native Son*, and *Pride and Prejudice*, to name a few.

Such assumptions about coming-of-age themes and teen reading inform the many lists of popular age-appropriate titles published each year, such as the Young Adult Library Services Association's (YALSA) annual top ten list for teens, as well as the International

Reading Associations.' (IRA) annual "Young Adult Choices" list published in the November edition of the *Journal of Adolescent and Adult Literacy*. These lists and the pedagogical scholarship mentioned above form a significant camp in the critical reception of coming-of-age literature and have had much to do with the use of coming-of-age texts in secondary school and college curricula.

This discussion of the pedagogical uses and significance of coming-of-age texts is an important contribution to the critical history of this theme. It is also important to the future of this genre, because the genre has been shaped significantly by the purchasing power of curriculum creators. School courses are often the venue through which individuals are first introduced to this theme in literature.

The critical history of the theme of coming of age in literature stretches out far beyond the major areas I have discussed here. But these areas resonate broadly and are central to many critical discussions of coming of age.

Works Cited

Ariès, Philippe. *Centuries of Childhood: A Social History of Family Life.* Trans. Robert Baldick. New York: Vintage, 1962.

Baxter, Kent. *The Modern Age: Turn-of-the-Century American Culture and the Invention of Adolescence.* Tuscaloosa: U of Alabama P, 2008.

Buckley, Jerome Hamilton. *Season of Youth: The Bildungsroman from Dickens to Golding.* Cambridge: Harvard UP, 1974.

Dalsimer, Katherine. *Female Adolescence: Psychoanalytic Reflections on Works of Literature.* New Haven: Yale UP, 1986.

Ericson, Bonnie, ed. *Teaching Reading in High School English Classes.* Urbana, IL: National Council of Teachers of English, 2001.

Gallo, Donald R. "How Classics Create an Aliterate Society." *English Journal* 90.3 (Jan. 2001): 33–39.

Garber, Marjorie. *Coming of Age in Shakespeare.* New York: Methuen, 1981.

Gillis, John R. *Youth and History: Tradition and Change in European Age Relations, 1770–Present.* New York: Academic, 1974.

Griswold, Jerome. *Audacious Kids: Coming of Age in America's Classic Children's Books.* Oxford, Eng.: Oxford UP, 1992.

Kaywell, Joan, ed. *Adolescent Literature as a Complement to the Classics, Volumes 1–4.* Norwood: Christopher-Gordon, 1992–1997.

Labovitz, Esther Kleinbord. *The Myth of the Heroine: The Female Bildungsroman in the Twentieth Century: Dorothy Richardson, Simone de Beauvoir, Doris Lessing, Christa Wolf*. New York: Lang, 1987.

LaLonde, Christopher A. *William Faulkner and the Rites of Passage*. Macon: Mercer UP, 1996.

LeSeur, Geta. *Ten Is The Age of Darkness: The Black Bildungsroman*. Columbia: U of Missouri P, 1995.

Medovoi, Leerom. *Rebels: Youth and the Cold War Origins of Identity*. Durham: Duke UP, 2005.

Mintz, Steven. *Huck's Raft: A History of American Childhood*. Cambridge: Belknap, 2004.

Peck, David. *Novels of Initiation: A Guidebook for Teaching Literature to Adolescents*. New York: Teachers College, 1989.

Salzberg, Joel, ed. *Critical Essays on Salinger's* The Catcher in the Rye. Boston: Hall, 1990.

Savage, Jon. *Teenage: The Creation of Youth Culture*. New York: Viking, 2007.

Sizemore, Christine Wick. *Negotiating Identities in Women's Lives: English Postcolonial and Contemporary British Novels*. Westport: Greenwood, 2002.

Trites, Roberta Seelinger. *Disturbing the Universe: Power and Repression in Adolescent Literature*. Iowa City: U of Iowa P, 2000.

White, Barbara A. *Growing up Female: Adolescent Girlhood in American Fiction*. Westport, CT: Greenwood, 1985.

In Search of Mildred Taylor's Womanists: Feminist Agency in the Logan Family Novels_____

Rachelle D. Washington and Michelle H. Martin

In Mildred Taylor's Newbery Medal-winning novel, *Roll of Thunder, Hear My Cry* (1976), protagonist Cassie Logan gets revenge on one of her white peers, Lillian Jean Simms, for humiliating her in the town of Strawberry. After Cassie gains Lillian Jean's trust by carrying her books, listening to her gossip about her friends, and pretending to befriend her for weeks, Cassie lures her into a heavily wooded area and soundly thrashes the incredulous Lillian Jean. When the white girl threatens to tell her father, a man who wields a great deal of power in town, Cassie promises her that if she tells anyone, "everybody at Jefferson Davis [School] is gonna know who you crazy 'bout and all your other business . . . and you know I know. Besides, if anybody ever did find out 'bout this fight, you'd be laughed clear up to Jackson. You here going on thirteen, getting beat up by a nine-year-old" (Taylor, *Thunder* 181). Certainly, Cassie is "feeling her womanhood," an oft-used expression inside of Africanist communities, when she ventures into such a subversive and bold act in a society in which such behavior could lead not only to revenge but to the lynching of Cassie and other members of her family.

In Alice Walker's groundbreaking essay, "In Search of Our Mothers' Gardens," she coins the term "womanist" and describes a womanist as a "black feminist or feminist of color [who is] committed to survival and wholeness of [an] entire people, male and female" (xi). The term also delineates the differences between feminism and womanism. Patricia Hill Collins (2000) holds that central to black feminism is the fact that racism and sexism were and are used to oppress African American women. Black feminism acknowledges that historically, feminism identified gender as the prominent issue, and African American women were encouraged to put aside racial concerns to focus on gender issues in the fight against patriarchy or male-dominated society. Thus, to identify as feminists, black women often had to put aside or suppress racial, ethnic, class, and color differences. Within this context, African American women battled with the importance of affirming their culture since their experiences were framed not just by gender but also by race, class, and color.

Collins relies on the early work of Maria Stewart, who in 1831 spoke up for the rights and freedoms of "the fair daughters of Africa" (qtd. in Collins 1). According to Stewart, African American women's self-definition provided an essential ingredient in their freedom, and she advocated for them to "use their special roles as mothers to forge powerful mechanisms of political action" (2). Further, Stewart argued that none of this could be accomplished without education, "for knowledge is power" (2). Black feminist theorist bell hooks notes: "Generations of Black Americans living in a white-supremacist country have known what it means to see education as the practice of freedom, have known what it means to educate for critical consciousness" (63). Collins therefore concludes: "This dialectic of oppression and activism, the tension between the suppression of African-American women's ideas and our intellectual activism in the face of that suppression, constitutes the politics of U.S. Black feminist thought" (3). Hence, "Black feminist thought aims to empower African-American women within the context of social injustice sustained by intersecting oppressions" (22). Black feminist thought, then, represented by theorists such as Collins, hooks, and Walker, encourages African American women to define themselves within particular sociopolitical and sociocultural contexts to validate their positions in society and serve as vehicles for social change. In light of these ideas, this essay will investigate the role of womanist agency in the Logan series.

In Mildred Taylor's Logan family novels—*Roll of Thunder, Hear My Cry* (1976), *Let the Circle Be Unbroken* (1981), *The Road to Memphis* (1992) and *The Land* (2001), and the novellas *Song of the Trees* (1975), *Mississippi Bridge* (1990), *The Well: David's Story* (1995), *The Friendship* (1997), and the more tangentially related *The Gold*

Cadillac (1998), set primarily in racist rural Mississippi in the 1930s—
she creates a matriarchal family system that consists of many womanists, including Cassie Logan and even her great-grandmother, who sur-
vived slavery, emancipation, and reconstruction. Through the power
of story—and specifically through the stories Cassie's elders share—
Taylor reifies oral traditions heralded in Africanist communities and
provides spaces for intergenerational exchange and lived experiences.
The knowledge gained through the oral telling of true family (hi)sto-
ries plays a significant role in motivating Cassie and her siblings to
become agents of change in the oppressive society in which they live.
Furthermore, the relationships within this family teach the children familial support, fortitude, self-determination, and hope. Given that the
narrative arc of these novels conveys primarily the significant events
in Cassie Logan's childhood and young adulthood, they illustrate both
how strong Cassie's female family members are and how those who
help to raise her contribute to her womanist perspective.

One might question what form womanism takes when the protagonist, especially in the earlier novels, is not yet a woman. Walker
offers womanism as an identity embracing the spiritual and cultural
experiences of African American women. Walker further defines a
womanist as "outrageous, audacious, courageous, and willful," someone who always questions and learns (xi)—descriptors that certainly
fit the character of Cassie Logan. Furthermore, Walker indicates that
"womanish" evolves from the "folk expression of mothers to female
children, 'You acting womanish,' i.e., like a woman . . . 'You trying
to be grown'" (xi). Although Walker uses this term to refer to black
feminism, given that "womanish" originally referred to girls who were
overly sure of themselves in the presence of female elders, this term
might be even more appropriate for young Cassie Logan than for some
of the matriarchs in her family. Furthermore, as Cassie negotiates her
power both within and outside of the protection of the African American family and community in which she lives, her maturation relies
heavily on her growing self-definition in the context of the "intersect-

ing oppressions" she experiences as a result of her race, gender, and socioeconomic status (Collins 22). Taylor's texts embody a womanist perspective through their investment in African roots and traditions, as well as their advocacy of resistance and social justice. To be sure, Taylor's texts illuminate womanism and demonstrate myriad ways her black female characters, particularly a young African American girl, navigate their lives within the binaries of a divided and dichotomous black and white America. It should also be noted that Taylor's post-civil-rights perspective and agenda, which she liberally inserts into the lives of her post–Civil War and pre-civil-rights characters, sometimes create ahistorical political dynamics and unrealistic outcomes. Readers should approach the novels and novellas aware of this characteristic within her works of historical fiction, but it is precisely because of this disjuncture that we can discuss how womanism—a concept originating in the 1970s—manifests itself in the Logan novels.

In the Logan family saga, Cassie crafts her own form of African American womanism from the stories her family members tell her about her ancestors; from the assertive and somewhat subversive behavior of her mother, Mary; from her cautious, politically aware, somewhat fearful grandmother, Big Ma; and even from her dapper but fiery-tempered Uncle Hammer. As she experiences conflicts of her own, Cassie learns to balance her pride and willful aggression with a more tempered means of functioning in a racist society. While womanism adds a rich texture to the work of black feminist writers like Taylor and uncovers the uniqueness of living life as an African American female, the goal of black feminists is to be *womanish* enough to ask bold questions and make bold statements. For Cassie, womanism means embracing her own agency at a time and place when agency or self-empowerment in a young black girl could mean danger or death. Cassie demonstrates her agency through sacrificing her own individual needs for the economic and physical survival of her family and by upholding the core values of the proud and resilient Logan family.

Agency in Taylor's Female Characters

Since the agency of female characters in general and of Cassie Logan in particular will constitute a significant portion of this essay's focus, we would like to offer a more thorough explanation and illustration of what agency means in the Logan family novels before delving into the primary argument. Mildred Taylor's family stories abound with African American women who attend to their own agency. By this, we mean that they take their circumstances into their own hands and effect change for a better outcome. In Taylor's work, this often becomes what Tamara Beauboeuf-Lafontant, author of *Behind the Mask of the Strong Black Woman* (2009) calls the "costly performance" of being an African American woman—particularly in the Jim Crow South where laws challenged these performances and whites brutally punished blacks who did not comply. When discussing black women in general and African American women in the South in particular, Taylor has her womenfolk exhibit agency despite social, familial, and institutional complexities surrounding the racist, classist, and even sexist treatment they receive.

One of the most salient examples of female agency comes from Cassie's great-grandmother, Ma Rachel. In *The Well: David's Story*, set during Hammer and David's childhood, a drought has hit the area, but the Logans' well remains one of the few that has not gone dry. The family, for the most part, generously shares their water with surrounding neighbors, regardless of their race, allowing them to get water when they need it. When conflict arises between thirteen-year-old Hammer and fourteen-year-old Charlie Simms (who would later become Lillian Jean's father), the Simms brothers, in an act of vengeance, poison the water by killing and cutting up a skunk and several other animals that they throw down into the well. In the background of all of this, David's grandmother, whom the family acknowledges to be suffering from dementia, resents having white people—especially those whom she despises—come onto their land for water. Having been born a slave, she holds an age-old grudge against her master's family for an offense committed at her birth, and because she cannot distinguish between past and present in her state of dementia, she blames all white people for this transgression.

The reasons for her feelings are many. Among them is having had a piece of her personhood and her very identity–her name–stolen when her mother gave birth to her. Ma Rachel repeatedly accuses the whites whom she sees on her property ("They done took my name") and threatens to run them off of the property with a shotgun (Taylor, *Well* 17). It is true that dementia perhaps interferes with Ma Rachel's reason in that she threatens violence against individuals for an offense that was committed by others generations earlier, but the fact that she recalls this conflict is significant: the historical injustice surrounding a conflict between a white plantation mistress and her black slave about the birth of their respective children remains in the forefront of Ma Rachel's mind for decades. This injustice happened to Rachel's *mother*, which means that her mother made sure her daughter knew of the conflict and made efforts—privately and among the slave families only—to recover the name that the slave master and mistress stole. This agential naming—using the name "Rachel" even though forbidden by the master's family—constitutes an act of defiance that would surely have led to physical punishment. Readers can be relatively sure of this because when the mistress realized that Rachel's mother was using the forbidden name, she whipped her mercilessly. When Rachel's mother still refused to stop using the name, the mistress threatened to whip the baby also, putting an end to the mother's outward resistance but certainly not to her covert defiance. This act of rebellion embodies the kind of subversive acts integral to the Logan family.

Despite the fact that the family considers Ma Rachel a little "touched in the head," the Logan women of the 1930s and 1940s imitate her rebellion by participating in risky behavior to protect their land, their families, and even the intangibles, like names, that represent their personhood and inalienable rights as human beings (Taylor, *Well* 15).

Self-Sacrifice for Economic and Physical Survival

For Cassie and for the Logan family, economic and physical survival go hand in hand. Were it not for the family's ownership of land, they would be in the same untenable and powerless situation as the African American sharecroppers who live in their community. In *Song of the Trees*, the first of Taylor's novellas and the first publication in the Logan family series, Cassie refuses to remain quiet either with the family matriarchs or with white people when she knows of a threat to the family's land. Cassie and her brothers, Stacey, Christopher John, and Little Man, realize that Mr. Andersen, a wealthy white man, has marked dozens of trees on their land with the intention of logging them for his own economic gain. After the children realize that their land is in danger, Mr. Andersen comes to the Logan house to let Big Ma and Mary know of his plan while pressuring them to allow him to take as many trees as he wants for the flat price he plans to give them. While Mary resists Andersen's bullying, Big Ma, attempting to avoid confrontation that would put her family at risk, gives in to Mr. Andersen's demands. That night, however, Mary and Big Ma send Stacey on horseback to Louisiana, where Mary's husband David is working on the railroad, to inform him of what has transpired. Disgruntled with the passive way the matriarchs have handled the situation, Cassie and her two younger brothers physically assault Mr. Andersen and his men after Andersen shouts for them to "Get away from here" (*Song* 39). Cassie retorts: "We are home"; "You're the one who's on our land" (39). By the time David appears, Mr. Andersen has already begun to lash the children with his wide leather belt to teach them not to interfere with adult matters. David stops the punishment, telling Andersen: "Put the belt down, Andersen . . . Let the children go . . . Any teaching, I'll do it. Now, let them go" (45).

In this situation, David's intervention not only saves the children from what could have become a brutal beating by a white man who sees them as meddlesome and insubordinate, but it continues the approach that the children have taken. David's actions affirm what the children already know: Logans believe that integrity should trump fear and that money should never tempt them to compromise their principles. Taking control of this threat to his land, David tells Andersen: "One thing you can't seem to understand . . . is that a black man's always gotta be ready to die. And it don't make me any difference if I die today or tomorrow. Just as long as I die right" (49). In this scene, David teaches his children, by example, not only what is worth standing up for but how to do it. In many ways, however, David's actions model a male's open aggression. When Cassie attacks the men in the family's grove to protect the integrity of their land as well as when she beats up Lillian Jean Simms in the grove of trees, she fights openly like David; more often than not, however, and much more often as she matures into young womanhood, she relies on a womanist approach to agency—an approach that involves defending her family or her rights verbally or more subversively.

Cassie's verbal assertiveness both within and outside of the realm of family and the African American community often gets her into trouble, but it also gains her a reputation as one unwilling to accept mediocrity and discrimination. Acting as a leader for her younger siblings, Cassie defies Ma and Big Ma's orders to steer clear of the grove of trees while the logging is taking place and attacks Mr. Andersen and the loggers while Stacey goes to get David. Furthermore, her emotional connection with the trees—which both she and David believe sing— gives her even more reason to fight for them. The text earlier in the novel foreshadows that Cassie will opt to fight those who threaten the family's land rather than obey the elders' orders. When Mr. Andersen visits Big Ma to "negotiate" about the trees, Cassie and her siblings, who should certainly be seen and not heard in this context, become "whistle blowers" when Stacey interrupts the conversation between Mr. Andersen and Big Ma to tell Big Ma that Andersen is "gonna cut them all down" rather than logging selectively. Cassie further interjects: "I won't let him cut them . . . I won't let him! The trees are my friends and ain't no mean old white man gonna touch my trees" (29).

Mr. Andersen criticizes Mary for her lack of control over her children, but this is usually the way Cassie operates. Her bold statements—bold for an African American, especially a young black girl in the 1930s—could cost her dearly, yet she refuses to be silenced.

In *Mississippi Bridge*, Cassie's outspokenness, which narrator Jeremy Simms mentions explicitly, gets her into trouble as she insists on equality for her grandmother, Big Ma. A novella published after *Song of the Trees* but set prior to *Roll of Thunder Hear My Cry*, *Mississippi Bridge* is narrated by Jeremy Simms, a sympathetic white neighbor boy who appears in most of the books. Jeremy describes Cassie in this way: "But that Cassie, she spoke right up; she wasn't closed mouthed as Stacey" (*Mississippi* 36). At this point in the novella, Jeremy has asked the four Logan children where they are going. Stacey does not want to tell him. Cassie, on the other hand, blurts out: "We goin' over to Miz Georgia's. We takin' her some milk" (36). Jeremy continues to comment: "Then she gone on strutting toward the bridge; she done had her say. That girl, she had plenty of mouth on her and she never paid me much attention one way or the other, 'ceptin' to speak her mind" (36). Cassie speaks her mind not just with children but with adults as well. Just prior to this interaction with Jeremy, Cassie and her siblings have helped Big Ma onto the bus for a trip to take care of her sister, who is ill. As Big Ma boards the bus and proceeds to walk to the back, passing empty seats near the front, Cassie, simultaneously innocent and defiant, meets a now-common visitor: Jim Crow.

"Wait up there a minute, Big Ma! Here's a seat. Here's a seat right here!"

Everybody on the bus turned eyes on them. Their grandmamma Caroline looked around, seen them eyes, and she let loose on Cassie. "Hush up, girl!" she snapped. "Ya hush up and come on!" Then she turned and kept on to the back of the bus where all the other colored folks was seated. But Cassie ain't let up. She ain't moved. "But what ya wanna sit all the way back there for, Big Ma?" she cried. "Can't see nothin' from *waaay* back there. This here seat much better'n . . ."

Stacey, he come behind her and he give her a good poke, then he grabbed her hand and jerked her on. She yanked back, fussin furious. "Boy, what's the matter with you?" she screamed. "You got no cause to be hittin' on me. . . ."

"Girl, hush!" Stacey hissed at her. "Them's *white* folks' seats!" (29, 31)

Cassie's befuddlement about the law cannot cajole her into acceptance. In this scene, which echoes Rosa Parks's defiance against unjust bus laws that sparked the civil rights movement, Taylor, who lived through and took part in this movement, reminds readers that children were an integral part of that change. Hence, whether in a low-risk situation such as the one at the bridge with Jeremy, or in a high-stakes conflict such as the one on the bus or in the grove of trees with Mr. Andersen and the loggers, Cassie *will* speak her mind. She is most persistent and vocal when the economic welfare of the family is at stake, but she also refuses to hold her tongue when political circumstances force her into personal conflicts.

In *Roll of Thunder, Hear My Cry,* during Cassie's first trip to the town of Strawberry, she has two personal encounters that bring her face-to-face with racism. Were it not for Stacey's intervention in the first situation and Big Ma's insistence in the second, Cassie would have continued to assume her womanist stance and would likely have suffered severely as a result. Despite these interventions on the part of family members, the encounters that Cassie has in Strawberry illustrate the problem mentioned earlier in the essay of Taylor's ascribing feminist behavior to a pre-feminist character. Taylor's choice to make Cassie as much of a womanist as she is, however, accentuates the lessons Cassie learns about racism and how personally and deeply she feels this oppression.

In Cassie's first encounter with racism in Strawberry, it is once again her verbal insistence that brings on the negative attention. Stacey, Cassie, and T. J. Avery, a friend and neighbor, enter the mercantile to purchase a few items that T. J.'s family wants. After some time spent waiting to be served, Cassie realizes that Mr. Barnett, the owner, has passed over them to serve a white girl in the store. This she finds intolerable.

> I spied Mr. Barnett wrapping an order of pork chops for a white girl. Adults were one thing; I could almost understand that. They ruled things and there was nothing that could be done about them. But some kid who was no bigger than me was something else again. Certainly Mr. Barnett had simply forgotten about T. J.'s order. I decided to remind him and, without saying anything to Stacey, I turned around and marched over to Mr. Barnett. (Taylor, *Thunder* 110).

Politely at first, Cassie reminds Mr. Barnett that he had been waiting on them before "this girl here, and we been waiting a good while now for you to get back" (111). When Mr. Barnett ignores Cassie, she moves to his side of the counter and tugs on his shirtsleeve. Mr. Barnett recoils at her touch, and after hearing her reminder, says, "Well you just get your little black self back over there and wait some more" (111). Cassie narrates: "I was hot. I had been as nice as I could be to him and here he was talking like this. 'We been waiting on you for near an hour,' I hissed, 'while you 'round here waiting on everybody else. It ain't fair. You got no right—.'" When Mr. Barnett asks, "Whose little nigger is this?" Cassie retorts, "I ain't nobody's little nigger!" When Stacey begins to pull Cassie out of the store, Mr. Barnett advises him to "make sure she don't come back till yo' mammy teach her what she is," to which Cassie responds, "I already know what I am!" (112). And indeed she does. Cassie's family has taught her to take pride in who she is and to expect fair treatment in all arenas—even, as is the case in this scene, to her own detriment.

Unfortunately, this expectation of fair treatment runs counter to the restrictive social situation in which they live in racist Mississippi. Cassie has intuited from both explicit and implicit lessons from her parents that threats to their economic and personal welfare should be met with uncompromising action. It is clear to her and to the reader in this encounter, however, that an overt response—like David's in the grove—would only get Cassie killed or badly beaten. Even her verbal defiance after being ignored in Barnett's Mercantile has incited a violent response. Hence, part of the lesson that Cassie learns from this conflict is that when open aggression results in retaliatory violence and when even verbal resistance brings a negative response, she must resort to more covert means. Notably, this instance in Strawberry does not destroy Cassie's spirit nor encourage her to give up fighting for social justice; it prompts her to take her aggressions underground. Her second encounter with racism in Strawberry occurs when Lillian Jean Simms gets offended when Cassie refuses to address her with respect, and Lillian Jean's father responds by slapping Cassie off of the sidewalk. Despite Cassie's desire for immediate revenge, she learns patience and more subversive means of retaliation—a lesson that culminates in her trouncing Lillian Jean privately after patiently and deviously pretending to be her friend and confidante for weeks. Through these circumstances, then, Taylor illustrates that though a womanist is "outrageous, audacious, courageous, and willful," a womanist is also smart enough to know when those characteristics will endanger her and her family and will change her tactics accordingly (Walker xi).

Upholding Core Logan Family Values

Cassie employs her agency to uphold Logan family values despite the many hurts she suffers from living in the Deep South. Protecting the integrity of the land the family owns at all costs stands as one of the Logans' primary core values. Closely related to that, however, is that each member of the family should obtain an education and should use it to improve himself or herself and the economic stability of the family, for, as Maria Stewart articulated in 1831, "knowledge is power" (qtd. in Collins 2). Educational inequities were commonplace during this time in history, and most of the Taylor women and even the girls confront them at some point in the series. When Cassie's turn to deal with educational injustice occurs, her behavior (as a young girl on the brink of adolescence) demonstrates that she understands the need for artful crafting—an additional trait of a womanist—as she resists social injustice and insists that others recognize her humanity.

In her fight for educational equity, fourth-grader Cassie riles her teacher when she and her brother, Little Man, question the condition of their school textbooks, which are *"Property of The Board of Education, Spokane County, Mississippi"* (Taylor, *Thunder* 25). These books, sent from the white schools, are marked with a chart that lists a date of issuance, the condition of the book, and the race of the student using the book each year. By the time the books from *"1922, New, White"* come to Great Faith Elementary, Cassie's school, they are marked *"1933, Very Poor, nigra"* (25). When Cassie's brother sees this insulting designation, Little Man refuses to take a book but opts to receive a whipping from his teacher, "Miz Crocker," instead. Cassie stands up for him, and for herself, by pointing out the word "nigra" to the teacher. Miss Crocker doesn't believe Little Man can read, but Cassie assures her that even though this is his first day of first grade, he can, indeed, read—an assertion that also points to the Logan family's emphasis on education even at the pre-school level. As Cassie draws her teacher's attention to the offensive label in the front cover of Little Man's textbook, she tells Miss Crocker, "S-see what they call us." Miss Crocker responds coldly: "That's what you are . . . Now go sit down." Cassie starts to return to her seat but changes her mind, turns back around, and tells the teacher, "I don't want my book neither" (26–27). The teacher commences to whip Little Man, who "had no intention of crying" (27). Afterward, Cassie gets the same.

While many readers mistakenly assume that Miss Crocker is white, because of the vehemence with which she defends the Board of Education's right to discriminate against the district's African American students and the swiftness with which she publically whips the two Logan children for their resistance to this racism, this is not the case. What Miss Crocker's behavior signals—perhaps the best example in the novel of the antithesis of a womanist—is Miss Crocker's own internalized racism, the result of years of being treated as inferior by whites. In other words, if, as Walker indicates, a womanist "is committed to the survival and wholeness of [an] entire people" (xi), Miss Crocker commits herself to the decimation of her own people: she has internalized white racist ideology so thoroughly that she encourages her impressionable black students to see themselves as "nigras" (an altered form of "nigger" rather than the then-proper term "Negro"). Collins cites black feminist activist Pauli Murray who explains that "a system of oppression . . . draws much of its strength from the acquiescence of its victims, who have accepted the dominant image of themselves and are paralyzed by a sense of helplessness" (Murray qtd. in Collins 99). Collins goes on to explain that "U.S. Black women's ideas and actions force a rethinking of the concept of hegemony, the notion that Black women's objectification as the Other is so complete that we become willing participants in our own oppression" (99). This is precisely the dynamic at work in the behavior of Miss Crocker—a participant in her own oppression—whom Mary forces to consider the hegemonic system oppressing them both.

When Miss Crocker goes to Mary to report on her children's behavior, Mary's noncommittal response further riles Miss Crocker, but Mary, unlike her colleague, teaches subversively and does all she can to educate her children and students while minimizing the damage that white racism attempts to inflict on them. This education includes teaching them both national and local African American history—lessons not sanctioned by the school board. Hence, when Miss Crocker confronts Mary with the news of her children's public defiance and rejection of the books, Mary takes the book from Miss Crocker and uses glue and brown paper to paste over the offending words so that her children can use them without constantly being affronted with the offensive words. Appalled by what she perceives as defacement, Miss Crocker warns Mary: "If somebody from the superintendent's office ever comes down here and sees that book, you'll be in real trouble"

(Taylor, *Thunder* 30). Mary, who performs the multiple roles of teacher, mother and radical, displays her womanist perspective as she laughs and says: "In the first place no one cares enough to come down here, and in the second place if anyone should come, maybe he could see all the things we need—current books for all of our subjects, not just somebody's throwaways, desks, paper, blackboards, erasers, maps, chalk . . ." (30). Mary's behavior in this passage reinforces her colleagues' belief that she is a "disrupting maverick" (30) whose "ideas were too radical" (31). Frightened and bewildered, Miss Crocker notes, "Well, if anyone ever does come from the county and sees Cassie's and Little Man's books messed up like that, I certainly won't accept the responsibility for them." Mary quips, "It will be easy enough for anyone to see whose responsibility it is, Daisy, by opening any seventh-grade book. Because tomorrow I'm going to 'mess them up' too" (31). In her womanist, verbally assertive approach to Miss Crocker, Mary uses her agency—as dangerous as it might be to deface school board property—to help her children advance their education by learning from the books while she also models for them how to subvert a system that does not value them as students or as human beings. Hence, in light of Mary's response, the reaction of Cassie and Little Man to the books makes sense. They have been raised to maintain the integrity of the Logan family's respect for education, despite the cost.

This high regard for education rests not just with the parents in the Logan household but also with Big Ma, the matriarch. In *Roll of Thunder, Hear My Cry,* Cassie and her siblings must walk to school since "the county would not provide school buses for its black students" (44). And every day on their way to school, the white bus driver "liked to entertain his passengers by sending us slipping along the road" as he attempts to force the children off of the narrow dirt road into the mud and brush. As Cassie and her siblings wish aloud that they, too, had a bus to ride to school, Big Ma advises: "So ain't no use of frettin' 'bout it. One day you'll have a plenty of clothes and maybe even a car of yo' own to ride 'round in, so don't you pay no mind to them ignorant white folks. You just keep on studyin' and get yo'self a good education and you'll be all right" (45). In this passage Big Ma teaches the children that acquiring an education is worth even the humiliation they are suffering at the hands of the white bus driver and his riders. Furthermore, she does not advocate open retaliation for the humiliation to which the white bus driver is subjecting them; rather, she teaches them that they can educate themselves beyond the narrow community in which they live and thereby escape oppression. Unbeknownst to the adults, the children find a more immediate—though subversive—way to get back at the bus driver and his white riders, but Big Ma advocates for a non-violent, patient, but highly effective way to best their oppressors. Notably, Big Ma has mellowed in her reaction to prejudice. Her refusal in *The Well* to publicly beat her sons, David and Hammer, to the extent that Old Man McAlister Simms (grandfather of Lillian Jean) demands shows that she, too, has openly resisted at times, even if she, as a grandmother years later, advocates more tempered means of resistance.

When David brings the children books for Christmas, it becomes clear that they, too, have thoroughly absorbed these messages about the importance of an education. David has carefully chosen *The Count of Monte Cristo* for Stacey because he learned from the seller that the Frenchman who wrote it, Alexander Dumas, was a mulatto whose father was a slave and whose grandmother was a slave in Martinique. When the seller tells him that the books might be too difficult for his children to read, David retorts: "I told him he didn't know my babies. They can't read 'em now, I said, they'll grow into 'em" (153). Despite the fact that the children each receive nice new clothes and "a sockful of once-a-year store-bought licorice, oranges and bananas," Cassie remarks, "But nothing compared to the books" (153). Given her excitement over the Christmas books as well as her willingness to submit to a spanking in front of all of her schoolmates because of the conflict over Little Man's textbook, Cassie understands that gaining literacy has a cost and comes only with sacrifice. As a preteen, she is preparing herself to do what is necessary to succeed, and as readers learn in *The Road to Memphis,* when teenaged Cassie leaves home to pursue a higher education, she needs all of the strength and determination she can muster as she seeks to come of age as a well-educated and strong African American young woman in a racist, sexist society.

Conclusion

Chronicling black women's lives, as Taylor has aptly done in the Logan family novels, reduces the tendency for readers to view black women as one-dimensional characters or victims, as Tamara Beauboeuf-Lafontant describes in *Behind the Mask of the Strong Black Woman.* She notes:

> They [African American women] resist constructions of their singularity for erecting a deceitful pedestal that renders them into spectacles to be admired or harshly critiqued, but always from a distance. As they question such fixed contrasts between themselves and all other race-gender groups, they become able to speak of both fulfillment and vulnerabilities. (150)

Furthermore, black feminism and womanism can provide a means by which African American women's lives and experiences can be included in the collective narratives of the larger culture and society. Specifically, the Logan series belongs to a genre that helps foster societal values at their roots: children's literature. Taylor's Logan family women put a "face" on Walker's theory of womanism, as women like Ma Rachel, Big Ma, Caroline, and Cassie fight for what they value most and celebrate African Americans' history of resistance, persist in their womanish ways, and reveal themselves as human beings deserving of the rights and freedoms due to every American. It may even be fair to say that as Cassie progresses from being a girl to being a woman, she leaves behind her father's and Uncle Hammer's overt, threatening ways of dealing with racial conflict and discrimination and more thoroughly embraces the womanist approach of her female role models.

This is not to say that teenaged Cassie doesn't have the fire and vitality of the younger Cassie, but she does become a wiser and more discerning character who understands that accusing a white man in his own store is not the way to get better service.

As Cassie observes her closest role models and absorbs how they negotiate the power systems that attempt to control and suppress African Americans, she decides what sort of young woman she will become—opting for a personhood crafted not out of fear or self-enslavement, as evidenced through characters like Miss Crocker, but out of courage, determination, and the will to live a life of equality as she grows toward adulthood. Bell hooks says: "Certainly for black women, our struggle has not been to emerge from silence into speech but to change the nature and direction of our speech, to make a speech that compels listeners, one that is heard" (6). As Cassie learns the boundaries of Southern racist society, the agency and vocality that she has always had gets tempered as she learns to negotiate the rules of Jim Crow, and in doing so she begins to operate in subversive modes that will allow her to succeed. This subtlety will protect her but will also draw less negative attention to her as she continues to fight injustice.

Works Cited

Beauboeuf-Lafontant, Tamara. *Behind the Mask of the Strong Black Woman: Voice and the Embodiment of a Costly Performance*. Philadelphia: Temple UP, 2009.

Collins, Patricia Hill. *Black Feminist Thought: Knowledge, Consciousness, and the Politics of Empowerment*. 2nd ed. New York: Routledge, 2000.

hooks, bell. *Talking Back: Thinking Feminist, Thinking Black*. Boston: South End, 1989.

Taylor, Mildred. *The Friendship*. New York: Scholastic, 1997.

_____. *The Gold Cadillac*. Illus. Michael Hays. New York: Puffin, 1998.

_____. *The Land*. New York: Fogelman, 2001.

_____. *Let the Circle Be Unbroken*. New York: Dial, 1981.

_____. *Mississippi Bridge*. New York: Dial Books for Young Readers, 1990.

_____. *The Road to Memphis*. New York: Puffin, 1992.

_____. *Roll of Thunder, Hear My Cry*. New York: Dial, 1976.

_____. *Song of the Trees*. New York: Bantam, 1975.

_____. *The Well*. New York: Dial Books for Young Readers, 1995.

Walker, Alice. *In Search of Our Mothers' Gardens*. San Diego: Harcourt, 1983.

Coming of Age in History_____

Steven Mintz

Literature does not necessarily represent life as it actually is; rather, it reveals how life is experienced, felt, and understood. But if literature does not provide readers with an accurate blueprint or roadmap, it does reveal the expectations, conventions, ideals, and fantasies that color the way readers lead their own lives. It is from fiction—novels, movies, and television shows—that we learn what it means to grow up and embrace an uncertain future.

In literature, as in reality, the passage from boyhood and girlhood to adulthood is life's unsurpassed drama. During the liminal stage between childhood and full adulthood, the young must separate from their family of origin, define their identity, find their calling, establish more mature and intimate relationships, and grapple with profound spiritual and sexual issues. An odyssey of discovery and self-fashioning, this passage requires protagonists to pass through a series of trials, temptations, and rites of passage as they struggle to achieve mature status.

Literature has treated the passage to adulthood through a number of archetypal patterns, themes, and motifs. Literary treatments of coming of age often center on education (or apprenticeship or self-fashioning) or on rebellion against a father, on sexual initiation, or on the experience of first love. Some coming-of-age stories are tales of loss—especially the loss of innocence, naiveté, and spiritual faith. Others are tales of maturation, forged out of a hard-won experience, in which a young person grows cognitively and emotionally, developing a sense of autonomy, establishing a distinctive identity, and acquiring a sense of purpose and direction. Still others depict deepening alienation—often estrangement from parental values and from such institutions as schools or churches. All, however, emphasize the young person's agency, regarding their protagonists not as passive victims but as active agents who, for better or worse, make profoundly consequential choices. In these works, we can enter into their psyche; hear young people's voices—cynical, vulgar, humorous, and prematurely wise; and eavesdrop on their fantasies, desires, and dreams.

This essay will provide the historical context against which literary accounts of coming of age can be understood. It will discuss the shifting pathways to adulthood—paths that have taken very different form in various geographical settings and historical eras, and which have varied markedly by gender, ethnicity, and class.

Myths about Coming of Age

Historical perspective lays to rest several popular myths. Contrary to what many people assume, young people in the past did not enter adulthood at a very young age. While it is true that in classical Greece, many girls were married at or near puberty (to husbands perhaps a decade older), during the Christian era, most young people did not marry until their mid- or even late twenties or early thirties, about the same age as today (Flacelière 59).

Furthermore, navigating the path to adulthood has never been easy or seamless. To be sure, some young people followed in their mothers' and fathers' footsteps. But most did not. From the Middle Ages through the Early Modern Era up until the nineteenth century, a majority of young people left home for protracted periods of time, sometimes traveling extremely long distances, before attaining the emblems of adulthood, including marriage. In short, the transition to adulthood has almost always been as circuitous and conflict-riven as it is now (McClure 167).

Nor are youth cultures or youth organizations recent developments. Over the centuries, young people participated in a variety of informal and formally organized youth groups. Although young people in the past spent more time with adults than they do today, they did take part in a wide range of activities with peers: frolics, games, festivals, and sports.

Equally important, there was never a time when there was a single path to adulthood. Young women and men followed many disparate pathways before becoming adults, often involving a variety of work experiences outside the home and short- or long-distance migration. Indeed, perhaps the most important historical development in the process of coming of age is that over time the path to adulthood has become narrower and more circumscribed, more prescriptive and clearly defined. Contemporary society is distinctive in that it prefers a single path to adulthood, involving higher education (Graff xiii).

Above all, history makes it clear that the stage of life known as youth has always been a source of anxiety for adults and a period of uncertainty and ambiguity for young people. Coming of age is problematic precisely because young people occupy a profoundly indeterminate and ambiguous status.

Youth in European and American History

Prior to the twentieth century, Western societies identified a distinctive stage of life, known as youth, lying between childhood and adulthood. Vaguer and more amorphous than the modern category of adolescence, youth extended from the age of eight or so into the middle or even late twenties, divided into two stages at some point between the ages of fourteen and seventeen, when most young people exited the parental household. Young people in this transitional status were neither children nor full adults. After leaving their parental home, most lived in a dependent status as servants, apprentices, or farm laborers, or in the case of wealthy sons, as pages, serving as attendants in a court (Chudacoff 9).

European society strongly disapproved of early marriage, generally requiring couples to wait until a young man inherited land or achieved economic independence, which typically was not until he reached his late twenties or early thirties. Strong efforts were made to prevent young women and men from pairing up prior to marriage. One striking example involves dancing; instead of dancing as couples, men and women participated in group dances in which they danced in one or more lines or rows (Gillis, *For Better, For Worse* 274).

Delayed marriage meant that young people spent many years outside the parental home. Within their workplaces, young peoples' lives were strictly regulated, and any violation of their master's or mistress's orders could result in harsh physical punishment. Outside the workplace, the young socialized in same-sex peer groups, ranging from informal gangs to village groupings and more formal fraternal or sororal organizations. In continental Europe, these latter groups were known as brotherhoods or sisterhoods (or in France as youth abbeys or youth kingdoms). Sometimes, these groups enforced community norms. For example, in England, informal groups known as charivari enforced communal values, publicly deriding cuckolds (men whose wives had committed adultery), serenading those who broke sexual customs with "rough music," and symbolically hanging straw dolls to stigmatize women considered sexually promiscuous (Thompson 304).

Like adolescents in the twenty-first century, young people were widely regarded as rude, unruly, and disrespectful. Not surprisingly, many youths felt frustrated by the long delay before attaining full adult status. To deal with youthful discontent, their societies created escape valves that allowed young women and men to release their frustrations. These included activities such as dances, singing, competitive games, and carnival-like festivities in which the young could mock their elders.

During the eighteenth century, young people faced more choices than ever before. As the number of occupations expanded, young men faced greater challenges in choosing a vocation. As geographical mobility increased, young women as well as young men had greater freedom to decide where to live. Most strikingly, an increasing number of young people asserted the right to choose a marriage partner based on love and affection, rather than on practical, pragmatic considerations or upon parental preference (Mintz, *Huck's Raft* 50–51).

The expansion of choice made the process of coming of age increasingly problematic. In colonial America, rates of premarital pregnancy and illegitimacy shot upward during the eighteenth century, reflecting a breakdown of parental controls over youthful sexuality. In the early nineteenth century, a growing number of young women elected not to marry. As unmarried women's opportunities to work outside the home expanded—especially as mill girls or schoolteachers who could work alongside other young women their same age—a striking number viewed marriage as a closing off of freedoms that they had enjoyed in girlhood.

The Industrial Revolution of the nineteenth century had far-reaching consequences for growing up, intensifying class differences in young peoples' experience. Household production declined sharply, accompanied by a sharp shift from family labor to wage labor. There was a marked increase in office occupations as well as in factory employment (Mintz and Kellogg 49–52).

Growing affluence allowed the rapidly expanding middle class to keep its children in the parental home into their late teens or early twenties. Prior to the late nineteenth century, youths of different classes worked side by side in farms, on ships, or in small workshops. Youths, regardless of class, sporadically moved in and out of the parental home. But with the growth of white-collar employment, the middle class increasingly embraced schooling as the route to a successful career and kept their children at home into their late teens or even into their twenties. Prolonged schooling, delayed entry into the workforce, and delayed marriage became defining attributes of middle-class life. Upward mobility hinged on delaying many forms of gratification and postponing entrance into full adult status until young men were fully established economically. A code of values emphasizing self-improvement, self-control, and respectability was embraced by many middle-class youth (Mintz, *Huck's Raft* 88–89).

At the same time, working-class youth entered the wage labor force at a very young age, often before reaching their teenage years, giving them a greater measure of economic independence from parents. Older mechanisms that had regulated the lives of laboring class youths, such as apprenticeship or indentured servitude, broke down. In cities, there was a rapidly growing population of free-floating young men and women living outside a master's household and in boarding houses in distinct working-class neighborhoods (*Huck's Raft* 139).

Contrasting youth cultures emerged among middle-class and working-class youth and among young women and men. Many middle-class young men participated in debating societies, literary clubs, and the youth affiliates of reform organizations, which provided young people not only with peer support, but with opportunities to develop organizational and oratorical skills that proved valuable in later life. Many middle-class young women joined church and missionary societies, which provided a sense of sisterhood. The highest rates of religious conversion were found among middle-class women in their late teens and early twenties (*Huck's Raft* 88).

Meanwhile, many young urban men participated in boisterous, rowdy activities, joining voluntary fire companies or gangs with such names as Dead Rabbits and Plug Uglies. Also challenging middle-class conventions of propriety and deportment were growing numbers of urban, working-class women who promenaded on urban streets wearing eye-catching clothing purchased with their own earnings, and who openly socialized with men in public (Stansell 86).

Rowdy and disorderly youthful behavior became an increasing source of concern. A common student ritual was to "bar out" their teachers, locking them out of their own schoolhouses. Youthful gang violence was common; so, too, was violence on college campuses. During the 1830s, one University of Virginia professor was horsewhipped, another stoned, and yet another murdered (Hitchcock 51–52).

Beginning in the 1840s, educators and youth workers made concerted attempts to restructure the path to adulthood, creating a host of new institutions—including high schools and YMCAs—to shield middle-class youth from contamination from the "dangerous classes," the corruptions of the urban life, and stresses that accompanied industrialization. Anxiety over the unstructured nature of youthful experience—involving young people moving sporadically in and out of school,

---

jobs, the parental home—prompted efforts to rationalize, standardize, and institutionalize the transition to adulthood. Casual, unstructured contacts with adults were to be replaced with age-segregated institutions (Chudacoff 35–36).

A host of reformers wanted to universalize a middle-class ideal of the passage to adulthood. There was also a deepening fear that if working-class youth started to work too soon, without adequate schooling, they would be trapped in dead-end jobs. The goal was to construct an institutional ladder that would allow the young to attain adulthood in measured steps. A previously haphazard system of education was replaced by age-graded classrooms, the creation of the high school, and a regularization of college entrance requirements. In turn, the extension of schooling paved the way for a landmark event in the process of coming of age: the discovery, or more accurately, the invention of adolescence (Chudacoff 66–68).

The "Discovery" of Adolescence

Adolescence is not a timeless concept; despite the word's Latin roots, adolescence is an age category that only dates to the early twentieth century. It was not until 1904, when American psychologist G. Stanley Hall published an influential two-volume work entitled *Adolescence: Its Psychology and Its Relations to Physiology,* that the term began to be widely used to refer to a phase of life, marked by such psychological traits as defiance and risk taking, around the time of puberty. Although Hall was not alone in identifying adolescence as a distinct phase of life, he was instrumental in linking this stage to awkwardness and emotional turmoil (Chudacoff 66–68).

Hall encouraged adults to view children's cognitive, emotional, physiological, and social development in terms of discrete stages tied to particular ages. Convinced that adolescents "grew up too quickly" and were expected "to make too many of their own choices," he believed that teens needed to be sheltered in institutions, such as high schools, that would meet their special needs for camaraderie, competi-

tive athletics, and adult supervision. At the turn of the century, a majority of young people dropped out of school between the ages of twelve
and fourteen to enter the labor force or to assist their mothers in the
home, but by 1940, educators, psychologists, and youth workers succeeded in universalizing a middle-class conception of adolescence, in
which a majority of young people spent their early and middle teen
years in high school. These reformers succeeded in outlawing child
labor and extending the age of compulsory school attendance in most
states to sixteen. It was Depression-era unemployment that made adolescence a normative experience. To remove teens from the workforce
and provide job opportunities for adults, the Fair Labor Standards Act
of 1938 abolished child labor. By the end of the 1930s, for the first time
in US history, a majority of sixteen- and seventeen-year-olds were in
school, where they inhabited a culture radically separate from that of
adults (Lindenmeyer 238–40).

Within high schools, a distinctive peer culture took hold. High
school students generated their own lingo, clothing styles, customs,
and celebrities, like Frank Sinatra, Mickey Rooney, and Judy Garland.
A new word, "teenager," arose to describe high-school students. Unlike
adolescence, which referred to a biological and psychological stage of
life, "teenager" referred to a culture and a market (Mintz, *Huck's Raft*
252).

The early post–World War II era was the golden age of the teenager,
with its own musical style—rock 'n' roll—and symbols, like James
Dean and Elvis Presley. The teenage years had an intensity that has
since abated, since a majority of women married by their twentieth
birthday and most men by the twenty-second birthday (often after
serving a stint in the military). During the early post–World War II era,
the young wed, bore children, entered a full-time career, and purchased
a house earlier than at any other time in US history. By the end of the
1950s, however, this era was coming to an end. College enrollment in
the United States, already surging because of the GI Bill, expanded
still further as growing numbers of young women enrolled. Very early

marriage—in which half of women married by the age of twenty—started to give way to later marriage (Mintz and Kellogg 203–4).

A key development of the mid- and late 1950s and the 1960s was the growing self-consciousness of the young as a distinctive social group, marked off from the rest of society by distinct forms of dress, hairstyle, music, demeanor, and even political activity. "Youth" no longer simply referred to a stage of life; rather, it began to refer to a collectivity with its own unique outlook. Young people increasingly developed a collective self-consciousness with an oppositional flavor, antagonistic to the values of adults. During the 1960s, social commentators spoke of a generation gap, a lack of communication between young people and their parents, reflecting fundamental differences in values and attitudes, especially involving sexuality and gender. Campus upheavals and anti-war protests prompted debate over whether a youth rebellion had begun (Mintz, *Huck's Raft* 312–13).

Careful studies revealed that the generation gap was grossly exaggerated and that young people's political attitudes did not diverge sharply from their elders'. Nevertheless, profound shifts in behavior, indeed, in the nature of coming of age, were taking place. During the 1970s, the age of first intercourse fell sharply; meanwhile, women and men began to socialize with one another much more informally than in the past. Since the 1970s, youthful identities have become increasingly diverse. Young people are free to fashion a distinctive self and to choose among a variety of youth cultures.

Physiologically, the young mature earlier than ever before, reaching sexual maturity as early as the age of twelve or even earlier—perhaps four years earlier than in the nineteenth century. But achievement of the markers of full adulthood—marriage, an independent household, and a full-time job—takes place later than ever. After graduating college, many twenty-somethings move in and out of their parental homes. The transitional period once known as youth has become an odd mixture, involving a vacillation between autonomy and childhood dependence, between continued parental oversight and periods of self-indulgent irresponsibility.

Rites of Passage

In classic works of ethnography, anthropologists reported that the process of coming of age in small-scale societies involves a series of rituals, rites of passage, and experiences involving the crossing of thresholds. These rites of passage separate the young from their previous identity and environment, situate them temporarily in a threshold status outside conventional social categories, and then reintegrate young people into society with a new status. These rituals often involve physical tests or ordeals and the acquisition of a new name, denoting a new social identity. The purposes of these rites of passage include managing conflict between generations, defining gender and distinguishing the realms of the sexes, and assisting the young in the passage from dependence to adult responsibilities (Turner 93–94).

In many seventeenth- and eighteenth-century Native American societies, for example, the young went through a variety of rituals of separation, transition, and incorporation. Thus, at the time of first menstruation, a girl might go into seclusion to a special menstrual hut and reemerge as an adult member of her society. Boys, too, achieved adult status after undertaking a rite of passage. In many Native American societies, boys experienced a "vision quest," fasting and seeking a vision from a guardian spirit on a mountaintop or in a forest (Mintz, *Huck's Raft* 35–36).

The passage to adulthood in contemporary Western societies bears scant resemblance to this earlier pattern. For one thing, the transition to adulthood is an unusually protracted process, occurring over the span of a decade and a half. Equally striking is the paucity of formal public rites of passage. To be sure, a few such rituals remain. These include high school and college graduation ceremonies, as well as the bar mitzvah and bat mitzvah celebrations among Jews and religious confirmation among Catholics and Protestants—though these latter ceremonies tend to mark the transition to adolescence rather than to adulthood. There are also a small number of more secular rituals such as the sweet sixteen party and the quinceañera, a Hispanic celebration of a girl's fifteenth birthday. In addition, hazing rituals—which often require a person to undertake an ordeal—exist among gangs, fraternities and sororities, sports teams, and military units to initiate newcomers into the group. Hazing rituals have become highly controversial, since they often subject initiates to bullying and humiliating sexual or physical abuse.

In contrast to many non-Western societies, in which an individual's transition to maturity is public and social, in contemporary Western societies, the process is individual and inward. A young person's odyssey is as much a voyage of psychological self-discovery and identity formation as it is a matter of physical movement. As in small-scale societies, coming of age is a time of uncertainty and risk. It is a period when the young begin to detach from parents, abandon older loyalties and form new ones, and experiment with adult forms of behavior. But this process occurs primarily on a personal, not a collective or communal, level.

Many of the most culturally significant signposts of coming of age—a driver's license, a first drink, a first cigarette, or sexual initiation—are private matters, experienced solely by young people themselves. This fact has led some observers to suggest that the difficulty many young people experience in making the transition to adulthood may be related to a deficiency of public rituals that mark off the maturational process. In her classic 1928 ethnographic study, *Coming of Age in Samoa*, anthropologist Margaret Mead contrasts the supposedly easy and effortless passage to adulthood in Samoa and the conflict-riven process in the United States. She argues that the stormy familial struggles that American society experienced were not inevitable products of human biology, but were effects of a culture that provided young people with few ways to express their growing maturity and competence and which inhibited expressions of adolescent sexuality and kept the young psychologically and economically dependent far too long.

Today, many young people view adulthood with ambivalence or even disdain. Adulthood, once equated with maturity and wisdom, now often evokes images of stagnation, depression, and "selling out." Scarcely any young person today says that "life begins at forty" or that adulthood is the prime of life—at least not without irony.

In the past, it was taken for granted that the young wanted to grow up and assume the privileges of adult status. But in contemporary society, it is now possible to enjoy adult privileges without the burden of adult commitments and responsibilities. This has led some social critics to decry the prevalence of "extended adolescence," "arrested development," "failure to launch," and "the Peter Pan syndrome," attributing the trend toward delayed marriage and entry into adult careers to an increase in immaturity, narcissism, and commitment phobia. In actuality, these delays are primarily due to broader economic changes—including the need for advanced education and declining real wages for those without a college degree. Nevertheless, as a growing group of young people have come to regard conventional adulthood with scorn and condescension, the meaning of coming of age has shifted: No longer a discrete passage with a clear objective and endpoint, it may well have become an end in itself.

Works Cited

Abbot, Mary. *Life Cycles in England, 1560–1720: Cradle to Grave.* New York: Routledge, 1996.

Ben-Amos, Ilana Krausman. *Adolescence and Youth in Early Modern England.* New Haven: Yale UP, 1994.

Boydston, Jeanne. *Home and Work: Housework, Wages, and the Ideology of Labor in the Early Republic.* New York: Oxford UP, 1994.

Bradley, Keith R. *Discovering the Roman Family: Studies in Roman Social History.* New York: Oxford UP, 1991.

Burguière, André, Christiane Klapisch-Zuber, Martine Segalen, and François Zonabend. *A History of the Family, Volume I: Distant Worlds, Ancient Worlds.* Cambridge, MA: Belknap, 1996.

Burnett, Mark Thornton. *Masters and Servants in English Renaissance Drama and Culture: Authority and Obedience.* New York: St. Martin's, 1997.

Calcutt, Andrew. *Arrested Development: Pop Culture and the Erosion of Adulthood.* London: Cassell, 1998.

Cantú, Norma E., and Olga Nájera-Ramîrez, eds. *Chicana Traditions: Continuity and Change.* Urbana: U of Illinois P, 2002.

Chudacoff, Howard P. *How Old Are You? Age Consciousness in American Culture.* Princeton: Princeton UP, 1989.

Cross, Gary S. *Men to Boys: The Making of Modern Immaturity.* New York: Columbia UP, 2010.

Dixon, Suzanne. *The Roman Family.* Baltimore: Johns Hopkins UP, 1992.

Flacelière, Robert. *Daily Life in Greece at the Time of Pericles.* New York: Macmillan, 1965.

Friedenberg, Edgar Z. "The Generation Gap." *Annals of the American Academy of Political and Social Science* 382.1 (Mar. 1969): 32–42.

_____. *Coming of Age in America: Growth and Acquiescence.* New York: Random, 1965.

_____. *The Vanishing Adolescent.* Boston: Beacon, 1960.

Gillis, John R. *For Better, For Worse: British Marriages, 1600 to the Present.* New York: Oxford UP, 1985.

_____. *Youth and History: Tradition and Change in European Age Relations, 1770–Present.* New York: Academic, 1974.

Goldberg, P. J. P., and Felicity Riddy. *Youth in the Middle Ages.* Rochester: Boydell, 2004.

Golden, Mark. *Children and Childhood in Classical Athens.* Baltimore: Johns Hopkins UP, 1990.

Goody, Jack. *The Development of the Family and Marriage in Europe.* Cambridge, Eng.: Cambridge UP, 1983.

Graff, Harvey. *Conflicting Paths: Growing Up in America.* Cambridge, MA: Harvard UP, 1995.

Griffiths, Paul. *Youth and Authority: Formative Experiences in England, 1560–1640.* New York: Oxford UP, 1996.

Hanawalt, Barbara. *Growing Up in Medieval London.* New York, Oxford UP, 1995.

Hine, Thomas. *The Rise and Fall of the American Teenager.* New York: Harper, 2000.

Hitchcock, Susan Tyler. *The University of Virginia: A Pictorial History.* Charlottesville: U of Virginia P, 1999.

Hymowitz, Kay S. *Manning Up: How the Rise of Women Has Turned Men into Boys.* New York: Basic, 2011.

Just, Roger. *Women in Athenian Law and Life.* New York: Routledge, 1989.

Keniston, Kenneth. *The Uncommitted: Alienated Youth in American Society.* New York: Harcourt, 1965.

_____. *Young Radicals.* New York: Harcourt, 1968.

_____. *Youth and Dissent: The Rise of a New Opposition.* New York: Harcourt, 1971.

Kiley, Dan. *The Peter Pan Syndrome: Men Who Have Never Grown Up.* New York: Avon, 1984.

Kett, Joseph F. *Rites of Passage: Adolescence in America, 1790 to the Present.* New York: Basic, 1977.

Kimmel, Michael. *Guyland: The Perilous World Where Boys Become Men*. New York: Harper, 2009.

Lacey, W. K. *The Family in Classical Greece*. Ithaca: Cornell UP, 1984.

Lindenmeyer, Kriste. *The Greatest Generation Grows Up: American Childhood in the 1930s*. Chicago: Dee, 2005.

Maza, Sarah C. *Servants and Masters in Eighteenth-Century France*. Princeton: Princeton UP, 1983.

McClure, Peter. "Patterns of Migration in the late Middle Ages: The Evidence of English Place-Name Surnames." *Economic History Review* 32.2 (1979): 167–182.

Mead, Margaret. *Coming of Age in Samoa: A Psychological Study of Primitive Youth for Western Civilization*. New York: Morrow, 1928.

Mintz, Steven. *Huck's Raft: A History of American Childhood*. Cambridge, MA: Belknap, 2004.

_____. *Native American Voices*. Hoboken, NJ: Wiley, 2000.

Mintz, Steven, and Susan Kellogg. *Domestic Revolutions: A Social History of American Family Life*. New York: Free, 1988.

Mitterauer, Michael. *A History of Youth*. New York: Blackwell, 1992.

Nuwer, Hank. *The Hazing Reader*. Bloomington: Indiana UP, 2004.

Orme, Nicholas. *Medieval Children*. New Haven: Yale UP, 2003.

Palladino, Grace. *Teenagers: An American History*. New York: Basic, 1997.

Pomeroy, Sarah B. *Families in Classical and Hellenistic Greece: Representations and Realities*. New York: Oxford UP, 1996.

Rawson, Beryl. *The Family in Ancient Rome: New Perspectives*. Ithaca: Cornell UP, 1987.

Rorabaugh, W. J. *The Craft Apprentice: From Franklin to the Machine Age in America*. New York: Oxford UP, 1988.

Ross, Dorothy. *G. Stanley Hall: The Psychologist as Prophet*. Chicago: U of Chicago P, 1972.

Rotundo, E. Anthony. *American Manhood: Transformations in Masculinity from the Revolution to the Modern Era*. New York: Basic, 1994.

Sealey, Raphael. *Women and Law in Classical Greece*. Chapel Hill: U of North Carolina P, 1990.

Stansell, Christine. *City of Women: Sex and Class in New York, 1789–1860*. Urbana: U of Illinois P, 1987.

Thomas, Keith. *Age and Authority in Early Modern England*. London: British Academy, 1976.

Thompson, Edward P. "'Rough Music': Le Charivari anglais." *Annales. Économies, Sociétés, Civilisations* 27. 2 (1972): 285–312.

Transition to Adulthood. Spec. issue of *The Future of Children* 20.1 (Spring 2010): 1–234

Turner, Victor. *The Forest of Symbols: Aspects of Ndembu Ritual*. Ithaca, NY: Cornell UP, 1967.

Van Gennep, Arnold. *The Rites of Passage*. Trans. M. B. Vizedom and G. L. Caffee. London: Routledge, 1908.

Wallach, Glenn. *Obedient Sons: The Discourse of Youth and Generations in American Culture, 1630–1860*. Amherst: U of Massachusetts P, 1997.

"Not Now. . . . Not Yet": Developmental Difficulties in *Jane Eyre* and *Wide Sargasso Sea*_____

Beth A. Wightman

> Their world . . . is, as I always knew, made of cardboard. I have seen
> it somewhere before, this cardboard world where everything is colored
> brown or dark red or yellow that has no light in it. As I walk along the pas-
> sages I wish I could see what is behind the cardboard. They tell me I am
> in England but I don't believe them. We lost our way to England. When?
> Where? I don't remember, but we lost it.
>
> (Rhys, *Wide Sargasso Sea* 180–81)

These words are spoken by Bertha Antoinette Mason, the madwoman
in Edward Rochester's attic in *Jane Eyre*, describing her situation after
marrying Mr. Rochester. But you will not find these words in Charlotte
Brontë's 1847 novel that tells the story of an orphaned, middle-class
girl named Jane and her development from a stubborn child to a governess for a wealthy member of the English gentry to a contented, married heiress. Bertha says this some eighty years later, in *Wide Sargasso
Sea* (1966), a prequel to *Jane Eyre* written by Jean Rhys. The chronology alone indicates the complexity of the relationships between
these two novels: Brontë's text lies both in *Wide Sargasso Sea*'s past
(Brontë's novel was published before Rhys's) and in its future (the story in Rhys's novel precedes the story in Brontë's); the story of Bertha
in Britain[1] happens in the Victorian present in *Jane Eyre*, but "Not now.
. . . Not yet" in *Wide Sargasso Sea* (90)—not until the third section of
the book. The novels are further connected by genre as examples of
the bildungsroman, or, as it has become more popularly known, the
coming-of-age novel: these novels chronicle the maturation of young
female characters, linked by literary and British colonial history in the
nineteenth century, into adulthood.

The intertwined stories of Jane and Bertha are dizzying, funhouse
mirror images. In Brontë's work, Jane famously struggles with her

---

temper. As an orphaned child taken in by a reluctant aunt, mocked and abused by her cousins, Jane refuses to let their injustices go unanswered. After one such incident, "the mood of a revolted slave still bracing me with its bitter vigor," she is locked up in a creepy, red bedroom ("alas, no jail was ever more secure"), looks in the mirror hanging in the room, and sees a "a strange little figure . . . half fairy, half imp" looking back at her from the glass (Brontë 11). Years later, as a grown woman about to be married, Jane looks in another mirror and this time sees a "savage" face reflected, with "red eyes and the fearful blackened inflation of the lineaments" (242). The face looking back is that of another angry, desperate woman, Bertha Mason, who is already married to the man Jane plans to marry, lives locked away in the attic above Jane's room, and will eventually throw herself from the roof of Rochester's house after setting it on fire. In *Wide Sargasso Sea,* Antoinette Cosway, known as Bertha while growing up in the West Indies,[2] escapes from her burning Jamaican home and looks into the face of Tia, her sometime playmate who stands with the former slaves who most likely caused the fire. Tia has just thrown a rock at Antoinette's face; Antoinette is bleeding, and Tia is crying. "It was as if I saw myself," Antoinette tells the reader. "Like in a looking glass" (Rhys 45). Jean Rhys takes up Charlotte Brontë's images of fire and mirrors, weaving them back into the early life she created for Bertha. "She seemed such a poor ghost, I thought I'd like to write her life," Rhys once said (Rhys, "Interview").

These textual connections also suggest how these carefully crafted literary portraits of young female protagonists depict aspects of British social and political history. Both novels invoke the bildungsroman, a popular nineteenth-century genre with a specific history that traditionally depicts the development of middle-class boys into socially acceptable men. The bildungsroman's interest in the maturation of the protagonist means that it is largely driven by character. However, many novels in this genre are just as interested in historical realities: Dickens's novels, for instance, place characters like Pip within comprehensively detailed depictions of nineteenth-century Britain, using the young man's experiences to comment on specific aspects of British society in a specific time. Mikhail Bakhtin's study of the bildungsroman identifies this relation to history as a feature of a particular subset of the genre, where the protagonist "emerges *along with the world* and . . . reflects the historical emergence of the world itself" (23; emphasis original). For Bakhtin, the bildungsroman protagonist can represent a variety of historical forces as they develop and influence the human social world, and so a bildungsroman itself can demonstrate the processes of history. *Jane Eyre* illustrates the conundrum of unmarried, middle-class British women's lives and the strictures of British evangelical religious life in the nineteenth century. *Wide Sargasso Sea* represents the twentieth-century legacy of British colonialism in the Caribbean. In identifying the figure of Bertha as a West Indian Creole, a white woman of European ancestry born in the West Indies, Brontë raises the issue of Britain's colonial exploits, including its participation in the slave trade.[3] Rhys takes up that thread, directly addressing what Brontë's novel acknowledges only obliquely: that is, the economic and political implications of British colonial history and the conundrum of accurately representing the British colonies that usually had been explained solely in terms of imperial ideas about them. The bildungsroman form enables *Jane Eyre* and *Wide Sargasso Sea* to (re)tell conventionally masculine stories of British and colonial history.

Neither text is only or simply a bildungsroman. *Jane Eyre* also uses elements of the romance genre, particularly its gothic incarnation, and both the gothic and postmodernism figure in Rhys's work. And neither novel is "only" a fiction or "merely" a thinly veiled slice of history; they are both highly wrought aesthetic texts that represent and interrogate incidents and ideas defining particular historical moments. This essay looks at how these last two aspects of the novels combine, focusing on how these narratives of development (re)write the narrative of Britain's imperial "coming of age," which is bound up with a tangled set of social and cultural anxieties in nineteenth- and twentieth-century Britain.

Two Tales of Young Women

Elizabeth Rigby's often-cited 1848 review of Brontë's novel indicts Jane Eyre for being "throughout [the book] the personification of an unregenerate and undisciplined spirit." Rigby charged that "the tone of mind and thought which has overthrown authority and violated every code human and divine abroad, and fostered . . . rebellion at home, is the same which has also written *Jane Eyre*" (173, 174). Eventually, however, Jane does conform to conventional Victorian and Christian standards of female behavior, marrying Edward Rochester and bearing his children: "I am my husband's life as fully as he is mine. No woman was ever nearer to her mate than I am; ever more absolutely bone of his bone and flesh of his flesh. . . . I am still his right hand" (Brontë 384). Jane's allusion to the biblical book of Genesis (bone of his bone, flesh of his flesh) signals to the reader (if not to Ms. Rigby) that Jane has, in fact, submitted obediently by the end of the novel.[4]

The ways in which Brontë's novel links Jane and Bertha, setting them up as examples of the possible outcomes for headstrong young women in the nineteenth century, have been discussed by various scholars.[5] In these readings, the adult Bertha stands as the logical outcome of uncontrolled, un-Victorian feminine behavior. Rochester describes himself as "a man bound to a wife at once intemperate and unchaste," "cheated" into marrying a "mad" woman, arguably in both the senses of "insane" and of "angry." Jane describes Bertha's laugh as "demoniac" (126, 249, 261). Like Jane in the red room, Bertha cries out from her imprisonment on the third floor of Thornfield Hall—a "savage" and "fearful shriek" that Jane hears in the night (175). But unlike Jane, Bertha is not rescued or released. Bertha exists in Brontë's novel as the unredeemed standard by which Jane's growth will be measured.

Wide Sargasso Sea opens, like *Jane Eyre*, with a young girl's formative experiences and promises the tale of her development into womanhood. However, the protagonist here is a lonely, even somewhat docile Bertha. Born on the island of Jamaica, Antoinette Cosway Mason watches her mother attempt to keep their home and plantation after Antoinette's father's death. Her family endures the antipathy and violence of former slaves after Emancipation, and her mother declines into madness after the death of Antoinette's brother in the fire that burns their house. Alone and vulnerable, Antoinette accepts her stepbrother's arrangement of her marriage to a young British gentleman. This novel depicts how that marriage falls apart, rewriting the story of Bertha's experience at Thornfield Hall largely in Antoinette's voice (as opposed to Jane's). In Rhys's version, Antoinette, like Jane, struggles to "be good" and tries to meet the expectations of those around her in the face of social (and legal) injustices.

Brontë's imagery of "fire and ice"—red rooms, desolate Arctic landscapes, and red and white dresses—reappear in Rhys's novel and are transformed into the imagery of emotional darkness and colonial racial politics. As noted already, Rhys also uses *Jane Eyre*'s central image of the mirror to reiterate Antoinette's connection to Jane and her novel, but in *Wide Sargasso Sea*, the mirror also indicates just how divergent Bertha/Antoinette's *Bildung* (her development, formation, and experiences in the world) will prove. Trapped in the attic at the end of *Wide Sargasso Sea*, Antoinette (now "Bertha" to Rochester) explains that

> there is no looking-glass here and I don't know what I am like now. I remember watching myself brush my hair and how my eyes looked back at me. The girl I saw was myself yet not quite myself. Long ago when I was a child and very lonely I tried to kiss her. But the glass was between us—hard, cold, and misted over with my breath. Now they have taken everything away. What am I doing in this place and who am I? (Rhys 180)

As Gayatri Spivak has noted in a pivotal essay, where *Jane Eyre* sets Jane and Bertha up as doubles and alternatives, Rhys further sets Antoinette against herself; she is her own double, her own awful alternative, the other image that seems no longer herself looking back from the mirror (250). Antoinette here echoes Jane's experience with the distorting and alienating mirror, when she sees the "strange little figure" looking back that she does not recognize as herself; but while Jane's character eventually coheres around a Victorian middle-class ideal, Antoinette's narrative ends with her preparing to destroy Thornfield Hall and herself. Brontë's story of Jane's progress to acceptable middle-class mores becomes Rhys's narrative of Antoinette/Bertha's emotional degeneration and dissolution. Thus, in a crucial sense, *Wide Sargasso Sea* inverts the conventional trajectory of the bildungsroman, instead depicting how and why Antoinette's *Bildung*, unlike Jane's, must fail.[6]

From the outset, the bildungsroman was invested in "notions of linear progress and coherent identity . . . a purposeful youth advancing toward some clarity and stability of being" (Fraiman ix). The bildungsroman—also referred to at different times as the "novel of development," "novel of formation," and "apprenticeship novel," and, more recently, "coming-of-age novel"—emerged in Germany in the late eighteenth century, most visibly in *Wilhelm Meister's Apprenticeship* (1795–96) by Johann Wolfgang von Goethe, and was a prominent European form by the nineteenth century.[7] Derived to some extent from the quest plots of the romance (an important precursor of the novel form), the bildungsroman depicted the development of young middle-class men into "complete" individuals and their entrance into the public and social worlds. The socio-historical context in which this genre developed prized forward movement and psychological growth toward these goals, valuing inevitable progress even in the face of inevitable obstacles. Vehicles for and evidence of reaching these goals, both in European life and in literature, included a particular type of romantic identity, fiscal security, and a suitable wife.

In the traditional bildungsroman, female characters usually indicate various stages in the protagonists' development. They are minor figures who serve to define male *Bildung* (Fraiman 7). In the nineteenth century, this plot trajectory toward independent individuality did not fit easily onto the life of an ordinary, young, middle-class woman. Sandra Gilbert and Susan Gubar famously pointed out in 1979 that Jane's "story, providing a pattern for countless others, is . . . a story of enclosure and escape, a distinctively female *Bildungsroman* in which the problems encountered by the protagonist as she struggles from the imprisonment of her childhood toward an almost unthinkable goal of mature freedom are symptomatic of difficulties Everywoman in a patriarchal society must meet and overcome" (338–39).[8] Jane experiences repeated and thwarted efforts to "move forward" toward the economic and social independence that traditionally motivated the realist bildungsroman narrative. Every time she tries to escape constraining circumstances—at Gateshead Hall and Lowood Institution and, arguably, Thornfield Hall—she finds herself constrained all over again. When Jane leaves Lowood, she dares not even hope for freedom, instead asking only for "a new servitude" (Brontë 72).

The independence at issue in the bildungsroman was generally unavailable to middle-class women, whose conventional path led straight to the private world of marriage and child-rearing, and to a legal and social status that made them subordinate to and dependent upon their husbands. The concepts of primogeniture and entailment decreed that firstborn sons inherited the entire estate from their fathers and precluded women by definition from inheriting or owning property, the most secure source of wealth. Divorce was rare, but when it happened, or when a woman was widowed, she got nothing. Before the Married Women's Property Acts of 1870 and 1882, any property or money that a British woman brought to her marriage immediately became her husband's. Historical realities similarly undermine the concept of "mastery" at issue in the traditional bildungsroman narrative. The conventional male protagonist achieves maturity and gains mastery over himself and his future; he moves from apprentice to authority, a model for actual nineteenth-century middle-class men. The model for a nineteenth-century middle-class woman involved an appropriate marriage, in which her life was largely determined by her husband, who was socially and legally the "master" of the house and of all who lived within it. Being "mistress" of the household inherently involved submission, not authority. One critic has described this model as the life of "a perennial novice" (Fraiman 6).

*Un*married middle-class British women had a similarly limited range of choices about how to live their lives. While in the late eighteenth century a variety of occupations lay open to them, by the mid-nineteenth century, teaching (either in a school, or, like Jane Eyre, as a private governess) and dress- or hat-making were the most acceptable options (Poovey 127). The governess occupied a unique position in Victorian society, where the idea of women having paid careers outside the home breached middle-class values:

> [She was] the one exception to the rule that a well-bred woman did not earn her own living—if a woman of birth and education found herself in financial distress, and had no relatives who could support her or give her a home, she was justified in seeking the only employment that would not cause her to lose her status. She could find work as a governess. The position of governess seems to have been appropriate because, while it was paid employment, it was within the home. The governess was doing something she might have done as a wife under better circumstances. She avoided the immodest and unladylike position of public occupation. (Peterson 14–15)

In 1847, many unmarried middle-class women had "no relatives to support" them, a function of population demographics after the Napoleonic Wars (Peterson 15). At the same time, there were as many as 500,000 more women than men in Britain at mid-century, which meant a raft of unmarried women (Levitan 359). Those who could not find husbands were encouraged to emigrate, specifically to the colonies of the British Empire, where the gender situation was largely reversed.

Daughters of West Indian planters, like Antoinette Mason, presented a slightly different set of problems for the conventions of the bildungsroman, even as these young women appeared to offer a resolution to the economic difficulties of younger middle-class British sons. Since primogeniture and entailment ensured that only first-born sons inherited the family estate, younger sons presented a financial problem. Common solutions to that problem included joining the military or entering various professions. Wealthy wives were another solution, and the colonies provided a source of potential wives, daughters of the European families who had settled in the West Indies and in many cases made extraordinary fortunes from the slave-worked plantations. As Rochester, a second-born son, explains in *Jane Eyre*:

> It was [the elder Rochester's] resolution to keep the property together; he could not bear the idea of dividing his estate and leaving me a fair portion: all, he resolved, should go to my brother Rowland. Yet as little could he endure that a son of his should be a poor man. I must be provided for by a wealthy marriage. He sought me a partner betimes. Mr. Mason, he found, had a son and a daughter; and he learned from him that he could and would give the latter a fortune of thirty thousand pounds; that sufficed. When I left college I was sent out to Jamaica, to espouse a bride already courted for me. (260)

Bertha is thus a means to masculine economic ends, a marker on the path of Rochester's *Bildung*.

We know that Jean Rhys, whose family owned a plantation on the Caribbean island of Dominica,[9] found Charlotte Brontë's choice of Bertha as Jane's double and foil especially interesting. In a 1964 letter about the manuscript for *Wide Sargasso Sea*, Rhys wrote

> I believe and firmly too that there was more than one Antoinette. The West Indies . . . were . . . rich in those days *for* those days and there was no 'married women's property Act.' The girls (very tiresome no doubt) would soon once in kind England be *Address Unknown*. So gossip. So a legend. If Charlotte Brontë took her horrible Bertha from this legend I have a right to take lost Antoinette. (*Letters* 271)

Rhys wanted to recover Bertha from her position within Brontë's text, to pull her from the background of Jane's story and depict more fully and with greater sympathy the "lunatic . . . both cunning and malignant" that *Jane Eyre* rejects in Jane's journey to gain independence, mastery, and love (Brontë 264).[10] "I don't believe anybody has the 'feel' of the West Indies as they were in the 17th 18th and part of 19th century at all. Should say perhaps the 18th, 19th and part of the twentieth," Rhys wrote in 1957 (sic, *Letters* 144).

As a female protagonist, Antoinette Cosway is subject to all the gendered restrictions on the bildungsroman described above. Like Jane, Antoinette is socially and economically trapped and literally imprisoned in both *Jane Eyre* and in *Wide Sargasso Sea*. But if Jane, the middle-class Briton, is trapped by her gender and her class,[11] Rhys wants to make clear that Antoinette is trapped both by her gender and by the colonial status of the West Indies. Rochester tells Christophine, Antoinette's old nurse, who begs Rochester to free the distraught Antoinette and return to England alone, that all of Antoinette's property and money now belong to him, as her husband (Rhys, *WSS* 159). And as Spivak has suggested, when the British husband "violently renames [the West Indian] Bertha, Rhys suggests that so intimate a thing as personal and human identity might be determined by the politics of imperialism" (250). Spivak alludes to Rhys's analogy between the colonial practice of taking foreign lands, renaming them, and exploiting their natural resources for British ends and Rochester's treatment of his Creole wife, whose money he willingly takes while later subjecting her to his will and confining her to his attic.

Writing the West Indies

The nineteenth century saw a whole host of books, some of them coming-of-age tales, that were designed to teach British boys how to be successful imperialists: adventure novels (often about boys growing up on deserted islands) like *Treasure Island* by Robert Louis Stevenson and R. M. Ballantyne's *The Coral Island*, and stories by Captain Marryat, including *Masterman Ready*. These books emerged out of Britain's extensive colonial experience. Its initially lucrative West Indian colonies, established in the seventeenth and eighteenth centuries, had provided a steady and substantial income both for plantation owners and the British treasury, largely thanks to the slave trade, which provided a relatively cheap (if inhumane) source of labor. But when that trade was abolished in 1807, and slavery as a whole abolished in 1833, Britain increasingly focused its colonial efforts elsewhere—in India and Africa in particular. By the end of the nineteenth century, "the sun never set" on the British Empire; its colonial lands were that vast, spread out over every time zone.

Jane Eyre was written as Britain approached the apogee of its Empire, and it is not an accident that Jane compares herself to a "revolted slave" or that she describes Bertha as animal-like (Brontë 250) and her face as "savage." Language comparing Africans to savages and animals—and to children in need of British guidance for their successful "development" into acceptable humans—pervaded the discourse of colonialism and slavery. By becoming more Western, according to British imperial reasoning, slaves and other colonial natives could progress toward a more "adult" form of civilization (despite the fact that many colonized peoples came from civilizations that pre-dated Britain's by thousands of years). In Brontë's portrait of Bertha, *Jane Eyre* engages an entrenched set of ideas in circulation during Brontë's lifetime about colonies and those who inhabit them. Rochester explains to Jane that he "found [Bertha's] nature wholly alien to mine; her tastes obnoxious to me; her cast of mind common, low, narrow, and singularly incapable of being led to anything higher . . . a nature the most gross, impure, depraved I ever saw" (Brontë 261). His descriptions of Bertha's degenerate behavior in *Jane Eyre* manifest a long history of British attitudes toward whites who settled in the "inferior" tropical colonies (as opposed to the more desirable settler colonies in temperate zones like Canada and Australia). Tropical colonies were considered "unsuited to become the homes of white men," a belief that echoes a long paper trail of accounts of Caribbean life by British planters and travelers (Higham 249). The white Creole who lived in such places supposedly was possessed with a degree of supineness and indolence in their affairs, which renders them bad economists, and too frequently hurts their fortune and family. With a strong natural propensity toward the other sex, they are not always the most chaste and faithful of husbands. They are liable to sudden transports of anger; but these fits, like hurricanes, though violent while they last, are soon over and subside into a calm: yet they are not apt to forget or forgive substantial injuries. A lively imagination brings every circumstance present to their remembrance, and agitates them almost as much as if it had occurred but immediately. They are fickle and desultory in their pursuits; though unshaken in their friendships. . . . They are too much addicted to expensive living, costly entertainments, dress, and equipage. (Long 2.2.265)

Another common belief held that Creole women "in warm climates, are given to inordinate desires" (Atwood, qtd. in Raiskin 213). Such eighteenth-century sentiments about the moral (and physical) corruption of white settlers in the West Indies remain in play throughout the nineteenth and twentieth centuries and structure Rochester's relationship with and increasing doubts about his West Indian wife, both in *Jane Eyre* and in *Wide Sargasso Sea*.

Rhys was not alone in her attempt to address such attitudes, nor was she the first to do so. In fact, Edward Long's *The history of Jamaica or, General survey of the antient and modern state of that island* (1774) along with Bryan Edwards's *History, Civil and Commercial, of the British Colonies in the West Indies* (1793–1801) represent early attempts to correct commonplaces about the supposed corruption of white Europeans. Edwards felt, "in common with all the inhabitants of the British West Indies, a just sense of indignation at the malignant and unmerited aspersions which are daily and hourly thrown upon the planters" (I.xii). Long and Edwards objected to claims about the supposed moral degeneration attributed to the effects of West Indian sun. Edwards defended the settlers' character: "I cannot . . . admit that the Creoles in general possess less capacity and stability of mind than the natives of Europe, much less can I allow that they fall short of them in qualities of the heart which render a man a blessing to all around him." "Indolence," he acknowledged, "is too predominant among" Creoles, but "that they are deficient in personal courage, no man, who has the smallest acquaintance with them, will allow for a moment." Rather than succumbing to "those midnight assemblies and gambling conventions, wherein health, fortune, and beauty are so frequently sacrificed in the cities of Europe," Creole women in particular practice "an habitual temperance and self-denial" (II. 15, 16, 12). Nonetheless, colonial analysts and historians were still trotting out a variety of indictments against West Indian Creoles more than a century later.

Wide Sargasso Sea responds specifically to *Jane Eyre*'s imagery, to the history of British literature more generally, and to the cultural history of Empire. As one critic has put it, turning to the colonial beginnings of Rochester's marriage allows Rhys to illustrate how "Rochester maps out the process by which English men and women are made" and shows "how difference—the difference between English and Creole, white and black, man and woman—organizes what we know and how we know it" (Ciolkowski 343). On his honeymoon, Rochester comments on his wife's "Long, sad, dark, alien eyes. Creole of pure English descent she may be, but they are not English or European either?" (Rhys, *WSS* 67). Rochester's sense of Antoinette as "alien" in *Wide Sargasso Sea* alludes to a central paradox in Britain's relations with its colonies: these were places that Britain claimed as "ours" but that it simultaneously saw as inherently, and insurmountably, different—as "perennial novices," in fact. Colonies were places in some sense created by Britain but ultimately rejected as not British enough.

Just before returning to Britain with Antoinette, Rhys's Rochester describes his wife as "only a ghost. A ghost in the daylight. Nothing left but hopelessness. . . . She lifted her eyes. Blank lovely eyes. Mad eyes. A mad girl" (*WSS* 170). Rhys's novel connects *Jane Eyre*'s Bertha—the "ghost" that Antoinette has become—to the West Indian *zombi*. According to a book that Rochester finds in his West Indian bedroom, presumably written by a white European, "*A zombi is a dead person who seems to be alive or a living person who is dead. A zombi can also be the spirit of a place, usually malignant but sometimes can be propitiated*" (Rhys, *WSS* 107; emphasis original). Rhys suggests throughout *Wide Sargasso Sea* that Creoles like Antoinette and her mother are cultural zombies, the dead remnants of European identity living in and wandering among what remains of the British Empire in the West Indies. Rhys implies that the story of British imperialism is not one of "backward" colonies "maturing," but of lives and growth stifled and repressed, if never successfully. At the end of *Wide Sargasso Sea*, Antoinette is poised to burn down the English country house—long a metaphor for a functioning British nation—just as the former West Indian slaves burned her family's plantation house, another symbol of British "superiority." The corrosive ideas about West Indian Creoles existed long before the character called Bertha was "born" in 1847 and persisted after her fictional death. And rather than "maturing" into docile replicas of "advanced" Western nations like Britain, the West Indian colonies rebelled. They were beginning to gain independence while Rhys was writing *Wide Sargasso Sea*. But the problems wrought by the legacy of British colonialism persist even today. *Wide Sargasso Sea* asks readers to question the ideas of progress and development that lay behind the imperial enterprise.

History and Literary Form

The ideas at stake in the bildungsroman (personal, social, and historical progress) are thus evident in the content of *Jane Eyre* and *Wide Sargasso Sea*. However, the parallel between the bildungsroman's and the British Empire's interests in advancement—and the challenges to those interests—are also evident in the novels' form. *Jane Eyre* begins with Jane as a young girl and proceeds chronologically through her life, culminating in her successful marriage to Rochester. The many obstacles that thwart the expectations and conventions of the bildungsroman in Brontë's novel discussed above nonetheless occur with an organizing principle—linear development—central to the genre in the nineteenth century.

Wide Sargasso Sea initially may appear to conform to this structure as well. This novel begins during Antoinette's childhood and proceeds chronologically through her marriage and relocation to Thornfield Hall. However, Antoinette's three dreams interrupt and complicate that chronology. Alluding to Jane's dreams in the 1847 novel (Brontë 240–41), Antoinette's dreams specifically prefigure events that have yet to take place in her life. Some of them will take place, not in this book, but in *Jane Eyre*, a book written in a different time, by a different author. After her mother marries Mr. Mason, Antoinette dreams that she is in Jamaica "walking in the forest. Not alone. Someone who hated me was with me" (Rhys, *WSS* 26). Antoinette seems to anticipate her troubled relationship with Rochester. In her second dream, after Mr. Mason has arranged her forthcoming marriage, the Jamaican forest turns into "an enclosed garden, surrounded by a stone wall and the trees are different trees" (Rhys, *WSS* 60). Here Antoinette dreams about an English garden that she has yet to see. The third dream takes place in Thornfield Hall, a place that originates in another book, written years before Rhys's. In fact, Spivak has pointed out that Antoinette, a literary character created in the 1960s, *knows* that she is a character in that other book written in the 1840s (Spivak 250–51):

> Their world . . . is, as I always knew, made of cardboard. I have seen it somewhere before, this cardboard world where everything is coloured brown or dark red or yellow that has no light in it. As I walk along the passages I wish I could see what is behind the cardboard. They tell me I am in England but I don't believe them. (Rhys, *WSS* 180–81)

"The cardboard world" is the space bounded by a book's covers, and Antoinette *has seen it before* because, as a creation of the 1960s, she, like the reader, has access to that old book, and knows the other version of her life. Rhys undermines the chronological, linear trajectory of literary history (the later book's story precedes the earlier one's) and the linear chronology of a bildungsroman (Antoinette's fictional life is ruled and shadowed by events that are represented out of sequence and that erupt into the later book). *Wide Sargasso Sea* further challenges the conventions of fiction itself: the realist illusion that characters in a book represent actual people crumbles once Antoinette understands that she is a literary character whose "world" and experiences occur within and are defined by *books*. Breaking this illusion forces readers to consider what she represents, not who she supposedly is. *Wide Sargasso Sea* ends with Antoinette telling us about her third dream, which she says "has ended" (187). In the dream, she has already burned Thornfield Hall. In the last paragraph of Rhys's novel, she is about to act on her dream and burn Thornfield down but does not complete the act. The fire actually occurs only in Brontë's version. Antoinette's story, like those of the colonies she represents, does not end in Rhys's novel. What will happen to Antoinette, what her story's conclusion might be, isn't provided here. Only British literary history and a more conventional coming-of-age novel presume to do that.

Notes

1. With the Act of Union in 1707, the distinct geographic regions of England, Scotland, and Wales became a single political entity. However, it is still common (although problematic) to see the terms "England' and "Britain" used interchangeably.

2. Rochester calls the character "Bertha" throughout *Jane Eyre*, and according to legal documents produced by Richard Mason, her legal name is "Bertha Antoinette Mason" (Brontë 247). In *Wide Sargasso Sea*, Antoinette Cosway becomes Antoinette Mason when her mother remarries after her father's death. Rochester insists on calling her Bertha, a name she dislikes. In this essay, I will use "Bertha" when referring to *Jane Eyre*, "Antoinette" when referring to *Wide Sargasso Sea*, and "Bertha/Antoinette" when referring to both.

3. The term later came to designate racial and social mixture—the offspring of planters and slaves, for instance, or any mixed-race West Indian.

4. Nonetheless, critics have debated just how "conventional" the ending is. Gilbert and Gubar, for example, claim that Jane's newly acquired fortune and Roches-

ter's infirmities place Jane and her husband on equal footing, thus undermining "convention" (368–69).

5. See, e.g., Chase, Gilbert and Gubar, Baer, Williams, Thorpe, and Grudin.

6. Caroline Rody would disagree with the idea that *Wide Sargasso Sea* ultimately depicts failure, arguing instead that the novel changes readers' relationship to Bertha's story and thus encourages new kinds of feminist literary criticism (318).

7. Useful summaries of the bildungsroman tradition include Bakhtin, Moretti, and the Introductions to Abel et al. and Fraiman.

8. There are a number of critical studies of the "female bildungsroman." In addition to Gilbert and Gubar and Fraiman, see, e.g., Ellis, and Abel et al.

9. The region referred to in the twentieth and twenty-first centuries as "the Caribbean" was known as "the West Indies" throughout the sixteenth through nineteenth centuries, because Christopher Columbus stumbled upon them on a voyage to the East Indies (i.e., Southeast Asia). In this essay, I use the term "West Indies" when referring to the novels and to the eighteenth and nineteenth centuries.

10. At the same time, Rhys made it clear that "I have a very great and deep admiration for the Brontë sisters . . . How then can *I* of all people, say she was wrong? Or that her Bertha is impossible? *Which she is*" (*Letters* 271).

11. Important discussions of class in *Jane Eyre* include Eagleton and Fraiman.

Works Cited

Abel, Elizabeth, Marianne Hirsch, and Elizabeth Langland. Introduction. *The Voyage In: Fictions of Female Development*. Hanover, NH: UP of New England, 1983. 3–22.

Baer, Elizabeth R. "The Sisterhood of Jane Eyre and Antoinette Cosway." *The Voyage In: Fictions of Female Development*. Hanover, NH: UP of New England, 1983. 131–48.

Bakhtin, Mikhail. "The *Bildungsroman* and Its Significance in the History of Realism (Toward a Historical Typology of the Novel)." *Speech Genres and Other Late Essays*. Trans. Vern W. McGee. Ed. Caryl Emerson and Michael Holquist. Austin: U of Texas P, 1986.

Brontë, Charlotte. *Jane Eyre*. 1847. Ed. Richard J. Dunn. New York: Norton, 2001.

Chase, Richard. "The Brontës; or, Myth Domesticated." *Forms of Modern Fiction: Essays Collected in Honor of Joseph Warren Beach*. Ed. William Van O'Connor. Minneapolis: U of Minnesota P, 1948. 102–19.

Ciolkowski, Laura E. "Navigating the *Wide Sargasso Sea*: Colonial History, English Fiction, and British Empire." *Twentieth Century Literature* 43.3 (Oct. 1997), 339–59.

Eagleton, Terry. *Myths of Power: A Marxist Study of the Brontës*. New York: Barnes & Noble, 1975.

Edwards, Bryan. *The History, Civil and Commercial, of the British Colonies in the West Indies*. London: Stockdale, 1793–1801.

Ellis, Lorna. *Appearing to Diminish: Female Development and the British Bildungsroman 1750–1850*. Lewisburg: Bucknell UP, 1999.

Fraiman, Susan. *Unbecoming Women: British Women Writers and the Novel of Development*. New York: Columbia UP, 1993.

Gilbert, Sandra, and Susan Gubar. *The Madwoman in the Attic: The Woman Writer and the Nineteenth-Century Literary Imagination*. New Haven: Yale UP, 1979.

Grudin, Peter. "Jane and the Other Mrs. Rochester: Excess and Restraint in *Jane Eyre*" *NOVEL: A Forum on Fiction* 10.2 (1977): 145–57.

Higham, C. S. S. *History of the British Empire*. New York: Longmans, 1921.

Levitan, Kathrin. "Redundancy, the 'Surplus Woman' Problem, and the British Census 1851–61." *Women's History Review* 17.3 (July 2008): 359–76.

Long, Edward. *The history of Jamaica or, General Survey of the Antient and Modern State of that Island: With Reflections on Its Situation, Settlements, Inhabitants, Climate, Products, Commerce, Laws, and Government*. 3 vols. London: Lowndes, 1774.

Peterson, M. Jeanne. "The Victorian Governess: Status Incongruence in Family and Society." *Victorian Studies* 14.1 (Sept. 1970): 7–26.

Poovey, Mary. *Uneven Developments: The Ideological Work of Gender in Mid-Victorian England*. Chicago: U of Chicago P, 1988.

Raiskin, Judith L., ed. *Wide Sargasso Sea*. (Norton Critical Ed.) By Jean Rhys. New York, Norton, 1999.

Rhys, Jean. "Interview." *The Guardian* 8 Aug. 1968: 5.

_____. *Letters, 1931–1966*. Ed. Francis Wyndham and Diana Melly. London: Deutsch, 1984.

_____. *Wide Sargasso Sea*. 1966. New York: Norton, 1982.

Rigby, Elizabeth. "*Vanity Fair*—and *Jane Eyre*." *Quarterly Review* 84 (Dec. 1848): 153–85.

Rody, Caroline. "Burning Down the House: The Revisionary Paradigm of Jean Rhys's *Wide Sargasso Sea*." *Famous Last Words: Changes in Gender and Narrative Closure*. Ed. Alison Booth. Charlottesville: U of Virginia P, 1993.

Spivak, Gayatri. "Three Women's Texts and a Critique of Imperialism." *Critical Inquiry* 12.1 (Autumn 1985): 243–61.

Thorpe, Michael. "'The Other Side': *Wide Sargasso Sea* and *Jane Eyre*. *Ariel* 8.3 (1977): 99–110.

Williams, Judith. *Perception and Expression in the Novels of Charlotte Brontë*. Ann Arbor: UMI Research P, 1988.

CRITICAL READINGS

Coming of Age in Homer's Ithaca_____

William G. Thalmann

Near the end of the *Odyssey*, Odysseus has the last of a series of re-unions with members of his family, this one with his aged father Laertes. As in most of the poem's recognition scenes, Laertes cannot be sure that the man he sees is really his son, who has been gone from Ithaca for twenty years. So he demands proof. Odysseus offers two tokens: the scar on his thigh from a boar's tusk, and the trees in the orchard where he and Laertes are standing:

> . . . these trees—
> let me tell you the trees you gave me years ago,
> here on this well-worked plot [. . .]
> I begged you for everything I saw, a little boy
> trailing you through the orchard, picking our way
> among these trees, and you named them one by one.
> You gave me thirteen pear, ten apple trees
> and forty figs—and promised to give me, look,
> fifty vinerows, bearing hard on each other's heels,
> clusters of grapes year-round at every grade of ripeness,
> mellowed as Zeus's seasons weigh them down. (24.336–43; pp. 47–79)[1]

Here we have a glimpse of Odysseus as a boy following his father around the farm, long before he became a man famed for his exploits in the Trojan War and on the difficult ten-year journey home. We are reminded of his life's trajectory from childhood through the transition to adulthood, and then through the gaining of experience, skill, and maturity, to this moment when, once he has dealt with the dead suitors' kinsmen, he can look ahead to a peaceful old age.

The trees—we will discuss the scar later—are Odysseus's patri-mony, having passed to him when he replaced his father as head of the family and household (as he seems to have done before he left for Troy). And so they are a material expression of Odysseus's social identity, which is centered on the household in the society Homer depicts. They are also a token of legitimate succession within the family from one generation of males to another (patrilineal succession). Soon after this reunion, males of three generations, representing three age groups, will stand together in armor to fight the suitors' relatives: Laertes, magically (and temporarily) rejuvenated by Athena; Odysseus; and Odysseus's son Telemachus, who has just had his first battle experience the day before and has taken an important step to full manhood. Laertes exclaims, "What a day for me, dear gods! What joy— / my son and my grandson vying over courage!" (24.514–15; p. 484). It is not only property that is passed from one generation to another, but also a code of attitudes and behavior; for the elite in a class society like the one Homer depicts, property and values go together.

Within the family, and in Homeric society generally, there are hierarchies of age and gender and clearly defined roles that depend on where a person belongs in those hierarchies. Recognizing what these roles are is important to understanding the process of coming of age in the *Odyssey*. Old men are not expected to be physically active, but they are honored for their experience and wisdom; younger men receive their advice with marked deference, although the epics are attentive to the afflictions of old age as well (Falkner 5–14). Their mature sons are expected to sustain the elderly and protect them from enemies. A man in his prime has unquestioned authority over his family members, slaves, and other dependants. He represents his household in society at large. He maintains and adds to its honor in various kinds of competition with other men. He increases its wealth and standing by overseeing farm work, by winning booty in wars and raids on neighboring communities, and by exchanging gifts with elite men from other regions.

A married woman is active within the house, where she oversees the household chores carried out by slaves and produces clothing for the family by weaving. She is expected to maintain a reputation for sexual chastity in order to preserve the family's honor and ensure the legitimacy of sons. For this reason she rarely leaves the house or appears before men who are not relatives. The exchange of girls in marriage creates alliances among families. Upon marriage—which, at least in later periods, could happen shortly after puberty—the bride goes to live in her husband's house. Before marriage, it seems, the girl, like her mother, stays mainly in the house and learns skills like weaving and doing laundry. In his early years a boy evidently is raised mainly by women, especially his mother and a nurse. But as he approaches adolescence he is taught by older men—not necessarily only his father—"to be a speaker of words and a doer of deeds" (*Iliad* 9.443). The *Odyssey* is attentive to these roles as part of its overarching concern to depict society at peace, define its values, and show their importance. The poem shows us why, after its hero's adventures with a ten-year war and various monsters, natural hazards, and seductive nymphs, a quiet life at home is a prize to be struggled for. The depiction of young people making the transition from childhood to adulthood in socially prescribed ways is an integral part of these larger themes.

As tokens of identity and succession, the trees in the orchard suggest the passage of time and the reproduction of society over time through generations. But at the beginning of the poem this process seems to have been blocked on Ithaca. Two decades have passed since Odysseus left, but there has been no purposeful activity. Its lack is perfectly expressed by Penelope's weaving of a shroud for Laertes by day and unraveling it at night. Life seems almost suspended. She is in a stalemate with her suitors, who engage in the same round of amusements and feasting day after day. Laertes has retired to his farm, and there is no political activity (there have been no public assemblies for twenty years). All Penelope can do is to keep the household going in case Odysseus returns; preservation is essentially the woman's role, and her husband, who is responsible for economic and social reproduction, is absent (Foley 13–14). Odysseus is trapped on Calypso's island, longing for home "since the nymph no longer pleased" (5.153;

p. 157). Telemachus seems thwarted as well. Unable to succeed Odysseus as head of the house without certainty that he is dead, responsible by default for dealing with the suitors but helpless against them, and ambivalent about the prospect of his mother's remarriage, Telemachus seems trapped in an artificially prolonged childhood even though he is old enough to start the transition to an adult status and role.[2] Odysseus has been absent for Telemachus's whole life, and with only the negative example of the suitors, Telemachus has no one to help him make the transition to adulthood (van Nortwick 28, 30).

Athena sets everything in motion at the beginning of the poem, and the passage of time becomes meaningful again. Not only does she prod Zeus to make Calypso release Odysseus (5.7–42; pp. 152–53); her first action narrated in the poem is a visit to Ithaca, disguised as an old friend of Odysseus, in order to rouse Telemachus from his frustrated idleness. The scene brilliantly portrays a youth who is between childhood and maturity, with impulses in both directions. We are introduced to Telemachus when Athena arrives at Odysseus's house:

> First by far to see her was Prince Telemachus,
> sitting among the suitors, heart obsessed with grief.
> He could almost see his magnificent father, here [. . .]
> in the mind's eye—if only *he* might drop from the clouds
> and drive these suitors all in a rout throughout the halls
> and regain his pride of place and rule his own domains!
> Daydreaming so as he sat among the suitors,
> he glimpsed Athena now . . . (1.113–18; p. 81)

Athena appears literally as the fulfillment of his dreams; ultimately, the events she is setting in motion will result in the killing of the suitors. But notice what he is daydreaming about: not what *he* might do to avenge himself on these usurpers, but about his father coming home and enacting bloody vengeance. Telemachus wants his father to solve his problems for him, and his dream is one of continued childlike dependency. Athena will play skillfully on this tendency as part of her strategy to nudge him toward adulthood (1.253–66; pp. 85–86).

But Telemachus immediately begins to fill a man's role. Seeing a stranger at the door, he brings him (Athena in male disguise) in, gives him food, inquires about his identity, and engages in conversation with him, in a scene that follows the pattern of typical hospitality sequences in the *Odyssey*. Giving hospitality was the duty of the adult head of the household. The suitors, however, are feasting there too. Telemachus has to hold his head near his guest's so that they cannot hear his words, implying that he is not fully in control of the house; still, he starts to fill in for his father.

Athena encourages him to take decisive action, partly by arousing an image of Odysseus in his mind and commenting on his own resemblance to his father, and partly by giving him practical advice after he complains about his situation. Tomorrow, she suggests, call an assembly and publicly order the suitors to leave your house; if your mother wants to remarry, send her back to her father's house so that he can marry her off; sail in search of news about Odysseus; if you hear that he is alive, come home and hold out for another year; if you find out that he is dead, come home and erect a tomb for him, give your mother to a new husband, and plot vengeance on the suitors (1.271–96; pp. 86–87). This is not entirely coherent advice, but it gets Telemachus started. "You must not cling to your boyhood any longer," she goes on; "it's time you were a man." And then she holds up to him the example of Orestes, who, after spending his boyhood in exile, returned and killed his mother Clytemnestra and her lover Aegisthus in revenge for their murder of his father Agamemnon, the leader of the expedition against Troy. As often happens in Homer, Athena uses an exemplary story to illustrate an ideal of conduct, urging Telemachus to live up to it. This is how to be a man: Be prepared to use violence if necessary to restore your family's integrity and honor after a deeply dishonoring crime against it.

Athena departs, but her words have clearly had an effect (Millar and Carmichael 60). Phemius the bard begins a song about the disastrous returns of the Achaeans from Troy (a subject of other epic poems), and Penelope, hearing it from her room, comes downstairs in tears and orders him to sing about something else (Odysseus is still suffering the most difficult of all returns from Troy). Telemachus intervenes, telling her that Zeus, not Phemius, is to blame for mortal sufferings. The singer was just doing his job: people like the newest songs. He then tells her to go back to her room and take care of her weaving. "As for giving orders, / men will see to that, but I most of all: / I hold the reins of power in this house" (1.358–59; p.89; the word translated "giving orders" can also mean "storytelling"). Astonished, Penelope obeys her newly assertive son. The scene beautifully captures a late adolescent's impatience with his mother (something not unknown today), which reflects both the process of his separation from her as he matures and his need for further growth.

Telemachus continues to assert himself. After Penelope leaves, he tells the suitors to go on feasting for now (he is again claiming authority in the house, although he is powerless to make them stop), and announces that tomorrow he will call an assembly to complain publicly about their behavior. "They all bit their lips, / amazed the prince could speak with so much daring" (1.381–82; p. 90). They are surprised at his new resistance and amused, bullies that they are, because they know he can do nothing as a single person against 108 of them. Prompted by Athena, then, Telemachus has taken the first steps toward assuming an adult role as head of the household. He still has a long way to go before he can make his claims stick, but the seeds are planted here that will blossom into his fighting the suitors alongside Odysseus.

The assembly scene in book 2 can be seen in the same light. By calling the assembly Telemachus is taking on a man's role in the community as well as the household, and it is an important detail that he sits in his father's seat (2.14; p. 93). The assembly accomplishes nothing if its goal is to get the suitors out of the house. But it is a public performance of claim and counterclaim by Telemachus and the suitors, and Telemachus puts the Ithacan community on notice that there is an injustice in his house that the people are abetting by doing nothing about it. What emerges is a public demonstration of the suitors' wrongdoing, reinforced by the omen of their destruction and the suitor Eurymachus's bluster against Halitherses, who interpreted the omen (2.146–207; pp. 98–99). Telemachus ends his first speech by throwing down the speaker's staff and bursting into tears (2.80–81; p. 95), but that is not necessarily childish behavior: Homeric heroes weep unashamedly, and in the first book of the *Iliad* Achilles, the greatest of them all, throws the speaker's staff to the ground during his quarrel with Agamemnon (*Iliad* 1.245–46). Telemachus's behavior might be part of his performance, meant to arouse his audience's sympathy, although we might wonder how skillful this tactic really is. Achilles ultimately makes his claims against Agamemnon stick, but Telemachus is no Achilles. He has not persuaded the Ithacans to take action, as his father, a consummately clever speaker, might have done. But Telemachus has begun to achieve a social identity; he has stood up to the suitors in public argument and acquitted himself, on the whole, rather well.

Telemachus, it seems, has entered a "liminal" or "threshold" state, in which a boy, having "radically detache[d] himself from his mother and the female-dominated world of his childhood," "identifies with his father and his father's world and absorbs ancestral traditions, rehearsing and eventually consolidating his role as a male adult" (Felson 70). In many premodern societies, rituals of initiation help boys make this transition. In these, the boy typically leaves home and women, goes out into a wild or at least unfamiliar region with other males, undergoes various trials or ordeals in which he might be wounded, and returns ready to assume a socially prescribed masculine role and behavior (Felson 70). Many scholars have argued that the journey on which Athena sends Telemachus in books 3 and 4, in exclusively male company (the crew of his ship, Athena in disguise as Mentor, and eventually Nestor's son

Pisistratus), is initiatory in nature (see especially Eckert, as well as Clarke 141–45).

Measured by one of its goals, the success of this trip is decidedly mixed. All Telemachus learns about his father is that, as Menelaus tells him, the sea god Proteus saw him stranded on Calypso's island (4.556–60; p.142). This information is no help to Telemachus in deciding what to do about the situation at home. But Athena has another reason for sending him on his voyage, as she says several times: so that he can gain *kleos*, "fame" or "glory." *Kleos* is what every Homeric hero strives for: to gain renown that will live on after death, enshrined in stories told by, for example, singers of epic poems (as Telemachus's fame is preserved in the *Odyssey*). The usual way of gaining *kleos* is through exploits on the battlefield, or by struggling home against massive obstacles and killing interlopers in one's house. But it seems that the arts of peace are also important: knowing how to deal with others in ways that earn their respect, thereby gaining honor, and manipulating social conventions in order to surpass others in various kinds of competition. This, at least, is the way men get *kleos*; women earn it by chastity and loyalty to their husbands, as Penelope does (24.192–202; p. 474). Odysseus is famed as both a warrior and a consummate social actor; and it is this latter skill that Telemachus gets an opportunity to learn and practice on his journey. Fighting will come later, against the suitors in book 22.

Telemachus visits Nestor (book 3) and Menelaus (book 4), friends of Odysseus and his comrades at Troy. Telemachus renews his father's relationships with them. That is, he substitutes for his father if Odysseus is alive, or replaces him if Odysseus is dead. He is, then, not only acting as an individual but also representing his family. This is another, and significant, step toward manhood. In the process, he is challenged to act in a way that fulfills this role well, and his hosts will measure him by their knowledge of Odysseus. Hospitality (as either guest or host), gift exchange, and guest-friendship are basic elements of elite society in Homer, because through them social relationships are created or renewed and each participant enacts a social identity. This is why becoming known outside Ithaca, and particularly to these prominent heroes, and measuring up to their standards will give Telemachus *kleos*.

Guest-friendship needs some explanation. It is a form of "ritualized friendship" (Herman) that is based in hospitality. One man (and it is a relationship between men) gives hospitality to another. When the guest leaves, the two exchange gifts (this is separate from the guest-gifts that a host routinely gives his departing guest) and clasp hands. The gifts are saved as tokens of an enduring relationship. The host can call on his former guest for hospitality if he ever travels to the latter's community, and each can call on his guest-friend for other kinds of help. Agamemnon and Menelaus drew on networks of guest-friendship when they raised the expedition against Troy, and Athena appears to Telemachus in book 1 disguised as Odysseus's guest-friend Mentes (1.187–90; p. 83). This relationship is passed down from father to son, as "Mentes" says he and Odysseus inherited their friendship from their fathers, so that time and succession are important here. Telemachus, as a son who will succeed Odysseus now or later, steps into his father's relationships. This is the context within which we should understand his visits to Nestor and Menelaus.

When they have arrived in Pylos and are about to approach Nestor, Athena/Mentor tells Telemachus not to be shy. Telemachus replies (in my translation):

> Mentor, how shall I go up to him? How shall I greet him?
> I am not yet experienced in closely reasoned speeches.
> And a youth feels shy about questioning an older man. (3.22–24)

In Homeric epics, the Greek word translated here as "shy" implies an anticipation of social disapproval that keeps people from crossing the boundaries of acceptable behavior. Telemachus might justly shrink from the presumption of approaching Nestor as an equal. We should remember the age hierarchy in Homeric society. Its effect is magnified here because Telemachus is about to have social dealings with a legendary hero, one who has outlived three generations and embodies the heroic tradition. His feelings may strike us as exaggerated, because our society holds old age and social standards in far less reverence. But Telemachus, lacking the confidence that an older man experienced in such transactions would feel, is facing a serious challenge, which stands as his introduction to conducting social relations by speaking appropriately.

And he passes the test! After a meal, Nestor asks who his guests are, and Athena inspires Telemachus with confidence "to ask for the news about his father, gone so long, / and make his name throughout the mortal world" (3.77–78; pp. 111–12). In the second line, Athena literally says, "and so that noble *kleos* attends him among humankind." At this critical moment, we are reminded of what this conversation means for Telemachus's maturation. Telemachus replies with a courteous speech, identifying himself as Odysseus's son and describing his mission, and he asks Nestor for news of his father (3.79–101; p.110). Nestor replies with a long speech that begins by describing the hardships at Troy and then Odysseus's distinguished role in the war, especially his cunning. He continues,

> Your father, yes, if you are in fact his son . . .
> I look at you and a sense of wonder takes me.
> Your way with words—it's just like his—I'd swear
> no youngster could ever speak like you, so apt, so telling.
> (3.123–25; p.111)

So Nestor acknowledges Telemachus as a worthy son—high praise from so revered a figure. At the same time, the last line implies that youth cannot rival age in speaking ability; Telemachus has distinguished himself—for a young man. Nestor ends his speech with an implied challenge to Telemachus, by mentioning Orestes' revenge of his father—a story he goes on to elaborate at Telemachus's request.

Once again a paradigm is held up to him of a youth who matured by taking on a painful duty (as his society defines it) and succeeding (see Eckert 56).

Nestor sends Telemachus, along with his own son Pisistratus, to Sparta, where he visits Menelaus. Again he acquits himself well, even though Pisistratus at first speaks for him after Helen recognizes him by his resemblance to Odysseus (4.138–67; pp. 128–29). At one point Menelaus compliments him on his appropriate speech ("good blood runs in you, dear boy, your words are proof," 4.611; p. 143). Telemachus also meets Menelaus's wife Helen, the most beautiful woman in the world and the cause, through her adultery with Paris, of the Trojan War. He seems to get exposed here to mature female sexuality (Felson 83)—an important step in a society in which men and women who are not kin see relatively little of each other. In the same way, through his contacts with Nestor and Menelaus, and through their stories about Odysseus, Telemachus is introduced to the masculine role models that have been missing in his life on Ithaca (Austin, "Telemachos" 56–57; Clark 133; van Nortwick 29, 32–33).

The narrative leaves Telemachus as the guest of Menelaus until book 15, when Athena urges him to set sail for home (Odysseus is now on Ithaca and she is engineering their reunion). After book 4, the focus shifts to Odysseus himself. There are many parallels between Odysseus's experiences in books 8–12 and those of Telemachus on his travels; both, for example, weep at the arousal of painful memories in their hosts' houses and hold their cloaks over their faces to hide their tears (4.113–16; p. 128, 8.83–86; p.194). In part, these parallels emphasize Telemachus's likeness to his father and his growing maturity. But there is a highly significant contrast. Just when Odysseus is on his way home, Telemachus travels away from Ithaca to the wider world. Whatever he will do in life is still before him; Odysseus, with his extraordinary accomplishments, is ready to come home (his killing of the suitors will cap his heroic career). The two voyages contrast youth developing into manhood with a maturity that has been tested over time—two distinct stages in a masculine life.

Two anecdotes about Odysseus's youth suggest that Telemachus is undergoing maturation experiences like those of his father before him and emphasize the theme of generational succession over time. The first has already been mentioned: the story of how Odysseus got his scar (19.392–466; pp. 403–5). His experience shows all the features of initiation. The young Odysseus left his home and society for the wilds, underwent a test or ordeal (the hunt), and returned changed and ready to assume an adult role (his new status is marked on his body by a scar). As we have seen, the narrative of Telemachus's journey also has overtones of male initiation. The other anecdote about the young Odysseus is the story of how he got the bow with which he will kill the suitors (21.13–41; p. 424). While still a young boy, he was sent by his father, Laertes, and the elders to collect a debt that the community of Messenians owed to the Ithacans. There he met Iphitus, son of the famous archer Eurytus, and formed a relation of guest-friendship with him. His gift from Iphitus was Eurytus's bow. Telemachus's mission in the interest of his household is roughly similar to Odysseus's public mission, and like his father he engages in his own right in formal social relations with members of other communities. In both stories, boys about to enter manhood carry out adult responsibilities and practice their future roles in society. Both missions are public displays of maturation.

Telemachus seems a young version of Odysseus, then, whereas his youthful expedition is the inverse of the mature Odysseus's journey home. In the last stage of that journey, Odysseus meets a female version of Telemachus: Nausicaa, the daughter of the Phaeacian ruler Alcinous (Belmont 3–9). Nausicaa is also a late adolescent making the transition to adulthood (with prompting by Athena), but she is preparing herself for the role that Homeric society prescribes for women: marriage, and the management of a household that goes with it.

Athena contrives Nausicaa's trip to the river mouth and seashore so that she will meet the outcast Odysseus and help him. The goddess sets events in motion by appearing to Nausicaa in a dream, and she plays on the girl's expectations about marriage:

> Look at your fine clothes, lying here neglected—
> with your marriage not far off,
> the day you should be decked in all your glory
> and offer elegant dress to those who form your escort.
> That's how a bride's good name goes out across the world
> and it brings her father and queenly mother joy. (6.26–30; p. 169)

When Nausicaa asks her father for a mule cart to take the laundry to the shore, she mentions only her brothers' need for clean clothes. She is too shy to bring up her own marriage, but Alcinous understands what is on her mind (6.66–67; p. 170)—naturally, for from the perspective of Homeric society, what else would a girl her age be thinking about?

Nausicaa's "journey" to the seashore is the female counterpart of Telemachus's voyage to Pylos and Sparta. Nausicaa leaves the city, with its clearly prescribed codes of conduct, and travels to a marginal place—a margin literally between land and sea and therefore between human civilization and untamed nature. There she confronts an unusual situation that calls forth certain qualities in her and allows her to practice an adult role. Her return to the city is a little different from her departure, because she brings a prospective husband with her. Whether or not we want to call this experience initiatory, it at least suggests a pattern of departure, a maturing experience, and a return, with the girl ready to be incorporated into society as an adult—that is, through marriage. Nausicaa's experience may seem tame, but possible dangers lurk under the surface. That these do not materialize is due to her and Odysseus's deft behavior, just as Telemachus is tested in dealings with others.

When Nausicaa plays ball with her slave women while the laundry dries, an elaborate simile compares them to Artemis and her nymphs (6.102–9; pp. 171–72). Artemis was the virgin goddess of the hunt who was accompanied in the wild by an exclusively female band of nymphs. So the simile implies virginity and a sheltered female society inaccessible to men. But Artemis was also associated with the margins and was patroness of rituals of young people's transition to adult social roles (Vernant 209, 217–19). So, in addition to sexual inviolability, the simile also suggests Nausicaa's prospective transition to mature sexuality in marriage. At this moment, a man emerges from the bushes, naked except for a strategically held olive branch. In Greek myth, when a man or a god meets a girl in the wild, the usual outcome is rape; and this danger is in the background of the situation here, as a contrasting simile emphasizes. Odysseus is compared to a lion driven by hunger in pursuit of cattle, sheep, or deer (6.130–36; p. 172)—helpless animals, as Nausicaa and her maids are helpless before this sexually mature man, with none of the structures of society to protect them. No wonder the slave girls run away.

But Nausicaa stands her ground. Together she and Odysseus create a version of human society in this marginal space by conforming to the institutions and constraints of their culture. Instead of forcing himself on her, Odysseus keeps his distance and formally becomes her suppliant. Nausicaa plays the adult—and usually male—role of accepting the suppliant and helping him (supplication is another essential institution of Homeric society). In the process, both give excellent social performances. Each has a private agenda. Odysseus needs food, clothing, and transport to Ithaca. Nausicaa is interested in him as a possible husband; she makes this explicit to her maids when he emerges from his bath in the river, his appearance enhanced by the ever-busy Athena (6.239–46; p. 176). These objectives are compatible only up to a point, but they unite to get Odysseus to Alcinous's house; and that suffices for now. Each advances his or her interest through a clever use of the conventions of social speech.

In his speech of supplication (6.149–85; pp. 173–74), Odysseus hits all the right notes. He asks if she is a goddess (a compliment to her beauty, although it also is dangerous for mortal men to meet goddesses in the wild). If she is mortal, her parents and brothers are blessed, but even more blessed is the man who will make her his wife. This is obviously a compliment on how well she fits society's ideals for women, but he is also indirectly raising the possibility that she might consider him for a husband. He then compares her to the famous palm tree on the island of Delos where, he says, he stopped when he commanded troops on the expedition that would bring him many trials. Here he hints that he has an interesting story in order to arouse her curiosity, and he conveys to her that he is a person of high standing back home (she would never consider an insignificant outcast for a husband). He then mentions, tantalizingly, his recent experiences and only then asks her directly for help. In return, he wishes her a harmonious marriage, which he describes in famous lines. So clearly defined are the roles for different age groups and genders that Odysseus can look at a girl and know what she is thinking about (just as Alcinous did), and make use of it.

The speech works, and Nausicaa accepts his supplication with a graceful speech of her own. Then, when they are about to leave for the city, she tells Odysseus not to follow her all the way into town for fear of what the sailors on the waterfront will say as they pass (6.255–303; pp. 176–77). This speech is as rich in indirect messages as his was; in fact, she seems to be responding to his hints. "Now who is that tall, handsome stranger Nausicaa has in tow," she imagines a sailor asking (implying, "I find you attractive, Odysseus"). Is he a prospective husband (an obvious suggestion)? Is he a god (a compliment that returns his to her)? She may as well find a stranger, she remarks, since all the best young Phaeacians are wooing her and she pays no attention (in other words, "I'm desirable and so far unattached, but you have competition"). So she tells Odysseus to enter the city after her and ask directions to her father's house. Anyone can point it out—it's the biggest house in town (meaning, "I'm rich"). Without a hint of flirtatiousness and without committing herself to anything, but by ventriloquizing her desires through the supposedly coarse sailors, Nausicaa has let Odysseus know of her interest in him. So, after Alcinous offers her as a wife to Odysseus and he takes the offer of transportation home instead (7.308–33; pp. 189–90), she can bid Odysseus a graceful, if slightly wistful, farewell (8.457–62; p. 206). She has said nothing to be ashamed of, and she has not been explicitly rejected. Like Telemachus, Nausicaa is coming of age by learning to confront the complexities of life and her social world by manipulating that world's codes and conventions in a way that matches the mature Odysseus's skill.

That is the last we hear of Nausicaa. Telemachus's story continues for the remainder of the poem. In book 16, having returned to Ithaca and avoided the suitors' ambush, he is reunited with his father in the swineherd Eumaeus's hut. In books 17–22, he supports Odysseus's intrigue as the latter enters his own house disguised as a beggar and tests the suitors by begging food from them. This demands discretion from Telemachus—he keeps the beggar's identity a secret even from Penelope—skillful deception, and self-control: following Odysseus's orders (16.274–77; p. 347), he restrains his anger when the suitors mistreat his father. Concealment, deception, self-control: these are some of Odysseus's preeminent qualities that Telemachus is now internalizing and may have begun learning from Athena in book 1 (Austin, "Telemachos" 51–63; van Nortwick 33, 39). As before, he appears helpless against the suitors, but this helplessness is at least half an act now that his father is home. His daydream in book 1 is coming true, but with a difference. Odysseus will not fight the suitors by himself; Telemachus will help him, though in a subordinate role.

Another lesson Telemachus learns in these books is the importance of waiting for the opportune time for action, a pervasive theme in the *Odyssey* (Austin, *Archery* 87–88, 251–52). The right time comes in book 21, when Penelope sets the contest of the bow for her hand in marriage. At the beginning of the contest Telemachus tries three times to string Odysseus's bow, and fails. On the fourth try, he could string it but gives up on a signal from his father. To our post-Freudian sensibilities, this is a strikingly Oedipal situation: the son competes with his father for the mother. Potential competition, at least, is very much in the air here, but it is played out harmlessly. Telemachus is his father's equal, yet still his subordinate, and the hierarchy of authority within the family is thus preserved. In book 22, Telemachus fights the suitors at Odysseus's side, and the wound he receives fits the initiatory pattern we have been tracing (Eckert 54). He makes a serious mistake, however; he leaves a storeroom door unlocked and gives the suitors access to weapons. Even after the battle, Telemachus seems neither child nor adult. When he rebukes his mother for being slow to acknowledge Odysseus, she puts him firmly in his place by telling him that she and his father have secret signs by which they will know each other (23.96–110; pp. 458–59). Clearly three is a crowd here. Odysseus tactfully deflects his son by giving him something to do: the arrangement of a false wedding celebration so that the suitors' kin will not learn of their deaths too soon.

What, finally, can we conclude about Telemachus and his coming of age? He never completes the process of maturation during the poem's narrative, and despite the wonderful portrayal of that process, there does seem to be something unheroic about him (Clarke 137–40). His initiatory journey is a very easy and safe one under the vigilant care of Athena (13.420–24; p. 300). On his return he simply eludes the suitors' ambush and is never physically in danger. His wound in the battle with them is a minor one, on the wrist—very different from the gash in the thigh from the boar's tusk that was Odysseus's mark of initiation. The wrist is, in fact, an unheroic place to be wounded; that is where Diomedes wounds the almost comically unwarlike Aphrodite, goddess of love, in the *Iliad* (5.334–40). Perhaps Telemachus is depicted in this way because he must not overshadow his father in the struggle against the suitors (Clarke 137). Possibly the return of Odysseus marks the end of the age of heroes (Martin), and the son represents the beginning of a new and lesser age. Perhaps, more positively, Odysseus's return ushers in an age of peace on Ithaca, and peace demands qualities different from those required in war—the skills at social performance (including deception) that Telemachus has been learning. But these explanations beg a further question: Will Telemachus have the opportunity to grow up completely? Usually, epic heroes die in battle, and their sons compete with their memory; they are supposed to equal or outdo their fathers. What happens when the father returns? Tiresias has told Odysseus that he will live to a comfortable old age, surrounded by his people (11.134–37; p. 253). This does not sound like Laertes' enfeebled retirement. Will Telemachus be allowed to grow into the responsibilities of being Odysseus's successor?

In her splendid chapter on Telemachus, Nancy Felson argues that he will complete his maturation, and she suggests, appealingly, that when Telemachus chooses not to string the bow "he . . . provides a new paradigm for coming of age. It is more manly, his action asserts, to cooperate with your father than to compete with him" (86). Strong arguments can be made for this point of view. A slightly different perspective is that, although the text may be intended to suggest that he will come of age without difficulty, that moment with the bow exposes a problem that never gets resolved (Clarke 136–37; Thalmann 206–23). If Telemachus accepts a subordinate position now, will he ever not be subordinate until Odysseus's death, many years later? And can the competition latent in the father-son relationship be so easily overcome?

The *Odyssey* would not be the rich and challenging text it is if it were not open-ended in this and other ways. And poems do us good service by moving us to reflect on problems without necessarily arriving at complete resolution.

Notes

1. Except where noted, all translations from the *Odyssey* are by Robert Fagles. Passages are cited first by book and line number of the Greek text and then by Fagles's page number (his line numbers are different from those of the original).

2. How old is Telemachus? He must be at least between twenty and twenty-one, given the length of his father's absence, but he seems much younger. In Greece boys typically made the transition to adulthood in their late teens, around seventeen or eighteen. Possibly Telemachus's development has been arrested because of his situation and the lack of male role models. But Penelope says a beard has just begun to appear on his cheeks (18.269; p. 3840), and that would make him a teenager. I think we have to accept a contradiction here; but its existence shows how important it is to the poem to show Telemachus's maturation in progress, at the expense of strict chronology.

Works Cited

Austin, Norman. *Archery at the Dark of the Moon: Poetic Problems in Homer's Odyssey.* Berkeley: U of California P, 1975.

_____. "Telemachos Polymechanos." *California Studies in Classical Antiquity* 2 (1969): 45–63.

Belmont, David E. "Telemachus and Nausicaa: A Study of Youth." *Classical Journal* 63.1 (1967): 1–9.

Clarke, Howard W. "Telemachus and the Telemacheia." *American Journal of Philology* 84.2 (1963): 129–45.

Eckert, Charles W. "Initiatory Motifs in the Story of Telemachus." *Classical Journal* 59:2 (1963): 49–57.

Falkner, Thomas M. *The Poetics of Old Age in Greek Epic, Lyric, and Tragedy.* Norman: U of Oklahoma P, 1995.

Felson, Nancy. *Regarding Penelope: From Character to Poetics.* Princeton: Princeton UP, 1994.

Foley, Helene P. "'Reverse Similes' and Sex Roles in the *Odyssey.*" *Arethusa* 11 (1978): 7–26.

Herman, Gabriel. *Ritualised Friendship and the Greek City.* Cambridge, Eng.: Cambridge UP, 1987.

Martin, Richard P. "Telemachus and the Last Hero Song." *Colby Quarterly* 29 (1993): 222–40.

Millar, C. M. H., and J. W. S. Carmichael. "The Growth of Telemachus." *Greece and Rome* 1.2 (June 1954): 58–64.

Thalmann, William G. *The Swineherd and the Bow: Representations of Class in the Odyssey.* Ithaca, NY: Cornell UP, 1998.

Van Nortwick, Thomas. *Imagining Men: Ideals of Masculinity in Ancient Greek Culture.* Westport, CT: Praeger, 2008.

Vernant, Jean-Pierre. "Artemis and Rites of Sacrifice, Initiation, and Marriage." *Mortals and Immortals: Collected Essays.* Ed. Froma I. Zeitlin. Princeton: Princeton UP, 1991. 207–19.

Coming of Age in Shakespeare_____

Heather James

Coming-of-age stories fascinated William Shakespeare, who read avidly and found stories about this theme everywhere—in ballads, novellas, poems, histories, the Bible, moral fables, and myth. Each genre suggested a different perspective on the theme of coming of age, and Shakespeare snapped them all up for use in some of his best-loved plays, including the tragedies of *Romeo and Juliet* and *Hamlet*, the histories of *Henry IV, Parts I and II*, and comedies such as *A Midsummer Night's Dream*, *As You Like It*, and *Twelfth Night*. Of all genres and traditions that comment on the coming of age, however, ancient comedy is the one that predominates. Greek and Roman comedy focused on the concerns of youth. Its main themes were marriage, love, sex, and freedom—especially from overbearing fathers—and Shakespeare tapped and adjusted these themes to suit his own historical times and theatrical practices.

His success in adapting the theater of the ancients to the needs of modern times is astonishing: the coming-of-age plays were enormously popular in his own day and they also rank among the most studied, performed, and adapted plays today. Contemporary coming-of-age films, novels, and poems allude to Shakespeare's poetry and plays with a frequency that suggests Shakespeare has affected the very idea of what it means to come of age in modern times. Shakespearean allusions are privileged: they help to establish a genealogy of thought on topics of long-standing importance and, simultaneously, create an artistic resonance or aura that we might call the "Shakespeare effect."[1]

The Shakespeare effect can be powerful. A turning point in the movie *Clueless* (1995), for example, comes when the high-school heroine Cher corrects a pretentious college girl—and a potential rival in the love plot—who misattributes a famous line in *Hamlet*, "To thine own self be true," to Hamlet himself. The rival bridles at the idea of being corrected on "her Shakespeare" by a ditzy blonde, leading Cher to observe that while she may not know her Shakespeare, she does know her movie stars, including Mel Gibson, who starred in the 1990 film version of *Hamlet* directed by Franco Zeffirelli. Cher knows that Gibson/Hamlet said nothing of the kind: "that Polonius guy" did. And of course she is right. The apparently clueless heroine knows Shakespeare better than her college-age rival, who is only bluffing with the Bard to score points with a boy. Although Cher does not realize it, this is a turning point for her. This is the moment when she begins a remarkable evolution from a stereotype of the spoiled, rich girl in a high school farce: Cher may be clueless through much of the film, but in the end she has what it takes to be the witty and self-possessed heroine of a Shakespearean comedy.[2] She gains her newfound poise and confidence, moreover, when she realizes that it is better to feel clueless about life, from time to time, than believe you already have all the answers.

The scene in *Clueless* is a telling example of what happens when modern coming-of-age stories, comic or otherwise, tip their hat to Shakespeare: examples include Gus Van Sant's *My Own Private Idaho* (1991), Amy Heckerling's *Clueless* (1995), and Gil Junger's *Ten Things I Hate About You* (1999). At first glance the allusions suggest little more than the efforts of Hollywood filmmakers to gain cultural capital or prestige by quoting Shakespeare. This kind of allusion—as Amy Heckerling wittily suggests—is no different from the pretentious quotation of Shakespeare used by Cher's rival to impress her date. But the force of allusion goes further than the surface level of artistic boasting: it communicates to movie audiences, in unmistakable terms, that the young protagonists of these films deserve further thought and more respect from us. They may get utterly lost in the errors, deceptions, and wild machinations of a comic plot and they may have no clue about how to get out of the maze they are in. But this confusion turns out to be a good thing: the characters are learning by experience what it means to be, or try to be, true to themselves. And this is the point that is ironically lost on Cher's rival, who cannot rightly place the line in *Hamlet* about being true to oneself but is quick to put down a girl she thinks is beneath her.

The Shakespeare effect can be seen in films and novels in which the struggles of youth entail more than the challenges identified in ancient comedy, such as raging hormones, romantic idealism, and overbearing parents. Worse than all these things is coming of age in a world so stuffed with clichés about age, gender, class, and race that there is almost no escaping them. These ideas, prejudices, and social roles are altogether too easy to imitate or reproduce without thinking, since they are passed down right alongside of values so old and enduring that they seem to transcend time itself. It takes strenuous effort to resist them, in fact, because resistance requires young people, just at the time of life when they are rapidly assimilating information about the adult world, to slow down the very processes of learning that philosophers since Aristotle have described as a deep and innate pleasure in human beings. This pleasure is rooted in the ability to recognize forms, make connections and deductions, and then abstract general principles.

As Aristotle noted in his *Poetics*, however, ancient tragedy often contrasted the process of intake, deduction, and generalization with a strikingly different sort of recognition. Ancient tragedies tended to gather their strength for a pivotal *scene of recognition* that came at the crisis of a play and revealed to the protagonist that his or her situation was controlled by fates that cannot be altered by force of will.[3] The scene of tragic recognition in some ways resembles the scenes of recognition in ancient comedy, although the comic version may seem perfunctory, which is to say, like a mechanical means of advancing the plot to a necessary end. Like tragedy, ancient comedy devotes the body of the plays to a process of challenging social norms only to reach a catastrophe and reaffirm the status quo in the end.[4]

In comedy, the classic case is this. A young man pursues his love interest, heedless of the three strikes against her: she is lowborn, foreign-born, and at imminent risk of being snapped up by the play's pimp and slave trader. However, the case is miraculously altered at the end of the play, when certain items in her possession prove beyond a doubt that she is in fact the long-lost daughter of a wealthy and respectable citizen: problem solved. The young lover may have his girl without challenging social proprieties. By contrast, modern fiction and film often reverse the effect of ancient scenes of recognition: they generally focus on the inadequacy of external or surface views, which block the audience as well as the fictional characters from seeing alternatives to the status quo. Modern coming-of-age narratives tend to emphasize the courageous efforts of the young to extricate themselves from a fatalistic view of their worlds, to stop trying to "fit in" at all costs, and to try instead to find a voice and style of their own. These are the struggles that mark the coming of age. And these are the very struggles that Shakespeare introduced to the comic traditions that he inherited from antiquity.

Shakespeare took on the character types and dramatic situations of ancient comedy, but he altered the plots to focus on a new rite of passage, in which his young heroes and heroines accomplish two related tasks. They must test—to the very limit—both the conventions supplied by their roles in dramatic tradition and those at work in the social traditions of Shakespeare's day. The dramatic tradition, with its ancient roots in classical comedy, represents the long view on what it means to come of age and suggests an uninterrupted line of historical continuity. By contrast, the social traditions of Shakespeare's England present the foreshortened view of the here and now, in which change is both possible and desirable. The challenge facing Shakespeare's dramatic characters—much like Mike (River Phoenix) in *My Own Private Idaho*, Cher (Alicia Silverman) in *Clueless*, and Kat (Julia Stiles) in *Ten Things I Hate About You*—is to avoid repeating the mistakes and traumas of the past and, instead, create a story of their own to be passed down to future generations. The question that Shakespeare and his modern successors ask, in their dramatic fictions, is whether their characters will recognize and think through the more restrictive social conventions and, in the end, come down on the side of historical change.

The Resources of Ancient Drama

There was more than one type of comedy in antiquity. The one that Shakespeare and his contemporaries knew best was called "New Comedy," to distinguish it from the older and more rollicking type of comedy associated with Aristophanes. Old Comedy was often wildly inventive in its plots and boldly free with social and political references and lampoons (think of a cross between *Monty Python's Flying Circus*, *Saturday Night Live*, and *The Daily Show*). By contrast, New Comedy dealt strictly with general stereotypes and comparatively realistic scenarios, in the manner of classic sit-coms. New Comedy was developed by Menander in Greece and cultivated further by Plautus and then Terence in Rome to present an impressive array of stock characters caught up in a single plot (with variations), focused on the vicissitudes of getting married and staying well married. The character types include a "young lover," a "girl," an "angry father," a jealous wife or anxious mother, and a "clever servant" or slave, as well as a "pimp" or slave trader, a courtesan, a "braggart soldier," and a "parasite" or fawning sidekick.[5] Shakespeare's contemporaries knew these characters well from both the Latin that schoolboys studied in grammar schools and the plays that anybody might see staged in the London theaters.

Shakespeare took a great deal of pleasure in recycling and adapting these dramatic types. He sometimes doubled or multiplied a particular character type in a single play or even took it out of the context of comedy entirely. For example, just one history play, *Henry IV, Part I*, draws on the braggart soldier type to craft at least three different characters, all of whom represent some kind of threat to the play's young protagonist, Prince Hal: Hotspur (the rival to Prince Hal), the Earl of Douglas (the fierce Scot of the rebel camp), and Falstaff (the prince's broad-living, larger-than-life friend). In other plays, Shakespeare may take a character type, such as the courtesan, and use her not as an independent and fully realized character but as an idea that threatens all women. Many of Shakespeare's women characters, in fact, find themselves caught in the virgin-whore paradox (if they are not one, then they must be the other, as the cynical thought goes).

In *Othello*, for example, all three of the play's women find themselves denounced for sexual promiscuity and all three vigorously deny it: Bianca (Cassio's casual love interest), Emilia (Iago's loyal but pragmatic wife), and Desdemona (Othello's wife, who cannot bring herself even to utter the word "whore"). Another stock female character of New Comedy, the "jealous wife," also appealed to Shakespeare but, again, less as a character per se than as an accusation that a man levels against his wife.

Only one play, *A Comedy of Errors*—the most faithful of Shakespeare's experiments with New Comedy—presents a wife, Adriana, who stews over her husband's philandering and the damage it does to their marriage. But in no subsequent play does Shakespeare present a woman who can justly be called jealous or henpecking. Instead, infidelity and jealousy pervade plays from *A Midsummer Night's Dream* to *Othello* and *The Winter's Tale* more as suspicions and slanders than realities. In both *A Midsummer Night's Dream* and *The Winter's Tale*, for example, jealousy is an emotional tyrant found in men more than women. The cases of Oberon and Titania (the King and Queen of the fairies in *Dream*) and Leontes and Hermione (the King and Queen of Sicily in *The Winter's Tale*) reveal how dangerous this kind of emotional tyranny can be: it threatens to divide entire households and even undermine the stability of the social and natural environments.

Although Shakespeare had varying degrees of interest in the entire *dramatis personae* of Roman New Comedy, the collected ensemble had more character types than he needed for his favorite comic plot, which focuses on the business of marriage, and features a young lover, who relies on his imaginative and witty male servant to help him circumvent the efforts of his angry father to prevent him from marrying the girl of his dreams.[6] In his comedies, the "young lover" is rather less interesting to Shakespeare than the clever servant who is a born actor and generates both witty dialogue and entertaining turns on the plot. The servant has even more to gain or lose than his young master: if he fails he will be beaten, but if he succeeds he may gain the best possible reward, manumission, or freedom from slavery.

Fascinatingly, Shakespeare also focused a great deal of the dramatic interest on the emancipation of the "girl" of the marriage plot, whom he releases from the restricted role she plays in ancient comedy. Shakespeare's heroines are free to take the initiative in the love plot and pursue the object of their desires, as Helena does in *A Midsummer Night's Dream* and yet another Helena does in *All's Well That Ends Well*. Other heroines take the further step of disguising themselves as boys in order to pursue the marriage of their dreams: this way, they get to play the "young lover" and the "clever servant" as well as the "girl."

Shakespeare's more farcical comedies, such as *The Taming of the Shrew* and *A Comedy of Errors*, as well as the more introspective *A Midsummer Night's Dream*, recycle the stock characters from Roman New Comedy without insisting on many differences from the classic types. *Taming of the Shrew*'s Tranio is the quintessential clever servant, in service to a classic "young lover," Lucentio, who falls in love at first sight with a young woman who appears to be the perfect "girl" from comedy and a blank slate on which he may write the story of his own youthful desires: this is Bianca, whose very name means "blank" as well as "white" or "fair." In this case, Shakespeare lets the machinery of ancient comedy work without impediment and only gradually reveals the ways in which the story has gone awry: Bianca turns out to be no more colorless or pliable than her fiery sister Katherine, and Lucentio turns out to be a fool for judging by surfaces alone. *A Midsummer Night's Dream* goes further to expose the dark side of farce even in its first scene, which brings new meaning to the concept of a harsh father when an old man and citizen of Athens, Egeus, drags his daughter Hermia before Theseus, the Duke of Athens, and insists on his legal right to have her put to death if she marries Lysander (her choice) instead of Demetrius (her father's choice). He is among the first of many Shakespearean fathers—King Lear being the most famous—who feel that any independent-mindedness in their children is tantamount to betrayal and even treason.

Even Shakespeare's early experiments with farce suggest that he was curious about violence in the family and in the broader social relations inherited from New Comedy. A number of the romantic comedies, including *As You Like It*, *Much Ado About Nothing*, and *Twelfth Night*, explore dark themes about the victims and casualties of the rollicking comic plots. But the social and familial tensions of comedy also appear in places one might not expect to find them: the very heart of tragedy. In *Othello*, for instance, Shakespeare ironically and painfully develops the play's tragic matter out of the social tensions inherent in ancient comedy.[7] He does so through a series of inversions, the chief of which is Iago's resolve to play both the clever servant and flattering parasite in order to turn the business of the play from marriage and social integration to divorce, ruin, and death.

In the first act of the play alone, Iago stirs up the anger and prejudices of an initially rational father, Brabantio, in hopes that he will oppose and dissolve the marriage-by-elopement of his daughter, Desdemona, to Othello. Iago uses the power of stereotypes—social as well as dramatic—to frustrate the happiness of a couple that has deliberated with care and chosen to break strict social conventions. Othello is no young lover of comedy but is instead an experienced and aged African general, while Desdemona puts the cliché of the fair and passive girl to shame with her eloquence, passion, and determination. As the tragedy unfolds, the diabolically clever servant Iago busies himself with a plot to bring ruin on his "constant, loving, and noble" master (2.1.276) and the "exquisite" Desdemona (2.3.17). His main resource is not literal poison—the typically "Italian" way to do in one's enemies in Renaissance drama—but instead the power of language: specifically, the crushing language of stigma, stereotype, and convention. In this play, Shakespeare takes the wit of ancient comedy and lets Iago turn it "the seamy side without" (in the play's phrase for its villain's perverse imagination at 4.2.150). *Othello* recycles Roman New Comedy and rewrites it from the perspective of a fevered nightmare, where the familiar character types, scripts, and coming-of-age theme appear only to warp into strange and menacing forms.

Romeo and Juliet

Shakespeare's first extensive experiment with the dark side of comedy, *Romeo and Juliet*, is also the most beloved of his coming-of-age stories. In this play, Shakespeare uses the conventions of ancient comedy to suggest the ways in which his characters feel trapped by history: the people and city of Verona seem doomed to replay the violent scripts of the past, even if they do not entirely believe in them. Yet the city is also ripe for change: even old Capulet and Montague, the fathers of the two families that are locked in an ancient feud, would rather keep the peace than inflame ancient enmities. Montague regrets the violence of the first scene, which begins with the exchange of insults and rapidly escalates. For his part, Capulet aims to avoid a second scene of violence when he learns that the gatecrasher at his party is young Romeo and a Montague: although his hot-tempered nephew, Tybalt, itches to turn the festivities into a brawl, Capulet strenuously refuses. While the older generation seems weary of the feud (but unable or unwilling to end it), the younger generation is divided: Tybalt lives to fight, while Mercutio can see the point of an honorable fight, and Romeo curiously takes the most distanced and reflective view.

If there is one issue that Romeo seems to have thought through, even before he first enters the stage—late in the play's first scene, after the fight has ended—it is that the feud between his family and the Capulets is a pity, not an opportunity (as it is for Tybalt). Romeo steps into his role as the play's leading man, and wins hearts in the theater audiences, when he stops mooning in perfectly conventional terms about Rosalind (his first infatuation) and takes stock of the signs of the recent fight, which he sees as "brawling love" and "loving hate" (1.1.168).

Romeo takes his words from the amorous and erotic language of the love poets and sonneteers, who wrote of love as a set of warring opposites, such as hot snow and icy fire (Forster). But Romeo takes an unconventional step when he applies these terms to the ancient hatred between the Montagues and Capulets and voices his deep regret for the history of violence that ties the two families together in the tightest of bonds.

While Romeo reads the tragic signs of struggle and feels pity, his spiritual father, Friar Lawrence, goes further: he imagines comic resolution. When he learns that Romeo has fallen in love with the only daughter of his family's great foes, Friar Lawrence immediately envisions the blessing of a good marriage radiating outward to the families, the city, and the larger Christian brotherhood. He teases Romeo for having adored Rosalind only to change her for Juliet, but he quickly agrees to marry the lovers in hope that their "alliance may so happy prove, / To turn [their] households' rancour to pure love" (2.4.92–93). A great believer in happy endings, Friar Lawrence places his hopes and trust in the miraculous power of a comic plot to resolve ancient tensions. As he sees it, comic plotting and divine providence may yet come together. Friar Lawrence does not get his wish. The Montagues and Capulets are instead caught up in a tragic narrative that propels them toward a pattern of biblical atonement rather than providence and redemption. They will end the feud that divides their two families and their city, as the prologue tells us, but they pay a terrible price: the lives of their only children (terms of atonement that recall the vengeance taken by God against the Egyptians in Exodus).

While *Romeo and Juliet* is set on a tragic course, its dramatic materials are comic in a strictly technical sense: they come from Roman New Comedy. Just as the traditions of Roman New Comedy pervade *Othello*, without providing the promise of social integration, so do they also permeate *Romeo and Juliet*. The play is dominated by class conflict, gender struggle, and intergenerational conflict—themes lifted from comedy but with deadly rather than comic effect. The play also features character types of comedy, such as the angry father, the pimp or bawd, and the braggart soldier. But in the context of tragedy, these types have none of their usual ebullience and creative energy: they are instead terrible clichés, recycled through history, into which the play's relatively complex characters may fall as if into a trap. In short, the materials of Roman New Comedy suggest no future of reconciliation but return, to the contrary, to the violent scripts of the past.

Juliet's father, "old" and "rich" Capulet, quite tragically lives down to the stereotype of the angry father. He begins the play as a pleasure-loving figure of conviviality, inviting friends to supper and accommodating even enemies. What is more, he initially speaks progressive ideas about the upbringing of his daughter: he is careful to inform the rich, young count Paris that his daughter's marriage is not entirely in his hands—although this is his legal right—but is also a matter of her will and consent. By the middle of the play, however, Capulet has transformed into a terrifying version of the harsh father of New Comedy, who hurls terrible insults at his daughter and threatens her with physical violence: she is "green-sickness carrion!" and "baggage" (3.5.155), a "disobedient wretch!" (159) and a "hilding!" (166) if she does not view his wish as her own will.[8]

Once Capulet steps into the role of the angry father, he creates a domino effect in his own household: his wife becomes a reluctant servant to his rash will, as does Juliet's protesting Nurse, who is forced to perform the role of yet another pernicious stereotype from Roman New Comedy, the "bawd" who aims to prostitute the "girl." Although the Nurse loves Juliet as a daughter and willingly ventures into the marriage plot with her young charge, she changes sides: to Juliet's horror, her nurse advises her to forget the marriage vows she has sworn to Romeo and marry the Count Paris, as her father demands. For Juliet, this is an act of betrayal, which transforms her affectionate if ribald nurse into a figure of evil, an "Ancient damnation!" and "O most wicked fiend" (3.5.233). Unable to explain the change of loyalties, Juliet concludes that she has seen through the Nurse and found nothing but a bawd, the female type of the pimp and slave trader of ancient comedy.

It would be premature to conclude that Shakespeare uses ancient comedy to reveal latent vices in his characters. For Shakespeare, Roman New Comedy represents a slate of ingrained habits—roles that become second nature—rather than essential identities and deep truths. Neither Capulet nor the Nurse volunteers for the role of angry father or bawd: they act by compulsion. For the Nurse, Capulet is the trigger: he demands her compliance as part of his broad tyranny over all the women in his household. And Capulet is himself pushed into the role of the angry father when his nephew, the hot-headed Tybalt, challenges his authority as head of household at the party and can hardly be talked down from his bullying position. Capulet does not recover from this encounter. He becomes the "heavy" when he comes into direct conflict with another stereotype of Roman New Comedy: for Tybalt— proud, petty, and quarrelsome—plays the "braggart soldier" to the hilt.

While other characters in the play suffer gross reductions of character, Romeo and Juliet become increasingly vital and luminous. Neither character is free of convention—as if this were a possibility—but both stand apart from the larger community of Verona by trying to their utmost to test and hold at arm's length the conventions, clichés, and pieties of the past. The prompt is love, but consequence for the lovers is a strenuous and risk-taking resistance to the clichés of the past and their two families. Shakespeare makes the remarkable decision to distinguish his lovers from their dramatic prototypes, the "young lover" and "girl" of Roman New Comedy, by creating whole scenes—the love scenes—that focus not on the passions so much as the social bars to love. He submits his young lovers to moral and philosophical labor when he might have simply released them to the spirit of youthful rebellion that thrived in ancient comedy and in the morally prescriptive literature (including sermons) of his own day. It is both a delight and a curiosity that Shakespeare's most celebrated love scenes are also moral trials: Romeo and Juliet fall in love at first sight but they also spend every remaining minute of their lives thinking strenuously about moral action: when and how is it proper to follow custom or, on the other hand, to shun it? This question animates even first dialogues between the young lovers, when they meet at Capulet's party and meet after it in the balcony scene, which famously begins with Romeo listening in on Juliet as she privately wonders what exactly is in a name. Both characters come of age as they reflect on this question.

For Romeo, the question is what the names of the "beloved" and "friend" entail. He thinks, at the beginning of the play, that he understands the idea of the "beloved lady:" she is Rosalind, the woman on the pedestal. It seems unlikely that Romeo would remain in love with Rosalind for long: the merciless teasing of his friend Mercutio should eventually discourage him if the frustration does not get him first. Romeo in fact gives her up easily, once he meets Juliet: she loves him back, as Romeo explains to Friar Lawrence, and that is quite enough to convince Romeo that the name of the "beloved" is not the equivalent of "unattainable and untouchable idol." A harder lesson to learn is that "beloved" and "friend" may come into direct conflict. In this area—the arena of competing affections and loyalties—Shakespeare makes a striking change in the social template established by ancient comedy. In Roman New Comedy, the blocking figure in the young man's love plot was his father. In Shakespeare's play, the obstacles are the young man's friends. Benvolio, who is eager to draw Romeo into private and melancholy conversations about love, represents one kind of emotional appeal. Mercutio represents a competing claim on Romeo's emotions: Mercutio offers the love cure, a heady brew of cynicism about heterosexual love and idealism about the bonds between men.

Mercutio's position on love is honorable in Elizabethan society. The bond between men suggested an attraction between intellectual and physical equals, whereas heterosexual love was vulnerable to the charge that it is lust disguised as idolatry.[9] The attractions of male friendship were not at all lost on Shakespeare's audiences. In one of

---

his early comedies, male friendship represents the highest of emotional bonds. In *Two Gentlemen of Verona*, a young man named Valentine learns that his best friend is miserably in love with his own fiancée and he decides that the best thing to do is give her up to, and for, his friend. Romeo's choice is quite different. At a critical moment in the play, he gives up Mercutio for Juliet: in 3.1, when Mercutio and Tybalt are coming to blows, Romeo fails to second his friend in the skirmish—which was rash for Mercutio to enter into. He tries instead to stop the fight. The results are disastrous: Tybalt kills Mercutio under Romeo's sword, Romeo kills Tybalt (when he returns to the scene for yet more action), and Romeo is banished from Verona. The confusion of the scene as it unfolds on stage is remarkable, in part because the audience and not the characters understand how these events came about. Romeo chose Juliet not only as his lover but also as his friend. She affirms his choice when she learns of the catastrophe and still calls Romeo "my lord, my love, my friend!" (3.5.43). Mercutio presents one ideal of emotional bonds in the Elizabethan period, but Romeo chooses an alternative: the ideal of the companionate marriage, in which wives are esteemed friends rather than regarded as the material possessions of their husbands.

For Juliet, too, the passage to adulthood entails exciting and harrowing departures from the old scripts. She has much in common with the "girl" in the marriage plot of ancient comedy: the disapproval of an angry father (her own, not her lover's) and the threats of social stigma and even prostitution. But she has something that her prototype does not have: dramatic opportunity. Juliet has the means to speak her mind, choose her lover, and steal the show. The "girl" of Roman New Comedy can seem like little more than a structural device to advance the marriage plot, which focuses more extensively on the young lover and his clever servant and other flamboyant characters. The elements of this scenario that make the "girl" a challenge for modern readers and audiences—rather than a dramatic focal point—are precisely the features that keep her relatively safe in ancient comedy. She is exposed to many dangers, but she does not come under immediate threat from the single most forceful figure of opposition, the angry father. In *Romeo and Juliet*, Shakespeare changes that: he shifts the role of the angry father, the classic blocking figure, from the plot lines of the young man to those of the girl, especially as she transforms from an ancient stereotype to a young woman in the modern world. The "girl" of ancient comedy is often passive and silent: this is her default position in the genre. Juliet, by contrast, is first inspired and then forced to choose her words carefully. She speaks her mind freely and thoughtfully in her scenes with Romeo and her passionate soliloquies. And she scrutinizes every word she utters when she falls under the will of her father-turned-tyrant and inquisitor.

For Juliet, the process of coming of age means learning how to speak. In the narrowest terms of the plot, she must respond to the questions and demands of her angry father because the risks are so great: the lesser of her worries is that she will seem to deserve every damning insult that Capulet lets fly, if she reveals that she has married Romeo without his permission, while the worse possibility is that he will annul her marriage to Romeo and force her to marry Paris. In the larger social and political terms that the play invites us to consider, Juliet becomes a new kind of dramatic heroine when she faces a fundamental dilemma of citizens in a tyrannical government: she must choose between her conscience, which tells her to speak the truth and speak it boldly, and her modesty or obedience, which instructs her to hold her tongue and preserve social decorum. In this play, Shakespeare highlights the quite contemporary issues of the freedom of speech and the potential for opposition between a citizen's conscience and his or her obedience to authority. And he focuses these debates on his tragic heroine.

Women were not citizens in Shakespeare's England: while women had some legal rights and could take matters of property and reputation to trial, they lacked a voice in government.[10] As one writer put it, some thirty-five years after the publication of the play:

Women have no voyce in Parliament, they make no laws, they consent to none, they abrogate none. All of them are understood either married or to be married and their desires ar[e] subject to their husband, I know no remedy, though some women can shift it well enough. (T. E. *The Lawes Resolution of Womens Rights*)

As the last phrase suggests, some women were able to work within a system that was hostile to their wishes and will and still "shift" some things in their favor. Juliet seems to do just this, in her responses to her father: she cannot assert her will openly, but she can avoid saying anything that might violate it. In her father's view, the kind of speech that conceals dissent even as it outwardly complies is "chop-logic" (3.5.148). The other name for it in Shakespeare's day was "equivocation," the language used by religious dissenters who wished to create a separation of their (Catholic) faith and their political loyalties to the (Protestant) state of England. For English Catholics, the church and the state were tragically at odds and, as a consequence, their souls and lives were at risk.

Shakespeare draws on the contemporary language of religious and political division to animate the feud between the two leading families of Verona. The play reflects on a modern problem for Shakespeare and his audiences, and, simultaneously, the contemporary debates about religion and politics illuminate the dramatic stakes for Shakespeare's heroine. Juliet perceives herself to be the loyal but endangered subject of a hostile authority, her own father, and she responds by equivocating with him. This position is a strong, not a weak one. She assumes a position of considerable moral authority when she protects her thoughts (her marriage to Romeo) and yet speaks also from a position of loyalty (she does not accept that her marriage is treason).

Shakespeare's political and religious views remain mysterious and debated. His greatest pleasure as a playwright, however, is unmistakable: he can hardly be restrained from giving bold and open speech to his young heroine in ever greater measures. His Juliet learns to hold her tongue and keep her own counsel, but she also learns how to speak like the boldest love poets—poets, it almost goes without saying, who defy custom, cliché, and political authority in its more arbitrary and invasive forms. Her most famous soliloquy, for example, begins with urgent commands to figures from ancient mythology: "Gallop apace, you fiery-footed steeds, / Towards Phoebus' lodging. Such a waggoner / As Phaethon would whip you to the west, / and bring in cloudy night immediately" (3.2.1–4). Her wish, which echoes those of the greatest carpe diem poets before her, is that night will come and bring her lover to her, so that she may act out each one of her many passionate desires. She chooses, quite wonderfully, to imagine the sun rushing towards night, spurred on by the ardor and ambition of Phaethon, a young man of classical myth, who drove the chariot of his father, the Sun-God, to prove his own legitimacy.

In the earliest version of the play, this speech occupies just four lines. In the Folio version of the play, however, it runs to some thirty-one lines. Between the earliest and the later versions of the play, Shakespeare greatly expanded the play's most famous soliloquy and, in so doing, he greatly expanded the role of his heroine. In both versions, Juliet imagines herself as the mortal but "bastard" child of a god, who longs to have her way and prove her worth. In the boldest act of imagination in *Romeo and Juliet*, the dramatic character known as the "girl" in ancient comedy speaks her mind and comes of age.

Notes

1. For a discussion of this phenomenon, see entries for Robert Shaughnessy.
2. Amy Heckerling establishes a relationship to the farcical Roman comedy of Plautus and especially his play about clueless twins, *Menaechmi*, through the title of her film, *Clueless*. The allusion to *Hamlet*, which signals the generic turn from ancient farce to Shakespearean drama, comes directly after Cher's lowest moment in the film (literally—she was robbed and forced to lie face down in a parking lot).
3. For a useful student edition, see Aristotle, *Poetics*, trans. by Francis Fergusson (New York: Farrar, 1961).

4. For a fuller discussion of this point, see David Konstan.

5. The Latin terms for these character types are as follows: *adulescens* (young man), *puella* (girl), *senex iratus* (angry father), *servus callidus* (clever servant), *leno* (pimp), *meretrix* (whore), *miles gloriosus* (braggart soldier), and *parasitus* (parasite or fawning sidekick),

6. Northrop Frye, *Anatomy of Criticism: Four Essays* (Princeton: Princeton UP, 1957), discusses the angry father as the classic "blocking figure" of comic plots. See especially pp. 166–69.

7. For a more extended treatment of this play's relation to comedy, see especially Susan Snyder.

8. In his insults, Old Capulet wildly mixes his accusations, which range from disobedience to degeneracy and illegitimacy and from an unhealthy aversion to sexuality to an equally unhealthy addiction to it.

9. An excellent discussion of this topic may be found in Lorna Hutson.

10. An influential study of this topic may be found in Laura Gowing.

Works Cited

T. E. *The Lawes Resolution of Womens Rights*. London, 1632.

Forster, Leonard. *The Icy Fire: Five Studies in European Petrarchism*. Cambridge, Eng.: Cambridge UP, 1969.

Frye, Northrop. *Anatomy of Criticism: Four Essays*. Princeton: Princeton UP, 1957.

Gowing, Laura. *Domestic Dangers: Women, Words, and Sex in Early Modern London*. Oxford, Eng.: Oxford UP, 1999.

Hutson, Lorna. *The Usurer's Daughter: Male Friendship and Fictions of Women in Sixteenth-Century England*. London: Routledge, 1994.

Konstan, David. *Roman Comedy*. Ithaca: Cornell UP, 1986.

Shakespeare, William. *The Norton Shakespeare*. Gen. ed. Stephen Greenblatt. New York: Norton, 1997.

Shaughnessy, Robert. *The Shakespeare Effect: A History of Twentieth-Century Performance*. New York: Palgrave, 2002.

_____, ed. *The Cambridge Companion to Shakespeare and Popular Culture*. New York: Cambridge UP, 2007.

Snyder, Susan. *The Comic Matrix of Shakespeare's Tragedies:* Romeo and Juliet, Hamlet, Othello, *and* King Lear. Princeton: Princeton UP, 1979.

A Romantic Poet Comes of Age Over and Over Again_____

Richard Matlak

One would assume that "coming of age," if understood as a felt transition from innocence to experience, would happen once in a lifetime, as it often does in the narrative arts of fiction, film, and drama. But the big and single moment of transformation is not the formula for growing up in British romantic literature, which we can date roughly as the fifty-year period from 1780 to 1830. It is necessary to bring chronology and history into the discussion of a romantic coming of age, because an entire generation experienced the tribulation of the French Revolution in a personal way. The romantic era finds its moment of hopeful innocence in the French Revolution of 1789 and its period of disillusionment beginning with the Reign of Terror (1793) and ending with the crowning of Napoleon Bonaparte as emperor of France in 1804. Moving beyond political cynicism to reach a higher innocence in the natural world became a beautiful romantic paradigm of personal development in the poetry of William Wordsworth (1770–1850), but only temporarily. "Higher innocence" proved to be an illusion that the poet would have to overcome to reach his final coming of age with a fortitudinous acceptance of God's will.

Wordsworth describes the trajectory of his generation's experience in his poetic autobiography *The Prelude* (1805). "Bliss was it in that dawn to be alive," Wordsworth writes of the early days of the Revolution, "But to be young was very heaven"; for, he goes on, "Not favored spots alone, but the whole earth, / The beauty wore of promise" (*Prelude*, book X). It seemed to British sympathizers that something of biblical moment was occurring across the English Channel, even greater than their own Glorious Revolution of 1688, which resulted in the subordination of the monarchy to Parliament. The feeling and the belief were common that the Rights of Man, as civil rights and liberties were called at the time, would be assured if monarchical tyranny was restrained, or better yet, deposed. Charles James Fox, the leader of the Whig party in England, effused after France's political prison, the Bastille, was destroyed: "How much the greatest event it is that ever happened in the world! And how much the best" (Mitchell).

The fall of the Bastille occurred on July 14, 1789, and the Revolution was underway. The *London Times* declared that "the right hand . . . of tyranny is cut off." Joseph Priestley, the scientist who discovered oxygen and who was a leading radical and force in the development of modern Unitarianism, believed the Revolution to be a fulfillment of biblical prophecy. Richard Price, a Protestant minister and founder of actuarial statistics, exclaimed in a sermon before the radical London Revolutionary Society that he had "lived to see THIRTY MILLIONS of people, indignant and resolute, spurning at slavery, and demanding liberty with an irresistible voice" (Mellor and Matlak 9–10).

Bliss and youth were short-lived, lasting only until England went to war with France in 1793, and the government of Robespierre broke into the paranoid frenzy of the Reign of Terror. Bloodletting had begun with the September Massacres of 1792, when over one thousand priests, aristocrats, and common criminals were summarily executed after mob trials. And then King Louis XVI and Queen Marie Antoinette were decapitated in 1793 to commence the Reign of Terror, in an attempt to purge France of the suspected enemies of the Revolution. Tens of thousands were executed publicly by the guillotine.

Ironically, it was not the carnage that brought grief to the depths of Wordsworth's soul, but rather his own reaction to the behavior of England in goading France's leaders to murderous madness by declaring war in 1793. He recalls "Exult[ing] in the triumph of [his] soul"— in a chapel, of all places—"When Englishmen by thousands were o'erthrown, / Left without glory on the field, or driven, / Brave hearts, to shameful flight" (*Prelude*, X.261–64).

This internal confusion of hoping against his countrymen and the country he loved because of its betrayal of its own democratic ideals was "A conflict of sensations without name" (*Prelude*, X.266). For a great poet to be at a loss for words in naming a feeling is a significant rhetorical statement! In the meantime, matters in France got progressively worse, in the eyes of Wordsworth and English sympathizers, when France began its conquest of Europe, invading even the neutral country of Switzerland, and bungling an invasion of England in 1797 (Roe 248–62). Feeling betrayed and finding no hope in the institutions created either by national tradition or by human reason, Wordsworth "lost / All feeling of conviction, and, . . . / Sick, wearied out with contrarieties, / Yielded up moral questions in despair" (*Prelude*, X.898–900). He had hit rock bottom.

Although this historical, public tragedy is sufficient to explain Wordsworth's despair, there was an additional component that thickens the personal plot. He had a child by a French woman, Annette Vallon, during an extended stay in revolutionary France. He returned to England before the baby was born to raise money, but he was really in moral confusion about what to do next, and then the declaration of war between England and France separated him from his mistress and child for a decade. Wordsworth alludes to this debacle in a narrative in the *Prelude* of 1805 known as the Tale of Vaudracour and Julia, but it does not go beyond veiled comparison. On the other hand, Wordsworth's earlier verse often deals with abandoned women and children—"The Thorn," and "Ruined Cottage," in particular—which leads many to believe that his poetry is a locus for dealing with a reservoir of guilt.

The public narrative of the *Prelude* moves beyond despair to a higher innocence. With the intervention of his loving sister, Dorothy, and the inspiration provided by a kindred spirit, the poet Samuel Taylor Coleridge, Wordsworth worked his way out of despondency to find a new world of love and hope in nature. He concludes that his salvation was assured by "Nature's self, by human love / Assisted" (*Prelude*, X.921–22). He writes famously in *Lyrical Ballads* (1798) about his approach to experience in nature. If one can practice a "wise passiveness," that is, come to nature with an open mind and submit to a salubrious world of physical sensation, one can experience a profound and transformational education beyond the realm of books on moral reason:

> One impulse from a vernal wood
> May teach you more of man;
> Of moral evil and of good,
> Than all the sages can.
>
> Sweet is the lore which nature brings,
> Our meddling intellect
> Misshapes the beauteous forms of things,—
> We murder to dissect.
>
> Enough of science and of art;
> Close up those barren leaves;
> Come forth, and bring with you a heart
> That watches and receives. (*LB*, "The Tables Turned" lines 21–32)

Carl Woodring, who identifies a cluster of such poems in *Lyrical Ballads* as "doctrinal lyrics," believes that Wordsworth's gnomic pronouncements are "memorable exaggeration" (41). The question is, can "one moment" be transformative? Or does it just sound good to say so? This is a great challenge for understanding and interpretation and, really for an examination of one's own experience. To side with the poet in this instance, one could also ask if this belief in the power of nature is different from a younger man's belief in political power begetting promise for mankind. Or, perhaps it is as M. H. Abrams has posited in his *Natural Supernaturalism: Tradition and Revolution in Romantic Literature* (1971): poets, Wordsworth in particular, may have transferred their millennial hopes from politics to poetry (64–65) in the hope of implanting the principles of equality and democracy in the hearts of one reader at a time by a kind of natural osmosis.

Wordsworth develops his spiritual ideas more fully in the impassioned blank verse of "Lines Written a Few Miles above Tintern Abbey," concluding the great vacillation in *Lyrical Ballads* between poems of human suffering and poems infused with great joy in nature (Johnston). The poet has created a new world of worship. Here is one of the principal faith statements in "Tintern Abbey":

> And I have felt
> A presence that disturbs me with the joy
> Of elevated thoughts; a sense sublime
> Of something far more deeply interfused,
> Whose dwelling is the light of setting suns,
> And the round ocean, and the living air,
> And the blue sky, and in the mind of man,
> A motion and a spirit, that impels
> All thinking things, all objects of all thought,
> And rolls through all things. (*LB,* "Tintern Abbey" lines 94–103)

Wordsworth recapitulates his relationship to nature in "Tintern Abbey" as one of progressive maturation, moving from the "coarser pleasures of . . . boyish days" to the passionate highs of adolescence filled with its "aching joys" and "dizzy raptures" to the man of experience, now "A worshipper of Nature," who has listened carefully to the "still, sad music of humanity," in equipoise with the music of nature. The "burthen of the mystery" of man's inhumanity to man and "the heavy and the weary weight / Of all this unintelligible world" is now relieved by a "serene and blessed mood" experienced when he is "laid asleep / In body, and becomes a living soul" capable of "see[ing] into the life of things." It is a mystical step into an altered state of consciousness (Onorato), a kind of higher innocence that cannot account for evil but that knows how to go outside of the range of its power into the arms of nature. Indeed, it is a psychological way back to paradise for the poet and, potentially, for all of mankind.

Wordsworth follows through with the return-to-paradise motif as a challenge to John Milton's *Paradise Lost*, which concludes with Adam and Eve somberly leaving the gates of paradise after the Fall to travel the earth whichever way they will, with "Providence their guide" (*Paradise Lost*, XII.647). In his unpublished manuscript poem *Home at Grasmere*, Wordsworth and his sister Dorothy return to a paradise that Adam and Eve could never have understood. "[S]urpassing grace / To me hath been vouchsafed," the poet writes in his state of heightened awareness of the "one life" that sanctifies the universe:

> among the bowers
> Of blissful Eden this was neither given, possession of the good,
> Which had been sighed for, antient thought fulfilled
> And dear imaginations realized,
> Up to their highest measure, yea, and more. (*HG* lines 122–28)

Mind wedded to nature provides an entry into the paradise in nature available to those who come prepared to believe:

> Paradise, and groves
> Elysian, Fortunate Fields—like those of old
> Sought in the Atlantic Main, why should they be
> A history of departed things,
> Or a fiction of what never was?
> For the discerning intellect of Man,
> When wedded to this goodly universe
> In love and holy passion, shall find these
> A simple produce of the common day. (*HG* lines 47–55)

This wedding of mind to nature became the epic ambition of Wordsworth's "high argument" and the triumph of his maturity.

It may be that Wordsworth's emotional experience with the French Revolution marked him so deeply that he found it an appropriate grid for the big moments of his development: youthful hopes and understanding shattered, leaving him in crisis until a new source of strength, hope, and understanding could be found. I would like to consider three poems that follow this pattern, each dedicated to a different coming of age. The first poem, originally known as the "Leech Gatherer," was published with the title "Resolution and Independence" to reflect the leech gatherer's effect upon the poet's maturation in overcoming fears of economic survival. The second poem is "Ode: Intimations of Immortality Based upon Recollections of Early Childhood," and it concerns the poet's fear of losing faith in his youthful vision of nature and, thus, his power to create his visionary poetry. The third is "Elegiac Stanzas," a poem indirectly about the death of the poet's brother, John, but really about the demise of the poet's youthful belief in a loving nature and the poetry his belief inspired.

"Resolution and Independence" was written in 1802, prior to the poet's marriage. Although this personal circumstance is unstated, the poem builds on the understandable anxiety of an impoverished writer who is about to take on the responsibility of financially supporting a wife, a sister, and a coming family. Additionally, he is bound to do something for his mistress and child in France in compensation for moving on without them. Wordsworth had little income. He and Dorothy fished in a tarn for their dinner, had a vegetable garden, and shared a few dollars of invested inheritance. Poetry did not pay the bills.

Although a thirty-two-year-old man in the compositional present, the poet looks over his shoulder at the majority of mankind who work in the everyday world and admits to being different, "as happy as a boy," "a happy child of earth," who "walked far from the world . . . and from all care." It is a life that one might envy for a while. Like many a creative soul, however, this poet knows depression. His state of joy descends quickly into imaginings of another day, which may well hold "Solitude, pain of heart, distress, and poverty." He has lived his life as if "needful things would come unsought," because, being a good man, that is the way it should be. But then he remembers the fate of the poets he has loved, such as Thomas Chatterton, who committed suicide at the age of eighteen in poverty and neglect, and especially Robert Burns, whose life of dissipation led to his death at age thirty-four, leaving behind eight children born in and out of wedlock, the last of whom was born to his wife on the day he died:

> I thought of Chatterton, the marvelous Boy,
> The sleepless soul that perished in his pride;
> Of him [Burns] who walked in glory and in joy
> Behind his plough, upon the mountain side:
> By our own spirits are we deified;
> We poets in our youth begin in gladness;
> But thereof comes in the end despondency and madness.
> (*P2V*, "Resolution and Independence" lines 43–49)

Perhaps this prognosis seems melodramatic, but it may be the condition of a certain kind of mind in its maelstroms. The poet is also setting the stage for an important moment. Surely, his existential fears will be difficult to overcome without assistance. And just then, in the lonely woods of his morbid walk, as if "it were by peculiar grace, / A leading from above, a something given" (50–51), the poet meets an old man who is poking a pond with his staff looking for leeches, those aquatic bloodsucking worms used for bloodletting in eighteenth-century medicine. Could one imagine a less hopeful, indeed, a stranger, confrontation? In addition to being absolutely unpleasant for the reader to consider as a character, what could such a man have to teach a poet about survival?

It is necessary to say something about the kind of character the leech gatherer represents in Wordsworth's poetry and about the poet himself as a character in his poems. Wordsworth cultivated the appearance of such characters and the narrators who learn from them. It is very useful to distinguish those narrators as "Wordsworth," or the poet in the poems, as distinguished from the Wordsworth who writes the poems

(Waldoff). Wordsworth provides "Wordsworth" with many experiences of providential intercession from the most unexpected people in various places. Among these peculiar teachers are shepherds, an old peddler, a wanderer, a blind man begging on a London street, a female reaper singing a song in a language the poet does not understand, hikers along a Scottish lake, and this leech gatherer. They are sufficiently important as characters in Wordsworth's poetry for Jonathan Wordsworth, the poet's great-great-great-nephew and an important scholar of his ancestor's thought and works, to classify them as "Borderers," liminal presences who reside somewhere between life and death and appear when the poet is at a crisis point in his life (J. Wordsworth). Notice, in this case, how Wordsworth transforms the leech gatherer into one of these mysterious presences: "Such seemed this Man, not all alive or dead, / Nor all asleep." Geoffrey H. Hartman finds Wordsworth's obsession with this theme of personal salvation comparable to "the Puritan quest for evidence of election into the most ordinary emotional contexts" (5). And one might add, into the most extraordinary emotional contexts as well.

As we can now better understand, the leech gatherer of the poem and the dramatic situation are both staged by Wordsworth for "Wordsworth." Here is the biographical record of what happened to Wordsworth. William Wordsworth walking with Dorothy several years earlier had met an unfortunate soul on a road, who used to gather leeches until they became scarce. Dorothy reports in her *Grasmere Journal* for October 1800:

> Wm & I . . . met an old man almost double, he had on a coat thrown over his shoulders above his waistcoat and coat. Under this he carried a bundle & had an apron on & a night cap. . . . His trade was to gather leeches, but now leeches are scarce & he had not strength for it—he lived by begging. . . . He had been hurt in driving a cart, his leg broke his body driven over his skull fractured—. He felt no pain till he recovered from his first insensibility. (*Grasmere Journal* 24)

Wordsworth's description of the experience is included in the notes on his poems dictated to his friend Isabella Fenwick many years later: "This old man I met a few hundred yards from my cottage at Town-End, Grasmere; and the account of him is taken from his own mouth. I was in the state of feeling described in the beginning of the poem" (*P2V* 408). Obviously, the man's sheer will to exist against economic and physical odds remained with the poet as an example of fortitude, but the challenge for Wordsworth was to make him transcend the nitty-gritty of his pitiful experience into a special being: "like one" the poet had "met with in a dream; / Or like a Man from some far region sent / To give [him] human strength, and apt admonishment" (lines 117–19).

At first Wordsworth attempted to represent the real leech gatherer in the poem. It seems, to judge by the reaction of his first readers, that he was trying too hard to duplicate the actual speech of the old man on the road, as if reality, no matter how deeply felt, could translate into good art. The poet says in a letter to Sara Hutchinson and her sister Mary, who was soon to be his wife, that

> you speak of his speech as tedious: everything is tedious when one does not read with the feelings of the Author. . . . It is in the character of the old man to tell his story in a manner which an *impatient* reader must necessarily feel as tedious. But Good God! Such a figure, in such a place, a pious self-respecting, miserably infirm, and . . . Old Man telling such a tale. (*Letters* 367)

Nevertheless, Wordsworth took the criticism of tedium to heart in brilliantly shifting focus from the old man's speech to "Wordsworth's" state of consciousness while listening, or while he should have been listening. After inquiring what work the leech gatherer was doing, "Wordsworth" begins by listening but then experiences a reverie:

The Old Man still stood talking by my side;
But now his voice to me was like a stream
Scarce heard; nor word from word could I divide;
And the whole body of the man did seem
Like one I had met with in a dream;
Or like a Man from some far region sent;
To give me human strength, and apt admonishment. (*P2V*
lines 113–19)

"Wordsworth" slips deeper into fear for his future, as well he might in gazing upon the suffering creature before him:

My former thoughts returned: the fear that kills;
The hope that is unwilling to be fed;
Cold, pain, and labour, and all fleshly ills;
And mighty poets in their misery dead.
And now, not knowing what the Old Man had said,
My question eagerly did I renew,
"How is it that you live, and what is it you do?" (120–26)

"Wordsworth" picks up a few words about the scarcity of leeches and the man's perseverance, but again he drifts from the man to his vision of the man:

While he was talking thus, the lonely place,
The Old Man's shape, and speech, all troubled me:
In my mind's eye I seemed to see him pace
About the moors continually,
Wandering about alone and silently. (134–38)

When he returns to the man before him, who is still speaking "Chear-fully," "with demeanour kind," the narrator finally allows the reality of this "decrepit Man" to rebuke him and his dismal fantasies: "'God,' said I, 'be my help and stay secure; / I'll think of the Leech-gatherer on the lonely moor'" (146–47).

But what exactly is it that transforms the leech gatherer into the "Leech-gatherer?" He has been likened to the return of someone significant to the poet's consciousness, perhaps even a presence venturing from the unconscious. The "Leech-gatherer" comes from some "far region" and is "sent" by one who cares for the poet. His seeming to step out of a dream provokes a psychological interpretation of deep consciousness as that "far region." Is it Wordsworth's younger brother John, who was presently risking his life at sea as a mariner for the East India Company to support his brother's genius financially, as Irene Tayler speculates? Or perhaps it is his long-dead father, as Leon Waldoff has argued: "The speaker's longing to be comforted (or rescued) is ultimately gratified by his own imagination through a reinstatement of the reassuring image of a father-figure (Waldoff 94). These are brilliant theses that can only be hinted at here. As far as "coming of age" is concerned, here is what we can conclude: Although Wordsworth spiritualizes the "Leech-gatherer" as "Wordsworth" indulges his anxieties, finally it is the real leech gatherer's brute and factual presence—the suffering soul represented in Dorothy's *Grasmere Journal*—that grounds the poet's exquisitely wrought fears on a rock of real fortitude.

Not unrelated to Wordsworth's financial anxieties are the disturbing changes he was experiencing in his perception of nature, which had inspired his great nature poetry. He had written of his poetic vision and the responsibilities that came with his particular genius in *Home at Grasmere*:

> Unto me I feel
> That an internal brightness is vouchsafed
> That must not die, that must not pass away.
> . . . .
> Possessions have I, wholly, solely mine,
> Something within, which yet is shared by none—

Not even the nearest to me and most dear—
Something which power and effort may impart.
I would impart it; I would spread it wide,
Immortal in the world which is to come. (885–87; 897–902)

In the first four verse paragraphs of the "Intimations Ode," composed in March 1802, Wordsworth begins to explore this new crisis of imagination. "There was a time," he begins, when the objects of nature—meadows, groves, streams—seemed "Appareled in celestial light, / The glory and the freshness of a dream." But no longer. He concludes flatly: "The things which I have seen I now can see no more," for there "hath passed away a glory from the earth." He still feels and sees the joy of springtime and the gaiety of new and vibrant forms of life—birds in song, bounding lambs, the blooming of flowers, the warm sun, a "happy Shepherd Boy," a babe "leaping up on his mother's arm." "I hear, I hear, with joy I hear!" the poet exclaims:

—But there's a Tree, of many, one,
A single Field which I have looked upon,
Both of them speak of something that is gone:
    The pansy at my feet
    Doth the same tale repeat:
Whither is fled the visionary gleam?
Where is it now, the glory and the dream? (*P2V* 1–57 passim)

Is the Tree an allusion to the Tree of Good and Evil and the lost innocence of paradise? It can work that way in a poem about a youthful loss. "A single Field" is harder to explain, but it may be a personal allusion that any reader may have of losing a special feeling about something or a place that was once important. Such images are "concrete universals," very specific objects that can be understood symbolically as very big, or "universal." Clearly, however, what had been "appareled" in celestial light has had its glory removed, as if it had never been *in* the object itself, but had always been in the eyes of the perceiver (Brooks 126–27).

The poem ended in 1802 at this point, as if Wordsworth were stymied, incapable of answering the questions that meant so much to the artist who claimed to possess a prophetic vision of nature. His friend Coleridge, who felt that he was afflicted by a comparable dilemma, intensified Wordsworth's crisis with a response that poetic vision is an effusion of an internal state of joy. Coleridge's poem "Dejection: An Ode" begins one of the most famous poetic dialogues of literary history in response to the questions of Wordsworth's "Ode." There is a long line of criticism on the dialogic interplay between the poetry of the two poets, but Paul Magnuson's *Coleridge and Wordsworth: A Lyrical Dialogue* (1988), is the most comprehensive. Magnuson says that reading only one poem in a dialogue is like listening to one-half of a telephone conversation. The "unheard" poem is generative in advancing the conversation, i.e., the development of the "heard" poem, but we have to listen to both poems to fully understand the development of each.

Coleridge believes that a world "appareled in celestial light" is a function of unconscious projection. Addressing William as Edmund, a nickname of Coleridge's for Wordsworth, Coleridge writes:

> O EDMUND! we receive but what we give,
> And in our life alone does Nature live:
> Ours is her wedding garment, ours her shroud!
> And would we aught behold, of higher worth,
> Than that inanimate cold world allow'd
> To the poor loveless ever-anxious crowd,
> Ah from the soul itself must issue forth
> A light, a glory, a fair luminous cloud
> Enveloping the earth— (*Dejection* lines 48–56)

Coleridge explains that a sacred state of joy in the poet's soul spiritualizes the world he perceives:

> Joy, Edmund, is the spirit and the pow'r,
> Which wedding Nature to us gives in dow'r
> A new Earth and new Heaven
> Undream'd of by the sensual and the proud—
> Joy is the sweet voice, Joy the luminous cloud—
> We in ourselves rejoice. (67–72)

Coleridge's poem was published on Wordsworth's wedding day, giving the wedding metaphor of his gift-poem a literal kick. Here, then, was a friend functioning not as a Borderer to help the poet out of crisis, but as an abettor of the creative crisis.

Wordsworth focused on the word and Coleridge's concept of "Joy" when he returned to his ode. If Coleridge were correct, then Wordsworth's creative situation would be as comparably hopeless as Coleridge's, who claimed that "afflictions" were bowing him "down to earth," and every one of them "Suspends what nature gave me at my birth, / My shaping spirit of imagination (83, 86–87). It is as if Coleridge were saying that his problem is about growing old, but, as Lionel Trilling argues, Wordsworth's ode is really about growing up in a very unique way (Trilling 151). Wordsworth concedes that youth perceives a luminous world, because, at birth, we arrive "Not in entire forgetfulness, / And not in utter nakedness, / But trailing clouds of glory do we come / From God, who is our home" (*P2V* lines 62–65). As the child grows into manhood, "the light of common day" is all that remains; in other words, we are at the point of stasis that concluded the fourth verse paragraph of 1802.

At this point, Wordsworth thinks back upon the presence of the luminous world of infants and children as speculative evidence for a state of pre-existence, a state that we remember we have forgotten:

> O joy! that in our embers
> Is something that doth live,
> That nature yet remembers
> What was so fugitive! (*P2V* 132–35)

And then the poem gets quite mystical—many would say mystifying—in describing the insubstantiality of a child's world that proves him to be something of a Borderer who has come to save the poet. The child Borderer exists between the purely spiritual world of God and the physical pleasures of mother earth, who, like a "homely Nurse doth all she can / To make her Foster-child, her Inmate Man, / Forget the glories he hath known, / And that imperial palace whence he came" (81–84). But sometimes the child is astonished and frightened by the spiritual wildness of his boundary condition, and for this recollection of the child's experience, the poet is fortified in his faith:

> But for those obstinate questionings
> Of sense and outward things,
> Fallings from us, vanishings,
> Blank misgivings of a Creature
> Moving about in worlds not realiz'd,
> High instincts before which our mortal Nature
> Did tremble like a guilty Thing surpris'd:
> But for those first affections,
> Those shadowy recollections,
> Which be they what they may,
> Are yet the fountain light of all our day,
> Are yet a master light of all our seeing. (144–55)

When Wordsworth was questioned as to what these lines could possibly mean, he described his own childhood experiences:

I was often unable to think of external things as having external existence and I communed with all that I saw as something not apart from but inherent in my own immaterial nature. Many times while going to school have I grasped at a wall or tree to recall myself from this abyss of idealism to the reality. At that time I was afraid of such processes. In later periods of life I . . . have rejoiced over the remembrances, as is expressed in the lines 'obstinate questionings . . .' & c. (*P2V* 428)

The key to growing up? Reinterpreting the past to better explain the present, thereby asserting a coherent, though complex, life-narrative, rather than the threatened disruption and dismay of Coleridge's "Dejection." Admit what is gone, but appreciate fully what remains:

> What though the radiance which was once so bright
> Be now for ever taken from my sight,
> Though nothing can bring back the hour
> Of splendor in the grass, of glory in the flower,
> We will grieve not, rather find
> Strength in what remains behind,
> . . . .
> In the faith that looks through death
> In years that bring the philosophic mind. (178–83, 188–89)

The "Ode" ends with the poet feeling deeply for the emotions of the human heart. A sobering image of mortality in the clouds of the setting sun now colors his understanding of the pansy of 1802:

> Thanks to the human heart by which we live,
> Thanks to its tenderness, its joys, and fears,
>
> To me the meanest flower that blows can give
> Thoughts that do often lie too deep for tears. (203–6)

We share, or at least our bodies share, the fate of the mortal pansies. The "faith that looks through death" rests on the poet's recollected experience of intimations of immortality, the "obstinate questionings / Of sense and outward things, / Fallings from us, vanishings."

One would think the poet was now well fortified to deal with mortal vicissitudes. It did not prove to be so. "Wordsworth" was not Wordsworth. When the poet's younger brother John drowned at sea during a night storm in February 1805, Wordsworth felt blindsided by nature and responded with a poem entitled "Elegiac Stanzas, Suggested by a Picture of Peele Castle in a Storm, painted by Sir George Beaumont." It is a cumbersome title and a curious elegy, which was not for his brother, as one might have expected, but rather for the loss of a "power . . . which nothing can restore" (*P2V* line 35).

The principal trope of "Elegiac Stanzas" is a contrast between paintings: the painting of nature the poet would have created prior to his brother's death and the antithetical painting of nature created by Wordsworth's friend and patron Sir George Beaumont following John's death. Wordsworth's lesson for the maturation of "Wordsworth" is that the goal of the greatest art is correctly choosing a vision that will benefit mankind in times of greatest need. The great poetic vision of nature in *Lyrical Ballads* proved to be of no use to the suffering poet and his family in dealing with the tragedy their brother had suffered at sea.

The facts of the Wordsworth tragedy made for a complex poetic reaction. John Wordsworth was a mariner captain in the East India Company. He was considered less able academically than his elder brothers and went to sea at the age of fourteen, instead of to university. By the time he reached his late twenties, his experience and some family influence got him the captaincy of the *Earl of Abergavenny*, along with the most lucrative trade routes to India and China. He stood to become rich at a young age and it was his dream to financially support his poet-brother and their sister Dorothy. He also made an agreement with William prior to assuming his captaincy. John said he would "work for" his brother so that he could devote himself to "do[ing] something for the world."

John's dream of making a fortune, however, soon dissolved. His first voyage was profitless, leaving him in great debt to his investors. The financial outcome of his second voyage was even worse, and the third and fatal voyage was just about his last chance to recover from his earlier failures. In a wild night storm off the coast of Portland, England, John's vessel scraped bottom against an infamous reef and over the course of eleven hours its hull filled with water until the vessel sank. His crew and hundreds of soldiers bound for India bailed water to exhaustion, but it was hopeless. For unexplained reasons, other vessels in the convoy did not respond to repeated signals for assistance and the *Earl of Abergavenny* sank at around eleven o'clock at night, just two miles off shore. Two hundred and forty-six people died, including John, who, survivors reported, did not attempt to save his own life. He was also accused of irresponsibility in failing to use the ship's boats prior to the sinking to save lives in a ship-to-shore operation. The charges of suicidal despair and irresponsibility in the loss of so many lives greatly exacerbated the family's grief over the loss of their brother (Matlak).

William wrote several heart-wrenching elegies on John's death that remained unpublished because their grief was too raw, but when he first viewed Beaumont's painting *Peele Castle in a Storm* at a showing in the British Academy, he was stunned with a new understanding of the role of art in relation to tragedy.

Beaumont had been a friend and patron of Wordsworth's for several years. He and Lady Beaumont were among the poet's biggest fans. Beaumont said that "Tintern Abbey" had done him more spiritual good than a hundred sermons. Now, in attempting to offer the poet some solace following John's death, especially over its metaphysical meaning, which had left the poet in a moral quandary, Beaumont created an instructive oil painting depicting a vessel in distress, bow down, stern up, in a stormy sea. The vessel dips towards the light of the setting sun, sinking westward, as it were, with a bolt of lightning flashing near its stern. Positioned as it is, there is no possibility for including a visible human presence on the vessel. Opposite the vessel is a moldering castle, with one of its keeps standing alone and closer to the vessel than the main castle, all being buffeted by the wind and raging waves. In relationship to the vessel, the castle is extraordinarily prominent. Significantly, there is no human presence in the painting. In other words, there is no hint to be found of the messy human tragedy that beset the sinking of the *Abergavenny*. No inkling of John's suicidal end or of the panic that overcame the hundreds that drowned. Beaumont's scene rises to the metaphysical level of a fated, generic end for a vessel in distress, opposite an enduring edifice that has witnessed many such ends over the course of time. It had been reported by survivors that John's final words were, "God's will be done," and so Beaumont painted "God's will."

Wordsworth's idyllic painting of nature's sea and the castle on Peele Island, which he had visited as a young man at a time of great joy in his life, would have been quite different. But here again we must invoke "Wordsworth." Marjorie Levinson and others have criticized Wordsworth for pretending he was as morally naïve as he claims in "Elegiac Stanzas" prior to John's death. Of course he was not. He had experienced the traumatic deaths of his mother and father early in life (Onorato), but John's death and its associated allegations were sufficiently unique to require another "coming of age" for "Wordsworth" to move beyond a visionary world of higher innocence.

Addressing the castle, the "hoary Pile," of the second quatrain, "Wordsworth" imagines:

> Ah! THEN, if mine had been the Painter's hand,
> To express what then I saw; and add the gleam,
> The light that never was, on sea or land,
> The consecration, and the Poet's dream;
>
> I would have planted thee, thou hoary Pile!
> Amid a world how different from this!
> Beside a sea that could not cease to smile;
> On tranquil land, beneath a sky of bliss:

> Thou shoulds't have seem'd a treasure-house, a mine
> Of peaceful years, a chronicle of heaven—
> Of all the sunbeams that did ever shine
> The very sweetest had to thee been given.
>
> A picture had it been of lasting ease
> Elysian quiet, without toil or strife,
> No motion but the moving tide, a breeze,
> Or merely silent Nature's breathing life. (*P2V* lines 13–28)

Most importantly, because of the "fond delusion of [his] heart" he would have seen "the soul of truth" in his painting, and "A faith, a trust, that could not be betray'd" (32).

The poem shortly moves to its new understanding of art, as "Wordsworth" acknowledges that "Well chosen is the spirit" of Beaumont's painting. The illumination that the artist *chooses* "the spirit" of his work, rather than allowing himself to be led by the "fond delusion of [his] heart," is a major lesson. The castle is the symbol of that "spirit," which is fortitude:

> And this huge Castle—standing here sublime,
> I love to see the look with which it braves,
> Cased in the unfeeling armour of old time,
> The light'ning, the fierce wind, and trampling waves.
> (49–52)

The poet's past happiness in nature has been "blind," his heart had been "hous'd in a dream," at a distance from the suffering of mankind. Beaumont's simple painting has provided a stunning reversal of understanding and a new appreciation for the qualities required to deal with tragedy:

But welcome fortitude, and patient chear,

And frequent sights of what is to be borne!

Such sights, or worse, as are before me here.

Not without hope we suffer and we mourn. (57–60)

This last and latest lesson that Wordsworth teaches "Wordsworth" is perhaps the most important for his art. The break with the past that he tries so hard to prevent in the "Intimations Ode" is now embraced as the way to artistic maturity. Wordsworth was nothing if not honest with "Wordsworth" on matters of growing up. At the end of the journey, there is maturity, but without the refuge of higher innocence. Ripeness is all.

Works Cited

Abrams, M. H. *Natural Supernaturalism: Tradition and Revolution in Romantic Literature*. New York: Norton, 1971.

Brooks, Cleanth. *The Well-Wrought Urn: Studies in the Structure of Poetry*. New York: Harcourt, 1947.

Coleridge, Samuel Taylor. *Coleridge's Dejection: The Earliest Manuscripts and the Earliest Printings*. Ed. Stephen Maxfield Parrish. Ithaca, NY: Cornell UP, 1988. Cited as *Dejection*.

Hartman, Geoffrey H. *Wordsworth's Poetry: 1787–1814*. New Haven: Yale UP, 1971.

Johnston, Kenneth R. "The Triumphs of Failure: Wordsworth's Lyrical Ballads of 1798." *The Age of William Wordsworth: Critical Essays on the Romantic Tradition*. Ed. Kenneth R. Johnston and Gene W. Ruoff. New Brunswick: Rutgers UP, 1987: 133–59.

Letters of William and Dorothy Wordsworth, I, The Early Years 1787–1805. Ed. Ernest De Selincourt. Oxford, Eng.: Clarendon, 1967. Cited as *Letters*.

Levinson, Marjorie. *Wordsworth's Great Period Poems*. Cambridge, Eng.: Cambridge UP, 1986.

Magnuson, Paul. *Coleridge and Wordsworth: A Lyrical Dialogue*. Princeton: Princeton UP, 1988.

Matlak, Richard E. *Deep Distresses: William Wordsworth, John Wordsworth, Sir George Beaumont, 1800–1808*. Newark: U of Delaware P, 2003.

Mellor, Anne K., and Richard Matlak, eds. *British Literature: 1780–1830*. Fort Worth, TX: Harcourt, 1996.

Milton, John. *Paradise Lost*. Ed. Scott Elledge. New York: Norton, 1975. Cited as *Paradise Lost*.

Mitchell, Leslie. "Charles James Fox." *Oxford Dictionary of National Biography*. Online ed. 2007.

Onorato, Richard J. *The Character of the Poet: Wordsworth in* The Prelude. Princeton: Princeton UP, 1971.

Roe, Nicholas. *Wordsworth and Coleridge: The Radical Years*. Oxford, Eng.: Clarendon, 1988.

Tayler, Irene. "By Peculiar Grace: Wordsworth in 1802." *The Evidence of the Imagination: Studies in the Interaction between Life and Art in English Romantic Literature*. Eds. Donald H. Reiman, Michael C. Jaye, and Betty T. Bennett. New York: New York UP, 1978. 119–41.

Trilling, Lionel. "The Immortality Ode." *English Romantic Poets: Modern Essays in Criticism*. Ed. M. H. Abrams. New York: Oxford UP, 1975: 149–69. First published in Lionel Trilling, *The Liberal Imagination*, 1942.

Waldoff, Leon. *Wordsworth in His Major Lyrics: The Art and Psychology of Self-Representation*. Columbia: U of Missouri P, 2001.

Wordsworth, William. *Lyrical Ballads and Other Poems, 1797–1800*. Eds. James Butler and Karen Green. Ithaca, NY: Cornell UP, 1992. Cited as *LB*.

_____. *The Prelude*, 1799, 1805, 1850. Eds. Jonathan Wordsworth, M. H. Abrams, and Stephen Gill. New York: Norton, 1979. Cited as *Prelude*.

_____. *Home at Grasmere: Part First, Book First, of* The Recluse. Ed. Beth Darlington. Ithaca, NY: Cornell UP, 1977. Cited as *HG*.

_____. *Poems, in Two Volumes, and Other Poems, 1800–1807*. Ed. Jared Curtis. Ithaca, NY: Cornell UP, 1983. Cited as *P2V*.

Woodring, Carl. *Wordsworth*. Boston: Houghton, 1965.

Woof, Pamela, ed. *Dorothy Wordsworth: The Grasmere Journals*. New York: Oxford UP, 1993. Cited as *Grasmere Journals*.

Wordsworth, Jonathan. "Wordsworth's 'Borderers.'" *English Romantic Poets: Modern Essays in Criticism*. Ed. M. H. Abrams. Oxford: Oxford UP, 1975. 170–87.

The Varieties of Adolescent Experience: Coming of Age in Alcott's *Little Women*

Anne K. Phillips and Greg Eiselein

Introduction

In 1867, having observed the success of "boy books" by authors such as "Oliver Optic" (the pen name of William T. Adams), Thomas Niles of the Boston publisher Roberts Brothers asked Louisa May Alcott to write a "girls' book" (*Journals* 158). Although Alcott insisted that she did not enjoy writing it (*Journals* 158, 165), her finished novel, *Little Women* (1868–69), brought to life not only Meg, Jo, Beth, and Amy March but also their neighbor "Laurie" Laurence. Alcott's portrait of young adulthood attracted audiences as soon as the novel appeared in October 1868, and readers immediately wrote the author to suggest how she might continue the story. Alcott began writing the sequel in November 1868 and published it in April 1869. In its history of more than 140 years, *Little Women* has inspired readers' passionate identification with its characters. As Barbara Sicherman acknowledges, "reading the book has been a rite of passage for generations of adolescent and preadolescent females" (246).

Little Women humorously and vividly acknowledges the drama of the coming-of-age experience in its characterizations. Although inspired to some extent by Alcott's own family, the novel should not be read as autobiography but rather as a purposefully constructed and emotionally powerful account of the varieties of adolescent experience. It represents what adolescent psychiatrist Aaron H. Esman has identified as the central tasks of transitioning into adulthood. The characters must come to terms with their changing bodies and sexuality while also identifying and pursuing their chosen vocations. Additionally, they must negotiate changing familial and social relationships (Esman 31–32). In all three areas, *Little Women* provides profound insight into the transition from adolescence to adulthood.

Sexuality and the Body

Little Women offers five adolescent characters who transition from childhood to adulthood in noticeably different ways. It does not detail the physical experience of puberty in the direct fashion of later novels such as Judy Blume's *Are You There God? It's Me, Margaret* (1970), but it does represent the psychological, social, and physical changes of the characters as they grow into adulthood.

In the opening chapters of the novel, the oldest of the sisters, Meg, still squeals "with girlish delight" (27) at receiving an invitation to a New Year's Eve dance, but she is also clearly on the verge of becoming an adult woman in terms of her body and her sexuality. At the New Year's party, for example, Meg's "lovely" (27) if painfully "tight" (30) shoes signal her vanity and also a body that is outgrowing its adolescent wardrobe, just as the twisted ankle that results from dancing in those high-heeled, too tight, "silly things" (32) suggests the physical and social discomfort associated with the transition into womanhood. Later that year, while spending a fortnight with the fashionable Moffats (chapter 9), Meg seems even more self-conscious as she experiments with a tight, low-cut dress as well as make-up and fashionable accessories. The experience produces in Meg feelings of enjoyment and delight as well as embarrassment or shame, feelings that send "her heart beating" (77) as she looks at herself in the mirror and make her blush (79) when she realizes that Laurie is looking at her. Shame is a fascinatingly complex emotion made up of "interest and enjoyment" as well as an inhibition of those feelings and "the incomplete reduction of interest or joy" (Tomkins 134). Meg's blushing combines the experience of indignity at being discovered by Laurie as she flirts, drinks champagne, and wears clothes that are not hers with the pleasure she takes in being perceived as "a little beauty" (*Little Women* 76).

The "Vanity Fair" chapter also represents Meg's not-yet-successful efforts to think of herself as a grown woman. When Miss Clara and Miss Belle attempt to talk about a romantic connection between Meg and Laurie, Meg insists that he is "only a little boy" (75). Meg's attempt to distinguish her sixteen-year-old more adult self from Laurie's sixteen-year-old boyhood is, for readers, pure comedy. When Annie Moffat presses and wants to know why Laurie's flowers shouldn't be read as a lover's gift, Meg abandons adult pretensions: "My mother and old Mr. Laurence are friends, you know, so it is quite natural that we children should play together" (75). The concession allows the other young women to confirm, mockingly, that Meg has not yet come of age. Miss Clara says, "It's evident Daisy [Meg] isn't out yet." Miss Belle adds, alluding to Meg's psychosexual development, "Quite a pastoral state of innocence all around" (75).

Despite the setback in "Vanity Fair," it becomes clear in later chapters that Meg feels "grown up already" (119) and that she associates adulthood with romance and marriage, perhaps more than any other character. As she comes to terms with her feelings about becoming a woman, Meg tolerates the jests of the Moffats as well as Laurie's pranks (including the fabricated love letter from John Brooke in chapter 21), and she endures resistance from others to the idea of her growing up and marrying. Although most of Aunt March's objection to the idea of Meg marrying John Brooke is class prejudice and snobbery ("You ought to marry well, and help your family; it's your duty to make a rich match" [181]), she also believes the couple is too young to marry. While initially repelling/encouraging John's profession of love, Meg herself protests, "I'm too young" (180). Still, her clear delight in the possibility of a union with John conveys Meg's desire to assert her right to marry whomever she wants. Thus, Meg makes what is for her the most important decision of her life as a way to assert her independence: "as she was peremptorily ordered *not* to like him, she immediately made up her mind that she would" (181).

Jo's resistance to Meg's marriage stems in part from her conviction that Meg—and all of the adolescent characters—are too young to be thinking about courtship or marriage. Jo is fatalistic about the fact that they are becoming sexually mature; she says at one point to her mother, Marmee, "I wish wearing flat-irons on our heads would keep us from growing up. But buds will be roses, and kittens, cats,—more's the pity!" (162). While Meg seems preoccupied with coming of age and the possibility of marriage, Jo resists the changes that seem to be waiting for all of them. Part of her negative view of marriage stems from her belief that adult life means the dissolution of the bonds among the March sisters and their mother. The novel foregrounds Jo's passionate attachment to her female family members, from her devotion to Beth to her wish to "marry Meg myself [to] keep her safe in the family" (161) to her declaration to Marmee that "Mothers are the *best* lovers in the world" (341). Thus, for Jo, Meg's marriage means "an end of peace and fun, and cosy times, together" (161). In Jo's view, "I see it all! they'll go lovering round the house, and we shall have to dodge; Meg will be absorbed, and no good to me any more; Brooke will scratch up a fortune somehow,—carry her off and make a hole in the family; and I shall break my heart, and everything will be abominably uncomfortable. Oh, deary me! why weren't we all boys? then there wouldn't be any bother!" (161).

Jo's moan "why weren't we all boys?" suggests that she also sees marriage as the end of a young woman's freedom. The novel's third-person narrator seems to share this view. In volume 2, in the chapter titled "On the Shelf," the narrator explains how American society, in contrast to French society, provides freedom to its girls and young single women but not its married women:

In France the young girls have a dull time of it till they are married, when *"Vive la liberté"* becomes their motto. In America, as every one knows, girls early sign a declaration of independence, and enjoy their freedom with republican zest; but the young matrons usually abdicate with the first heir to the throne, and go into a seclusion almost as close as a French nunnery, though by no means as quiet. Whether they like it or not, they are virtually put upon the shelf as soon as the wedding excitement is over. (304)

Anxiety about being abandoned by those whom she loves most fills Jo with a sense of despair about the end of childhood and the process of becoming a woman. "It never can be the same again. I've lost my dearest friend" (184), says Jo shortly after the announcement of Meg and John's engagement. Hence she yearns for the "flat-irons on our heads." While her refusal to entertain the possibility of a romantic relationship with Laurie has provoked readers from the 1860s to the present, Jo's uneasiness about marriage is rooted in her fears about what it means for young women generally as much as what it means for her and her family.

Jo and Meg represent two ends of a continuum in the novel's portrayal of various ways of becoming a woman or, in the case of Laurie, becoming a man. In some respects, Amy is closer to Meg's end of the continuum. Although she is the youngest of the March sisters and the furthest from adulthood when the novel opens, she yearns to be older. Throughout the first volume, much of the novel's comedy involves Amy's attempts to act older than she is, whether managing social relationships among schoolgirls with pickled limes (chapter 7) or drawing up a will (chapter 19). In volume 2, however, Amy has matured, physically and emotionally, and in several ways, she appears more mature than both Jo (who sulks when having to conform to social expectations in the "Calls" chapter of volume 2) and Laurie (who lacks the discipline and concern for others that Amy demonstrates in the "Lazy Laurence" chapter).

In some respects, Laurie could be identified as a character midway between Meg and Jo. He does not fear adulthood as the loss of family and freedom, as Jo might. In fact, he shares Meg's preoccupations with what growing up means in terms of romance and sexuality. In chapter 21, Laurie is obsessively and inappropriately nosy about the possibility of a romance between Meg and John, and he mercilessly teases Jo about marriage. He is lovelorn after Jo's rejection of his attempts to court her. Although preoccupied with love and marriage in ways similar to Meg, he does not have her maturity. Even after college, in his twenties and six feet tall, he still seems childlike, which prompts Meg to say, "I wonder if you will ever grow up, Laurie" (196). Like Jo, but perhaps with less deliberate intention, Laurie holds on to his adolescence, even though his body is full grown; he is well into his twenties before he seems ready for an adult romantic relationship or marriage.

The possibility of and problems associated with sexual maturity and courtship are prominent in the development of Meg, Jo, Amy, and Laurie. The same cannot be said of Beth. In many respects, she resembles Jo in that she is not eager to grow up and leave her family. The novel overtly defines her in volume 1 in terms of her youth: "Beth was a child still" (38). While there is little attention drawn to her adolescent struggles or her sexual maturation, one of Alcott's larger purposes with Beth's character may be to depict someone whose adolescence is almost entirely overlooked by others. In what may seem an abrupt revelation in volume 2, we learn that Beth the child has become Beth the woman, when Jo says: "I think she is growing up, and so begins to dream dreams, and have hopes, and fears, and fidgets, without knowing why, or being able to explain them. Why, mother, Beth's eighteen; but we don't realize it, and treat her like a child, forgetting she's a woman" (254). Perhaps Alcott attempts to depict the kind of adolescent who quietly resists coming of age, rather than in Jo's dramatic fashion. Or perhaps Beth is a character who is so preoccupied with her own mortality that she pays little attention to the process of becoming an adult. Another important possibility might be the novel's attempt to draw our attention to a kind of sexual maturity that goes unnoticed, even by the members of one's own family.

Vocation

Although issues of courtship are central to each volume of *Little Women*, thinking about and preparing for a future profession is another essential aspect of the adolescents' experiences. *Little Women* highlights not only these possibilities but also the realities associated with pursuing a vocation. In the end, none of the protagonists attain precisely the professional occupation they envisioned as adolescents, yet an acceptance of their actual position becomes an indispensable element in the novel's happy (if not fairy-tale) ending.

To a degree uncommon among mothers in earlier coming-of-age novels, Marmee encourages her daughters to pursue their talents and avoid focusing on matrimonial matters. After Meg's experience at the Moffats', for example, Marmee reminds Meg and Jo that it is "better [to] be happy old maids than unhappy wives, or unmaidenly girls, running about to find husbands" (84). She knows that marriage is not the only option for them: "I am ambitious for you, but not to have you . . . marry rich men merely because they are rich" (84). She reminds them that she and Mr. March "hope that our daughters, whether married or single, will be the pride and comfort of our lives" (84).

Moreover, each of Marmee's daughters has her own set of special talents. Jo is the writer, while Beth's passion (like Laurie's) is music; Meg is "the best actress we've got" (14), and Amy devotes herself to drawing, painting, and the visual arts. This attention to the arts is one of the ways that the novel differentiates the characters from each other. Laurie longs "to be a famous musician" in chapter 13, "Castles in the Air," while Jo declares that she "shall write books" and Amy expresses her "modest desire" to become "the best artist in the whole world" (118). Despite their artistic talents and passions, Meg and Beth do not articulate their vocational aspirations in terms of a career in the arts but instead imagine their ideal future life in terms of homemaking. Meg wants to be a wealthy "mistress" of "a lovely house," though she fails to confess that she also dreams of "a splendid, wise, good husband, and some angelic little children" (118), to use Jo's words. Beth envisions herself "home safe with father and mother" (118).

None of these professional aspirations are fully realized, however. Alcott's decision to have her characters articulate but never achieve their adolescent vocational dreams might seem unusual or unexpected. Or perhaps this outcome is foreshadowed all along. In "Castles in the Air," Laurie complains about the career dilemma he faces. He dreams of a musical career, but his grandfather wants him to be "an India merchant, as he was" (119). Although Laurie melodramatically declares that he would "rather be shot" (119), he actually resigns himself that night to staying with his grandfather even if it means forsaking his artistic dreams: "Remembering the conversation of the afternoon, the boy said to himself, with the resolve to make the sacrifice cheerfully, 'I'll let my castle go, and stay with the dear old gentleman while he needs me, for I am all he has'" (121).

It is not solely his grandfather's insistence that alters Laurie's professional aspirations, however. In Europe, Laurie idles for months before pursuing a career as a romantic composer. He tries writing a requiem and then an opera. Though "he got on swimmingly for a time" (329), Laurie eventually realizes that "every one who loved music was not a composer" (329) and begins to contemplate other employment options. As he tells Jo after his return from Europe, "I'm going into business with a devotion that shall delight grandpa, and prove to him that I'm not spoilt. I need something of the sort to keep me steady. I'm tired of dawdling, and mean to work like a man" (354). By the novel's end, Laurie has become a businessman and philanthropist "doing lots of good with [his] money, and laying up the blessings of the poor, instead of dollars" (375).

Amy too realizes that she may not have the "genius" to become "the best artist in the whole world" (118). As she tells Laurie: "Rome took all the vanity out of me, for after seeing the wonders there, I felt too insignificant to live, and gave up all my foolish hopes in despair. . . . Talent isn't genius, and no amount of energy can make it so. I want to be great, or nothing. I won't be a common-place dauber, so I don't intend to try any more" (317). Laurie's later reflection on this speech leads him to realize that possessing talent is not sufficient reason for pursuing composing *as a career*. Other factors, such as family needs or perspective on where one might do the most good, are also critical in such decisions. At first, Amy ambiguously articulates her new vocational focus in terms of becoming "an ornament to society" (317).

By the novel's conclusion, however, it has become clear that her goal is to serve as a patron of the arts, "helping others fulfil their dreams of beauty" (379).

In many respects, Jo is perhaps the most successful of the book's adolescents who imagine an artistic life. While Amy and Laurie are learning the difference between talent (a certain artistic ability) and genius (the artistic passion and focus that help turn that talent into genuine creativity), Jo does "burn" (211) with genius: "when the writing fit came on, she gave herself up to it with entire abandon, and led a blissful life, unconscious of want, care, or bad weather, while she sat safe and happy in an imaginary world, full of friends almost as real and dear to her as any in the flesh" (211). Moreover, she publishes her literary endeavors, wins prizes, receives critical attention, and gets paid for her efforts. Jo seems destined to become the writer she wants to be. Despite her success as a writer, however, which seems even greater after her experiences publishing sensation stories in New York, Jo becomes dissatisfied with the work she is creating. While some critics attribute her dissatisfaction to Professor Bhaer's criticism of the sensation story genre as "bad trash" (280), the novel itself suggests that Jo's unhappiness has more to do with her recognition that her style and subjects are no longer her own. They have been determined for her by editors and a literary marketplace eager for "thrilling tales" (275). Her father had long advised her, "Aim at the highest, and never mind the money" (214). But in New York, Jo finds herself writing, it seems, simply for money. Looking at her accumulated stories, Jo admits, "I can't read this stuff in sober earnest without being horribly ashamed of it" (280). Although she then attempts other, more wholesome genres without much financial or artistic success, Jo temporarily sets aside her writing.

After marrying Professor Bhaer and inheriting her grandmother's estate, Plumfield, Jo then declares, unexpectedly, that she plans to open a boys' school. This second vocation, headmistress of a school, may appear to be a new idea. Yet Jo makes it clear that "that this isn't a new idea of mine, but a long-cherished plan" (374), a wish that pre-dates her decision to stop writing for the popular press, allowing her to meld her work life and her family life:

> Before my Fritz came, I used to think how, when I'd made my fortune, and no one needed me at home, I'd hire a big house, and pick up some poor, forlorn little lads, who hadn't any mothers, and take care of them, and make life jolly for them before it was too late. I see so many going to ruin for want of help, at the right minute; I love so to do anything for them; I seem to feel their wants, and sympathize with their troubles; and, oh, I should so like to be a mother to them! (374)

Her enthusiasm for her school stems in part from her realization that a career in writing would not be as fulfilling as she had imagined as an adolescent: "the life I wanted then seems selfish, lonely and cold to me now. I haven't given up the hope that I may write a good book yet, but I can wait, and I'm sure it will be all the better for such experiences and illustrations as these" (379). Although many critics and readers have attributed this change in vocation to the influence of Professor Bhaer and Mr. March, it may be Beth who most inspires Jo, urging her to care for her family: "you'll be happier in doing that, than writing splendid books, or seeing all the world; for love is the only thing that we can carry with us when we go" (327). In the sequels to *Little Women*, *Little Men* (1871) and *Jo's Boys* (1886), Jo turns again with some real success to writing and publishing, but she also continues to feel that the life of an author is somewhat annoying and unsatisfying, perhaps reinforcing the notion that Jo does not so much sacrifice her career as a writer as change her mind about the kind of vocation that would best produce the kind of life she wants to live.

Despite their own set of artistic talents, Meg and Beth never aspire to a vocation outside the domestic realm. Nevertheless, the novel represents even these aspirations as only partially obtainable. Meg yearned as a teenager to be the head of a wealthy household. However, she finds herself instead struggling to cope with a tiny cottage rather than the splendid mansion life she once imagined. Meg declares that her "castle was the most nearly realized of all" (379), and she does become a mother, wife, and homemaker as she had wished, yet she struggles in chapters like "Domestic Experiences" and "On the Shelf" to become "satisfied" (379) with her actual domestic life, highlighting the discrepancy between her adolescent wishes and her adult realities.

Finally, Beth has by far the most circumscribed vocational ambitions, wanting nothing more than to be "safe" (118) within the domestic life she already has. Yet the novel refuses to fulfill even this most humble calling, as Beth succumbs to the ill health that has afflicted her from her initial bout with scarlet fever, perhaps suggesting that even modest teenage dreams are not likely to come true, at least not in the ways one might expect.

Readers and critics have interpreted in various ways Alcott's reluctance to permit any of her characters to achieve the fairy-tale life they imagine. Some readers might perceive that the characters embrace instead vocations that allow them to devote themselves to a cause larger than the self. Self-denial and self-control are certainly among the key themes developed in the novel. Other critics might see the disappointments of the March girls as a commentary on the limited career options available to women within Victorian society. Still other readers may find in the abandonment of these adolescent aspirations a mourning for the loss of childhood—and all of the hope and play and creativity it entails—as each of the five central characters transitions from childhood to adult life.

While such interpretations have merit, the vocational themes in *Little Women*, when seen in terms of the conventions and development of the coming-of-age novel, are likely to reinforce our understanding of Alcott's book as an early masterpiece of American realism. As the five teenagers become adults, they become something different than they were in ways that are familiar but not always predictable. The novel may imitate Alcott's own life a little less than is often assumed: Alcott becomes the famous author, while Jo becomes the schoolmistress and wife. Nevertheless, *Little Women* ultimately represents and even celebrates the kinds of vocational options (teacher, businessman, homemaker) that would be familiar to her readers.

Relationships

Although courtship and vocational concerns contribute to the novel's realistic depiction of adolescence, *Little Women* does not neglect the importance of interpersonal relationships. When the novel begins, the adolescents' interactions are notably intense. They squabble, whether disagreeing about who will accompany Laurie to a matinee at the theatre or whining about having to complete household tasks. In particular, Amy and Jo are prone to conflict, culminating in Amy's destruction of Jo's manuscript. In response, Jo deliberately allows Amy to skate on thin ice. Their behaviors contrast with those of the better-behaved, overtly Christian protagonists found in earlier nineteenth-century American literature such as *The Wide, Wide World* (1850) and *Elsie Dinsmore* (1867).

Those intense relationships are, however, multifaceted. The protagonists memorably play together, rehearsing the Christmas theatrical, writing a newspaper, or pretending that they are pilgrims. Jo insinuates Laurie into the Pickwick Club, and he introduces a neighborhood post office, among other pleasures. As Meg acknowledges, "we make fun for ourselves, and are a pretty jolly set, as Jo would say" (12). Whatever their activities, they involve and rely on each other.

Marmee is the adolescents' guiding force, particularly while her husband is serving as a chaplain in the Civil War. An especially intense example lies in Jo's admission to her mother of her seemingly uncontrollable anger: "It seems as if I could do anything when I'm in a passion; I get so savage, I could hurt anyone, and enjoy it. I'm afraid I shall do something dreadful some day" (68). Marmee responds to this heart-wrenching confession with honesty: "I am angry nearly every day of my life, Jo; but I have learned not to show it; and I still hope to learn not to feel it, thought it may take me another forty years to do so"

(68). Marmee's admission inspires Jo: "She felt comforted at once by the sympathy and confidence given her; the knowledge that her mother had a fault like hers, and tried to mend it, made her own easier to bear, and strengthened her resolution to cure it" (68–69). Later in the novel, Jo witnesses her mother's struggle with her temper (aptly, incited by Aunt March); knowing what her mother is feeling, Jo is inspired to continue to control her own destructive impulses, and in the process she also obtains a more substantive perspective on adult interactions.

Dealing with the realities of their lives, particularly in volume 2, all of Alcott's protagonists find it necessary to assume more realistic perspectives on their abilities, their goals, and their primary relationships. As Esman acknowledges, the adolescent particularly "must also undergo significant changes in his relations with parents and other family members, as he tests out his capacity for autonomous living while learning to come to terms with residual dependent wishes and feelings of attachment to parents who are no longer seen as omnipotent, idealized figures" (32). Particularly for the March sisters and their closest friend, it becomes necessary to renegotiate their relationships to varying degrees with the adults who have most shaped and influenced them, as they establish more independent, self-sufficient adult identities.

Meg must learn to manage her own home and, more importantly, to communicate effectively with others. She and Sallie (Gardiner) Moffat remain friends, but Sallie's higher standard of living tempts Meg and makes her become dissatisfied. After she has overspent, throwing the family budget into chaos, Meg has the honesty to admit to Sallie that she cannot afford what she has purchased, and she stops shopping with her wealthy friend (226). With John, she needs to communicate more effectively that she needs his help in raising their children. Marmee is essential in helping Meg, particularly because she too has experienced difficulty in balancing marriage and motherhood. Lovingly sharing her experiences, Marmee helps Meg to understand the lesson she and Mr. March have learned: "Each do our part alone in many things, but at home we work together, always" (307). Applying her mother's advice,

Meg resolves her difficulties, enjoying an increasingly satisfying life "not as a queen, but a wise wife and mother" (313).

The other sisters move beyond their parents' watchful perimeter in resolving some of their transition issues. Amy manifests innate flair for navigating societal expectations in the "Calls" chapter and additional poise in response to May Chester's unkindness during the preparations for the charity fair in the "Consequences" chapter. As Amy explains to her family, "because they are mean is no reason why I should be. I hate such things; and though I think I've a right to be hurt, I don't intend to show it" (239). Separated from the family during her tour of Europe, Amy demonstrates further self-sufficiency when she writes that she intends to accept Fred Vaughn's proposal: "Don't be anxious about me; remember that I am your 'prudent Amy,' and be sure I will do nothing rashly. Send me as much advice as you like; I'll use it if I can" (253). Although she ultimately does not accept Fred's proposal, she marries as well as she had hoped. Significantly, she marries in Europe, surprising loved ones with her spontaneous and triumphant return as "Mrs. Laurence" (355).

Like Amy, Jo leaves home, taking a position as a governess at a boarding house in New York. She finds her sense of identity tested when she is introduced by a gentlewoman who lives in her boarding house, Miss Norton, to the leading artists, scientists, and philosophers of her era. Their pontifications begin to sway her long-held beliefs. However, she is supported by Professor Bhaer, who defends his principles, despite their unfashionable nature, when he is challenged by the other intellectuals: "Somehow, as he talked, the world got right again to Jo; the old beliefs that had lasted so long, seemed better than the new. . . . She felt as if she had solid ground under her feet again" (278). It would be easy for a young woman on her own for the first time to be uncertain of her beliefs and values. However, her proximity to kind and helpful adult friends such as Miss Norton and Professor Bhaer helps her emerge from her stint as a governess wiser and with greater self-knowledge.

Together, Jo and Beth demonstrate maturity and acceptance that transcends their parents' awareness. Jo realizes that Beth is not well when she returns from New York: "She wondered, and was thankful also, that her parents did not seem to see what she saw" (291). During a trip to the shore, Beth confesses that she has known for some time that she was not getting better but chose not to tell her family (293). Here, Alcott transfers the role of guide and mentor from Mr. and Mrs. March to higher authorities, explaining that Beth "asked no questions, but left everything to God and nature, Father and mother of us all, feeling sure that they, and they only, could teach and strengthen heart and spirit for this life and the life to come" (294). In her ensuing conversation with Jo, Beth charges Jo to explain her situation to their parents: "I've heard that the people who love best are often blindest to such things. If they don't see it, you will tell them for me. I don't want any secrets, and it's kinder to prepare them" (294). Esman's description of the process by which adolescents begin to recognize the limitations of parents who had previously seemed to be "omnipotent, idealized figures" (32), is poignantly embodied in the reactions of Mr. and Mrs. March upon Beth's return from the shore: "Her father stood leaning his head on the mantle-piece, and did not turn as [Jo] came in; but her mother stretched out her arms as if for help, and Jo went to comfort her without a word" (295).

Transitioning into adulthood, Jo must discover how to transform her adolescent bond with Laurie into a lifelong friendship, and her deep friendship with Friedrich into true love. After the tumult of her earlier refusal of Laurie's proposal, Jo fears that her friendship with him has been destroyed. On his return from Europe, however, they reestablish their friendship when Laurie, "with a manly gravity she had never seen in him before" acknowledges, "I never shall stop loving you; but the love is altered, and I have learned to see that it is better as it is" (346). Jo responds by confirming their newly adult status: "We can't be little playmates any longer, but we will be brother and sister, to love and to help one another all our lives, won't we, Laurie?" (346). This conversation is a necessary resolution of their adolescent upheaval, enabling Alcott's preservation of one of the most complex and interesting male-female friendships in literature.

Jo's courtship with Friedrich begins drolly. She is "mortally afraid of being laughed at" (363), and Laurie, though eager to tease, manages to rein in his pranks. When she forays into the city in search of her lover, she blunders and bumbles through her errands, sending so many conflicting signals to him that he isn't sure what to think. But when Friedrich confesses his love for her, she poignantly acknowledges that it is "the one precious thing I needed" (372). Further, when Friedrich and Jo discuss their future together, Jo demonstrates determination and self-knowledge when she insists, "I'm to carry my share, Friedrich, and help to earn the home. Make up your mind to that" (372). While some readers have resisted this "funny match" (Alcott, *Letters* 125), Jo and Friedrich's relationship is fascinating and perhaps even appealing to those who regard equality, intellectual exchange, and working together as essential aspects of marriage.

As the novel concludes, the protagonists emerge with greater self-knowledge obtained through experience and with emotionally rich and satisfying interpersonal relationships. They no longer squabble, although they still continue to play and to rely on their artistic abilities (in the final chapter, they serenade Marmee with a song written by Jo and set to music by Laurie). These now-adult characters have endured/survived adolescence in ways that allow them not only to maintain but to reconfigure and strengthen their relationships with each other.

Conclusion

In its emphasis on bodies, vocations, and relationships, *Little Women* resonates with the theory of adolescent development articulated by Esman. The novel's rich depiction of this coming-of-age experience may in part account for its enduring attraction for so many readers and its status as a classic within the American literary canon.

Despite its classic status as a coming-of-age narrative, *Little Women* sometimes deviates from the conventions of this form. While many coming-of-age novels focus on a lone (male) figure who defines himself in opposition to others, Alcott's adolescents define themselves in relation to one another. In contrast to the typically negative portrayal of maternal figures in eighteenth- and nineteenth-century novels (in which mothers are often foolish, weak, domineering, or dead), Marmee is wise, supportive, and loving, but she is also committed to a child-rearing method that emphasizes learning by experience and self-reliance. Moreover, the protagonists' quests in this novel are not usually actual journeys, like the epic quest of an Odysseus, the river adventure of a Huck Finn, or the literal pilgrimage of Chaucer's travelers. The important journeys in *Little Women* are spiritual and psychological: the March girls "playing pilgrims," Jo taming her temper, Beth gradually accepting her mortality, and so on. For Chaucer, the goal of the pilgrimage is salvation. For Alcott, the goal is growing up. Part of the novel's power, however, lies in the fact that it does not neatly resolve the issues raised by adolescence. Although in the final scenes of the novel these protagonists are clearly adults, they have not finished the process of becoming. Alcott's pilgrims are still moving along their paths.

Although the pilgrim motif allows Alcott to emphasize the development of individual identity, she does not position individuality in opposition to relationships and the family. Jo initially is apprehensive that coming of age will break up the family, but at the end of the novel the family has not fractured; rather, it has expanded to include the protagonists and their spouses and children, as well as the students who attend Plumfield. Coming of age, then, is not a separation or a severing of family bonds, as Jo once feared. Instead, from Alcott's perspective, coming of age is something that most effectively happens in relation to and with the support of the family. Thus, when Jo exclaims in the final chapter, "I do think that families are the most beautiful things in all the world!" (375), she is expressing Alcott's own belief that family is essential to the growth and development of individual identity.

Works Cited

Alcott, Louisa May. *The Journals of Louisa May Alcott*. Eds. Joel Myerson, Daniel Shealy, and Madeleine B. Stern. Boston: Little, 1989.

_____. *Little Women; or, Meg, Jo, Beth, and Amy*. 1868–69. Eds. Anne K. Phillips and Gregory Eiselein. New York: Norton, 2004.

_____. *The Selected Letters of Louisa May Alcott*. Eds. Joel Myerson, Daniel Shealy, and Madeleine B. Stern. Boston: Little, 1987.

Blume, Judy. *Are You There God? It's Me, Margaret*. 1970. New York: Delacorte, 2010.

Esman, Aaron H. *Adolescence and Culture*. New York: Columbia UP, 1990.

Finley, Martha. *Elsie Dinsmore*. 1867. New York: Dodd, Mead, 1896.

Sicherman, Barbara. "Reading Little Women: The Many Lives of a Text." *US History as Women's History: New Feminist Essays*. Eds. Linda K. Kerber, Alice Kessler-Harris, and Kathryn Kish Sklar. Chapel Hill: U of North Carolina P, 1995. 245–66.

Tomkins, Silvan. *Shame and Its Sisters: A Silvan Tomkins Reader*. Eds. Eve Kosofsky Sedgwick and Adam Frank. Durham: Duke UP, 1995.

Wetherell, Elizabeth [Susan Warner]. *The Wide, Wide World*. 1850. New York: Feminist, 1987.

Irony and Moral Development in *Adventures of Huckleberry Finn*

Roberta Seelinger Trites

Mark Twain's *Adventures of Huckleberry Finn* is perhaps the most famous coming-of-age story in American literature (Mintz 1). Ernest Hemingway calls it the most influential (22). The novel develops through a series of moral decisions that the protagonist, Huck Finn, must make regarding his friend Jim's escape from slavery. Thus, *Adventures of Huckleberry Finn* is a coming-of-age novel that defines moral development as a necessary part of growth to maturity.

In the novel's first paragraph, Huck brings to the reader's attention the importance of "truth" as a factor in moral development. Huck says, "You don't know about me, without you have read a book by the name of *The Adventures of Tom Sawyer*, but that ain't no matter. That book was made by Mr. Mark Twain, and he told the truth, mainly. There was things which he stretched, but mainly he told the truth" (1). Huck also assures readers that he is, like almost everyone he knows, himself a liar: "I never seen anybody but lied, one time or another" (1). Thus, in the first few sentences of the novel, Huck has called the reader's attention to the fact that he is a liar who nonetheless cares about issues of "truth."

Later in that same chapter, Huck contrasts truth and hypocrisy when he expresses discomfort with his living conditions. Although in *The Adventures of Tom Sawyer* he has been content to be a homeless boy and the son of the town drunk, in *Adventures of Huckleberry Finn* he has been adopted by the Widow Douglas, who requires Huck to dress well, eat a healthy dinner—and to do so politely. She prohibits him from smoking. "She said it was a mean practice and wasn't clean"— but Huck comments on her hypocrisy: "And she took snuff too; of course that was all right, because she done it herself" (3). The widow's sister, Miss Watson, provides a further source of irritation for Huck by reminding him to follow social conventions. After fussing at him for fidgeting and yawning and not sitting up straight, she asks, "why don't you try to behave?" (3). She then tries to frighten Huck into respectable behavior with the Christian concept of hell, where, in her belief system, sinners go after they die. Huck rejects her conventional morality and shocks the woman: "I said I wished I was there" (3). In one respect, Miss Watson is already making Huck's life a living hell—but Huck claims all he wants is a change of scenery: "all I wanted was a change—I warn't particular. She said it was wicked to say what I said . . . *she* was going to live so as to go to the good place. Well, I couldn't see no advantage in going where she was going, so I made up my mind I wouldn't try for it" (4, emphasis original). With that decision, six paragraphs into the novel, Huck has made his first moral decision: he is not going to try to go to heaven if heaven is populated by representatives of conventional morality, such as Miss Watson.

Conventional morality can be defined as the prevailing opinions, attitudes, and values in a given culture. Before the Civil War, for example, conventional morality among the majority of white landowners in the Southern states involved an acceptance of slavery. *Adventures of Huckleberry Finn*, however, was published in 1885, twenty years after the Thirteenth Amendment to the US Constitution abolished slavery in 1865. Why, then, would Twain write a novel that seems to protest the evils of slavery when slaves had already been freed? The answer lies in the difference between conventional morality and Huck's independent thinking about race and his subsequent moral development. As Huck grows throughout the novel, he rejects the conventional morality of Southern racism—and readers are invited to form their own views about social problems that are created by racism and class snobbery. As David L. Smith puts it, Twain was combating the *racial discourse* of his age (104). Discourse is an entire system of language that makes an institution like slavery or social class difference possible. Racist discourse is the systematic use of language to reinforce racism throughout a culture—ranging from daily conversations, media depictions, and common assumptions about race to the social structures of racism codified by economic and legal systems (Smiley 63–64). Twain's anti-racist discourse is intended to challenge the racism of his time—and that discourse still serves the same purpose in the twenty-first century (Smith 103–20).

One specific literary element is crucial to understanding Twain's contrast between the conventional morality of hypocritical racists like Miss Watson and the independent thinking of someone like Huck, who seeks to understand truth and then acts on it. That literary element is irony. Irony involves a reversal of some sort and can best be understood as language that means the opposite of what it appears to mean. Twain relies on at least four different types of irony to contrast Huck to the situations he finds himself in. When Huck says that it is "all right" that the Widow Douglas takes snuff, he means the exact opposite of what he is saying. In that example, he is employing *verbal irony*, which is using words intentionally to mean their exact opposite. When Huck says something naïve and the reader knows he is wrong, he creates *dramatic irony*, as for example, happens when he proclaims that he would rather go to "the bad place" than converse any more with Miss Watson. Nineteenth-century readers would have known that no one would intentionally choose to suffer in the flames of hell for eternity—and that no one was likely to go there just for fidgeting. Twain relies on dramatic irony because he wants readers to learn for themselves that Huck is sometimes wrong in his assessments of his society. As Albert Stone argues, Huck's innocence creates the basis for most of the novel's dramatic irony and subsequent social criticism (134–58). When Huck discovers that Miss Watson's slave, Jim, has run away from home and the two decide to escape south down the Mississippi River rather than taking the quicker path to the east to escape into the free state of Illinois, the plot of the novel begins to depend on *situational irony*. That is, Huck and Jim are in a situation that is the exact opposite of what it should be: a runaway slave is heading south, instead of north (Smiley 62–63). The final type of irony on which Twain relies is *comic irony*, which is the use of irony to create humor. For example, Huck narrates this: "Jim said bees wouldn't sting idiots; but I didn't believe that, because I had tried them lots of times myself, and they wouldn't sting me" (55). Huck is too naïve to perceive that he has just made a joke by calling himself an idiot. Twain's use of irony thus creates a narrative climate in which readers grow to understand that Huck himself can't be trusted as a narrator. If he is a liar, if he is an idiot, if he is too earnest to recognize a joke when he hears one, if the reader knows more than Huck, then Huck is an unreliable narrator. Huck cannot always be taken at his word. In fact, sometimes, Huck means the exact opposite of what he has said. Twain purposefully creates an ironic and unreliable narrator as a way to emphasize the difference between the conventional racist morality of the nineteenth century and independent thinking. Understanding irony is therefore essential to understanding Huck's moral growth.

Not long after Huck decides that he would rather go to the "bad place" than continue listening to Miss Watson's moralizing, Huck gets his wish to go "somewheres" else (4). Huck's father returns to town and kidnaps his son, hiding him away in a cabin in the woods and beating the boy repeatedly. During one of Pap's drunken rants, the man criticizes the US government for allowing a freed slave, who is a professor, to vote. Twain employs dramatic irony here, assuming that readers will recognize Pap's racist discourse as reprehensible. Pap claims he has decided he will never vote again, to protest the fact that this African American professor can vote—after Pap reveals that he was himself too drunk to vote during the last election, anyway. He falls ill with delirium tremens, a form of mental disturbance caused by alcohol withdrawal. While he is crazed, Pap believes Huck is the "angel of death" and tries to kill his son, so Huck escapes to Jackson Island by sawing an escape route through the bottom logs of their cabin and faking his death (36). This is the first time that Huck takes moral action. He knows he is no "angel"—of death or of anything—but he also knows he can no longer abide racist anger so profound that it leads his father to drunkenly abuse him.

Huck's next moral action occurs on Jackson Island, where he finds Jim, who has run away because Miss Watson is threatening to sell him downriver for a profit. Huck makes a moral decision not to betray Jim, even if "people would call me a low-down ablitionist and despise me for keeping mum" (52–53). He is, in that moment, rejecting the racism of conventional morality. When Huck realizes that two white men are planning to come to the island to search for Jim, he wakes the runaway up and urges him to escape: "Git up and hump yourself, Jim! There ain't a minute to lose. They're after us!" (75). Ironically, no one is after "us," as Huck claims. Everyone in the area believes Huck is dead because he faked his own death so successfully. With that one sentence, Huck has made a decision to join his fate to Jim's.

As the two head downriver, they fish from the raft to feed themselves—but they also steal, which Huck calls "borrowing," rationalizing the behavior in a way that helps the reader understand his moral immaturity. To salve his guilty conscience, Huck talks to Jim, and they decide on two things they won't "borrow" anymore: crabapples and persimmons. Twain again relies on dramatic irony, knowing that the reader will recognize the paucity of this moral decision: "crabapples ain't ever good, and the p'simmons wouldn't be ripe for two or three months yet" (80). The two runaways soon climb aboard an abandoned steamboat, the *Walter Scott*, where they discover a band of thieves in the process of double-crossing each other. Huck and Jim eventually escape the doomed riverboat, but between them, they have established a clear principle: it is wrong to steal another man's property.

This principle becomes the root of Huck's greatest moral dilemma. In the American South during this era, slaves were considered property, not citizens entitled to basic human rights. Before Huck collides with the competing principle of determining whether he should think of Jim as a person or a piece of property, Twain establishes Jim's humanity—and his dignity (Ellison 50; Henry 32). Huck and Jim get separated by a fog that is notable for the way its dense whiteness confuses people's thinking. This symbolic oppression of the forces of whiteness creates the situational irony that informs the rest of the novel: they miss the Ohio River—Jim's route to freedom—while they are separated by this befuddling whiteness. Once they are reunited, however, Huck plays a trick on Jim that demonstrates Jim is the more mature and principled character of the two:

> When I got all wore out, wid work, en wid de callin' for you, en went to sleep, my heart wuz mos' broke bekase you wuz los'. . . . En when I wake up en fine you back agin', all safe en soun', de tears come en I could a got down on my knees en kiss' yo' foot I's so thankful. En all you wuz thinkin' 'bout, wuz how you could make a fool uv ole Jim wid a lie. Dat truck dah is *trash*; en trash is what people is dat puts dirt on de head er dey fren's en makes 'em ashamed. (105, emphasis original)

Jim's moral indictment of Huck operates on two levels. First, the man is simply pointing out that Huck is immature to value a joke more than the feelings of a friend. But Jim also calls Huck "*trash*," alluding to Huck's poverty and poor social standing. Calling someone "white trash" was a serious insult that, in this case, is made more demeaning by the fact that a slave who supposedly has even less social standing than poor white trash is the one calling Huck the pejorative term. The situation parallels Pap's rant about the freedman who can vote: in both cases, the African American has superior judgment to the poor white male's, which defies the conventional thinking of the day. Unlike Pap, however, Huck can perceive his own immorality. He admits he was wrong and makes his apology: "I done it, and I warn't ever sorry for it afterwards, neither. I didn't do him no more mean tricks, and I wouldn't done that one if I'd a knowed it would make him feel that way" (105).

In the very next chapter, Huck makes another significant moral decision. Huck starts to feel guilty for not returning Miss Watson's property to her. "Conscience says to me, 'What had poor Miss Watson done to you that you could see her nigger go off right under your eyes and never say one single word? What did that poor old woman do to you, that you could treat her so mean?'" (124). He feels so guilty his conscience makes him feel "feverish" and "scorched" (123). Huck does not consider Jim's freedom to be a basic human right because he still views slaves as property. Eventually, Huck's "conscience got to stirring me up hotter than ever" (124). He experiences metaphorical fevers, scorching, and heat in a way that anticipates his eventual decision to go to hell for Jim's sake. But in this moment, Huck does not remember Miss Watson's greed in wanting to sell Jim away from his family in the first place, nor does he remember how much her hypocrisy has made Huck prefer "the bad place" to her company, so he falls prey again to the era's conventional morality. He chides himself because Miss Watson "tried to learn you your manners, she tried to be good to you every way she knowed how. *That's* what she done" (124). Nonetheless, after Jim calls Huck his best friend and says "[you] de on'y white genlman dat ever kep' his promise to ole Jim," the boy finds that he cannot turn Jim over to the authorities after all (125).

Huck shifts from feeling bad about stealing another person's property to feeling bad about not revealing that Jim is a runaway: "I knowed very well I had done wrong, and I see it warn't no use for me to try to learn to do right" (127). He laments his poor upbringing and asks himself this significant moral question: "what's the use you learning to do right, when it's troublesome to do right and ain't no trouble to do wrong, and the wages is just the same? I was stuck. I couldn't answer that. So I reckoned I wouldn't bother no more about it, but after this, always do whichever come handiest at the time" (127). In the book's first chapter, Huck has decided he "wouldn't try" to get into heaven or hell, but here he decides to be henceforth morally expedient. His morality has developed from "not trying" to "doing what is easiest." The morality is still a flawed morality, but it represents an important stage in his growth: he is at least willing to do something, to take action, rather than not trying anything at all.

In subsequent chapters, Huck experiences the consequences of living in the type of rigid and racist culture that values such concepts as "chivalry," "honor," and class difference as part of its conventional morality. Indeed, the first indication that such a culture might be doomed is the sinking riverboat the *Walter Scott*, symbolically named for an author popular with white readers in the South before the Civil War. Sir Walter Scott wrote romantic novels about class-bound but chivalrous characters, such as Robin Hood in *Ivanhoe*. Everyone aboard the *Walter Scott* drowns when it sinks, implying that anyone who believes Sir Walter Scott's romantic ideals about social class and the importance of honor as a concept with which to justify violent action is doomed to failure. In other words, the slave-holding upper class of the South is doomed to failure because its rigid sense of honor includes a conventional morality that is violent and racist. Another direct indictment of murdering in the name of the type of honor associated with the Southern aristocracy comes when Huck witnesses the feud between the Grangerfords and the Shepherdsons. The two families are destroying each other, like the two sides of the United States that have attempted to destroy each other during the Civil War. Ultimately, both families will sustain so many damages that even victory looks like failure. A third instance of the destructiveness of aristocratic notions of honor occurs when Colonel Sherburne shoots "the best-naturedest old fool in Arkansaw," in cold blood, even though Boggs is obviously too drunk to be held accountable for his actions and has "never hurt nobody, drunk nor sober" (184). Sherburne uses rhetorical control to manipulate the crowd when they want to lynch him: "The average man don't like trouble and danger. You don't like trouble and danger" (190). Sherburne is teaching Huck something about conventional morality: people are often unwilling to risk independent action when doing so would make them feel discomfort. As a factor in his moral development, Huck is learning that the arbiters of conventional morality in the antebellum South are violent, corrupt, and wrong in their willingness to prioritize concepts of honor above the life of any human being.

Huck and Jim then give refuge to two rapscallions who claim to be nobility—a duke and a king—although even Huck, in his naiveté, can tell that they are frauds. Huck gains an increasing respect for Jim when, late one night while the Duke and the King sleep, Jim tells Huck how ashamed he was when he hit his daughter, Elizabeth, one day. Jim has asked his daughter to close the door, which she does not do, so he strikes her, believing she is intentionally disobeying. But once he realizes that a recent bout of scarlet fever has left her deaf, his remorse demonstrates the depth of his humanity as a parent, which creates a commentary on the immorality of selling parents and separating them from their children: "O, Huck, I bust out a-cryin', en grab her up in my arms en say, 'O de po' little thing! de Lord God Amighty fogive po- ole Jim, kaze he never gwyne to fogive hisself as long's he live!' O, she was plumb deef en dumb, Huck, plumb deef en dumb—en I'd ben a treat'n her so!" (202) The reader has been instructed not only on the evil the slave trade creates in separating families but also on the ethics of taking advantage of people with physical disabilities.

In the very next chapter, the Duke and the King hatch an elaborate plan to make money by selling a family's slaves downriver while they rob that family of its money—including the wealth of a man who is deaf and dumb. Although Huck never consciously connects Elizabeth to William Wilks, who is deaf, Huck does decide that he cannot be party to taking advantage of Wilks's nieces, especially not Mary Jane. He says, "It was enough to make a body ashamed of the human race" (210). He cannot bear her pain at watching the slaves in her family being sold down river. Because his conscience weighs on him again, he makes his next moral decision: "I reckon a body that ups and tells the truth when he is in a tight place, is taking considerable many resks, though I ain't had no experience, and can't say for certain; but it looks so to me, anyway; and yet here's a case where I'm blest if it don't look to me like the truth is better, and actuly *safer*, than a lie" (239, emphasis original). Huck, who has been evaluating issues of lying and the truth since the first page of the novel, is demonstrating the type of dramatic irony on which his moral development is based. The reader recognizes—even if Huck does not—that he is doing the right thing when he helps Mary Jane.

The final stage in Huck's moral development occurs after the King and the Duke sell Jim back into slavery. Huck is astonished by their perfidy but decides it would be better to return Jim to Miss Watson, so he can "be a slave at home where his family was, as long as he'd *got* to be a slave" (268, emphasis original). After Huck writes a letter to Miss Watson explaining what has happened, he feels "good and all washed clean of sin for the first time I had ever felt so in my life, and I knowed I could pray, now" (269). Huck believes he is "clean of sin" when he adheres to conventional morality—but he still cannot pray. He remembers how good Jim has been to him, and he cannot "seem to strike no places to harden me against him, but only the other kind" (270). Huck thinks it over and then makes a decision he believes will have dire consequences: "All right, then, I'll *go* to hell" (271, emphasis original). When the novel opens, he has been unwilling to try to go to either heaven or hell, but now he is making a conscious decision to help free Jim, thereby defying conventional morality and choosing to burn in the flames of hell for eternity. For a nineteenth-century Protestant boy, the decision is a momentous indication of what he is willing to sacrifice for this friend, but more important, he is taking a firm action that defies social convention.

Almost immediately, Huck is falsely identified by Tom Sawyer's aunt and uncle—and he describes it as "like being born again, I was so glad to find out who I was" (282). Huck, however, has not been reborn into a clean, new soul; he has been "reborn" as the most corrupt character in the book, Tom Sawyer. Only as a conventional Southerner, talking to another conventional Southerner, can Huck utter the book's most callous line in answer to Aunt Sally's question whether anyone has been hurt by a steamboat accident: "No'm. Killed a nigger" (279). Huck is talking as he expects typical Southerners talk to each other. The indictment of racism is chilling.

The irony of Huck's rebirth as Tom helps explain the rapid shift in tone that occurs in the final chapters of the book. Several literary critics explain this change in terms of Twain's social criticism. Louis Budd, for example, sees Tom's shenanigans as a parody of Jim Crow laws, while Cecil Moffitt and Charles H. Nilon demonstrate that the ending parallels the corruption of government policies toward African Americans during Reconstruction. Steven Mailloux and Frederick Woodard and Donnarae MacCann, on the other hand, argue that the ending shows the impossibility of any nineteenth-century novel overcoming the "white supremacy myth" of that era's conventional morality.

Tom is certainly the embodiment of the corruption of that era's conventional morality. For example, when Tom reappears in chapter 33, Huck tells him he plans to rescue Jim from his entrapment. Tom says, "What! Why Jim is—" but he stops himself before he utters the words "free" (284). Tom would rather turn Jim into a plaything, into an object that allows Tom to recreate the type of class-based romantic entrapment narrative that Sir Walter Scott favored, rather than reveal the truth to Huck. Ironically, Huck tries to convince Tom not to sully himself by stooping to the level of helping a slave escape. Huck considers himself a lost soul already, but he cannot imagine why Tom would commit such an immoral act when he is

> a boy that was respectable, and well brung up; and had a character to lose; and folks at home that had characters; and he was bright and not leatherheaded; and knowing, and not ignorant; and not mean, but kind; and yet here he was, without any more pride, or rightness, or feeling, than to stoop to this business, and make himself a shame, and his family a shame, before everybody. (292)

Here, too, Twain relies on dramatic irony. The reader soon realizes that Tom is *not* respectable or well brought up. He is definitely not kind to Jim. Tom represents everything that is wrong with conventional morality, and although Huck has grown enough to risk going to hell for Jim, he has not grown enough to reject Tom's sense of morality.

Serving to emphasize Southern corruption, the King and the Duke are tarred and feathered and run out of town on a rail. (That is, they are dipped in hot tar and rolled in feathers so that the hot tar will stay on their skin, making it impossible for the second- and third-degree burns to heal. Then, they are tied naked onto a fence rail, straddling the sharp log, while men very likely pull down on each of their shoulders, pushing them onto the sharp edge of the fence rail. Men ridden out of town on a rail were typically jostled so roughly that their reproductive organs were severely injured.) Huck looks with horror on this scene and utters the book's most important theme: "Human beings *can* be awful cruel to one another" (290).

Yes, human beings can be awful cruel to one another—and the worst cruelty depicted in this novel is the cruelty of a racism so powerful that it allowed people to justify slavery, physical abuse of those slaves, and the separation of their families. Cruelty permeates the novel, including Pap's racist ranting and abuse of Huck; the treachery of the thieves aboard the sinking *Sir Walter Scott*; the Shepherdsons' and Grangerfords' cruelty to one another; Sherburne's cold-blooded murder of Boggs; and the Duke's and the King's many exploitations of various townspeople, the Wilks family, and ultimately, Jim. The King and the Duke receive a terrible punishment for their exploitative behaviors—they are tortured and possibly killed—but slavery and racism go virtually unpunished in the novel. Tom Sawyer spends several chapters torturing Jim with snakes and spiders and rats and games that appear at first to be merely silly but eventually become dangerous. Tom's callousness is just another manifestation of cruelty in this book. When Jim finally does try to escape, Tom is shot—and Jim sacrifices what he believes is his chance at freedom to nurse Tom.

The local doctor tells the crowd that is ready to lynch Jim how kind the man has been to both Tom and the doctor. The crowd softens, but Jim is placed in a more secure prison—until Tom recovers enough to return the book to its original concern with truth by confessing that he has been lying, all along. Tom commands his aunt, "They hain't no *right* to shut him up! . . . Turn him loose! he ain't no slave, he's as free as any cretur that walks this earth!" (356). Tom has known this and yet has been just as willing to exploit Jim as the King and the Duke have been. Tom never apologizes to Jim—he simply pays him off, "forty dollars for being prisoner for us so patient and doing it up so good" (360). Tom has reduced Jim to an object, but the man still retains his dignity in his relationship with Huck. It is Jim who tells Huck that his father is dead, which frees Huck to claim his own money and "light out for the Territory ahead of the rest" (362). Significantly, Huck has no plans to wait for Tom Sawyer, or even Jim, who can now work to free his family. Huck has made a decision to reject conventional morality and the women that want to "sivilize" him (362). He does not have the moral maturity to stay and fight slavery by joining with the Abolitionists, but he does have the maturity to recognize that he was in error when he believed his friend was a piece of property rather than a human being—and he has grown enough to crave independence from the strictures of conventional morality. Huck has grown, albeit into a maturity that requires him to reject his own culture. His coming of age is thus a scathing critique of racist Southern culture. Literary critic Myra Jehlen argues that *Adventures of Huckleberry Finn* became the first canonical novel in American literature because of the unique way it demonstrates this tension between individual rights and those of the community (113). But, she asks, if every individual were to reject conventional morality in order to mature as Huck does, how could any community ever cohere?

Irony drives the relationship between Huck's moral development and Twain's critique of racism. For example, Twain understood that the word "nigger" was offensive. He explains in the novel's "Explanatory" that he is recreating Southern dialects of the day—but he also uses this racial epithet to critique the racist attitudes of the region and era in which the novel is set (Fishkin 3–47). Moreover, in the preliminary

"Notice," Twain demonstrates the text's intended irony with the signature "By Order of the Author, Per G.G., Chief of Ordnance" (n.p.). During the Civil War, the Chief of Ordnance was the army officer charged with maintaining and protecting weapons and ammunition; in other words, he was the man responsible for keeping ammunition from blowing up at the wrong time. Twain knew his book was incendiary; he knew it was explosive. And with the "Notice," he is instructing readers to read ironically—and to expect their reading to yield to a volatile subject: racism.

In *The Elements of Moral Philosophy*, James Rachels defines a moral agent as

> someone who is concerned impartially with the interests of everyone affected by what he or she does; who carefully sifts facts and examines their implications; who accepts principles of conduct only after scrutinizing them to make sure they are sound; who is willing to 'listen to reason' even when it means that his or her earlier convictions may have to be revised; and who, finally, is willing to act on the results of this deliberation. (13–14)

Huckleberry Finn is not necessarily impartial about the interests of people who are affected by his actions; he is too worried about harming Miss Watson to be completely impartial. But in every other way, Huck fits this definition of a moral agent. He scrutinizes the principles of his conduct; he has to revise his earliest convictions; and he acts on the results of his careful deliberations. But because so many of Huck's deliberations are skewed by irony—especially verbal, dramatic, and comic irony—it is possible for readers to miss the fact that he has experienced the moral development required of the coming-of-age story. He does, nonetheless, come of age by developing as a moral agent, as someone who is capable of acting beyond his own self interest for the interests of others (Banta 191–207; see also Stephens 3).

The many coming-of-age novels that have been influenced by *Adventures of Huckleberry Finn* tend to share the following characteristic: they include an ironic and/or unreliable narrator who learns to separate himself or herself from conventional morality by thinking independently and rejecting the corrupt culture from which this conventional morality stems (Trites 144–46). *Catcher in the Rye, To Kill a Mockingbird, A Tree Grows in Brooklyn, The Outsiders*, and *The Absolutely True Diary of a Part-Time Indian* all follow this pattern, as do many other novels written for young adults. Mark Twain was the first author in American literature to link irony to moral development, an approach that has affected—and will continue to affect—generations of coming-of-age novels written in English.

Works Cited

Banta, Martha. "Rebirth or Revenge: The Endings of *Huckleberry Finn* and *The American*." *Modern Fiction Studies* 15 (1969): 191–207.

Budd, Louis J. *Mark Twain: Social Philosopher*. Bloomington: U of Indiana P, 1962.

Ellison, Ralph. "Change the Joke and Slip the Yoke." *The Collected Essays of Ralph Ellison*. Ed. John F. Callahan. New York: Random, 2003. 100–12.

Fishkin, Shelly Fisher. *Was Huck Black? Mark Twain and African American Voices*. New York: Oxford UP, 1993.

Hemingway, Ernest. *The Green Hills of Africa*. 1935. New York: Scribner, 1953.

Henry, Peaches. "The Struggle for Tolerance: Race and Censorship in *Huckleberry Finn*." *Satire or Evasions? Black Perspectives on* Huckleberry Finn. Eds. James S. Leonard, Thomas A. Tenney, and Thadious M. Davis. Durham: Duke UP, 1992. 25–48.

Jehlen, Myra. "Banned in Concord: *Adventures of Huckleberry Finn* and Classic American Literature." *The Cambridge Companion to Mark Twain*. Ed. Forrest G. Robinson. Cambridge, Eng.: Cambridge UP, 1995. 93–115.

Mailloux, Steven. "Reading *Huckleberry Finn*: The Rhetoric of Performed Ideology." *New Essays on* Adventures of Huckleberry Finn. Cambridge, Eng.: Cambridge UP, 1985. 107–33.

Mintz, Steven. *Huck's Raft: A History of American Childhood*. Cambridge, MA: Belknap, 2004.

Moffitt, Cecil L. "The Historical Ending of *Adventures of Huckleberry Finn*: How Nigger Jim Was Set Free." *American Literary Realism* 13.2 (1980): 280–83.

Nilon, Charles H. "The Ending of *Huckleberry Finn*: 'Freeing the Free Negro.'" *Satire or Evasions? Black Perspectives on* Huckleberry Finn. Eds. James S. Leonard, Thomas A. Tenney, and Thadious M. Davis. Durham: Duke UP, 1992. 62–76.

Rachels, James. *The Elements of Moral Philosophy*. 2nd ed. New York: McGraw, 1993.

Smiley, Jane. "Say It Ain't So, Huck." *Harper's Magazine* (Jan. 1996): 61–67.

Smith, David L. "Huck, Jim, and American Racial Discourse." *Satire or Evasion: Black Perspectives on* Huckleberry Finn. Eds. James S. Leonard, Thomas A. Tenney, and Thadious M. Davis. Durham, NC: Duke UP, 1992. 103–20.

Stephens, John. *Language and Ideology in Children's Fiction*. New York: Longman, 1992.

Stone, Albert E., Jr. *The Innocent Eye: Childhood in Mark Twain's Imagination*. New Haven: Yale UP, 1961.

Trites, Roberta Seelinger. *Twain, Alcott, and the Birth of the American Reform Novel*. Iowa City: U of Iowa P, 2007.

Woodard, Frederick, and Donnarae MacCann. "Minstrel Shackles and Nineteenth-Century 'Liberality' in *Huckleberry Finn*." *Satire or Evasions? Black Perspectives on* Huckleberry Finn. Eds. James S. Leonard, Thomas A. Tenney, and Thadious M. Davis. Durham: Duke UP, 1992. 141–53.

Stephen Dedalus and the Other: Interiority, Language, and Gender in *A Portrait of the Artist as a Young Man*

Vincent J. Cheng

For the young and developing consciousness, one of the real challenges of adolescence and coming of age is to learn how to reconcile interiority with exteriority—that is, how to negotiate the relationship between the internal "self" and the external "other," that challenging relationship between the images/visions in one's mind and the actual reality "out there." Such negotiation involves, of course, the developmental processes of socialization, individuation, and maturation into a "well-adjusted" adulthood. Negotiating external reality (and the tension between "self" and "other") is, of course, also the central topic of the traditional bildungsroman—that nineteenth-century novelistic genre ("the coming-of-age novel") tracing the development of the self, the *Bildung* of a young protagonist from early childhood to young adulthood.[1] This is a process of "socialization," the goal of which—in the realist tradition of the nineteenth century—is the achieved, harmonious alignment of the self with his or her society; that is, learning to make one's inner drives and realities conform to the external expectations of one's society and its external realities.[2] By contrast, modernism and modern literature increasingly focus on the nature of interiority and the internal vision, in opposition to external realities and external events. Indeed, Joyce's young protagonist Stephen Dedalus has, as we will see, a highly romantic and solipsistic internal vision that (to him) is often much more compelling and arguably "real" than his understanding of the external reality out there, the actual/factual "real world." This tension between interiority and exteriority is, of course, also the basis for the individual self's relationship to difference, to any "other" that is different from the "self." And one major manifestation of this tension for Stephen, in trying to come to terms with the world outside of the self, is how to understand the feminine Other. As he grows older,

Stephen will increasingly struggle—in his attempts to "socialize" and come of age—with the nature of the feminine and gender difference, trying to reconcile his internal visions of the feminine with the actual females he encounters. This essay will investigate the complex and suggestive ways by which Stephen Dedalus tries to negotiate these dynamics of "self" and "other," of interiority and exteriority, of language and experience, and—eventually—of male and female.

Early in the novel, Stephen, as a young schoolboy, tries to ground his sense of self by situating himself in the real world, writing in his flyleaf "himself, his name and where he was":

> *Stephen Dedalus*
> *Class of Elements*
> *Clongowes Wood College*
> *Sallins*
> *County Kildare*
> *Ireland*
> *Europe*
> *The World*
> *The Universe* (12)

Reading what he wrote, Stephen tries to convince himself that his identity can be thus constituted: "Then he read the flyleaf from the bottom to the top till he came to his own name. That was he" (13). Years later, walking around Cork with his father during a period in which "Nothing moved him or spoke to him from the real world," Stephen would similarly try to reassure himself that he could believe in a self grounded in external facts and external realities:

> —I am Stephen Dedalus. I am walking beside my father whose name is Simon Dedalus. We are in Cork, in Ireland. Cork is a city. Our room is in the Victoria Hotel. Victoria and Stephen and Simon. Simon and Stephen and Victoria. Names. (98)

More than such factual correspondences of places and names, however, it is language that allows Stephen a mode by which to try to understand external reality. Early in the novel, Stephen thinks about the word "suck" and how it corresponds onomatopoeically to reality:

> But the sound was ugly. Once he had washed his hands in the lavatory of the Wicklow Hotel and his father pulled the stopper up by the chain after and the dirty water went down through the hole in the basin. And when it had all gone down slowly the hole in the basin had made a sound like that: suck. Only louder. (8)

But for Stephen words have even greater powers and effects, as he goes on to articulate:

> To remember that and the white look of the lavatory made him feel cold and then hot. There were two cocks that you turned and water came out: cold and hot. He felt cold and then a little hot: and he could see the names printed on the cocks. That was a very queer thing. (8)

To Stephen, words seem to have their own reality, to be able to make you feel hot and cold just by reading the words "hot" and "cold": in other words, not only is a word a signifier, but it can become the very thing signified. This is an attempt to make language and external reality the same, the Word made Flesh—which is to say that, for Stephen, there is a correspondence and identification between the interior world of language and the imagination, and the exterior world of the physical senses. Language, signification, and interiority are indistinguishable to Stephen.

For example, Stephen first tries to understand girls and gender difference through words and phrases which his mind has seized upon, "Tower of Ivory, House of Gold," words describing the Virgin Mary (in the Litany of the Blessed Virgin Mary): "Eileen had long thin cool white hands too because she was a girl. They were like ivory; only soft.

That was the meaning of Tower of Ivory. . . . Her fair hair had streamed out behind her like gold in the sun. Tower of Ivory. House of Gold. By thinking of things you could understand them" (43). Stephen's ability to understand difference—here, a girl, Eileen Vance—depends on words. Increasingly Stephen's young mind tries to understand the real world through words, language, and literature: "Words which he did not understand he said over and over to himself till he had learned them by heart: and through them he had glimpses of the real world about him" (64). For the language and visions in his mind are more powerful than external reality, to the degree that Stephen tries to find in the world outside that which would make his internal visions actually become real. Fantasizing and brooding upon the image of the fictional Mercedes from *The Count of Monte Cristo*, the adolescent Stephen realizes "that he was different from others":

> He did not want to play. He wanted to meet in the real world the unsubstantial image which his soul so constantly beheld. He did not know where to seek it or how: but a premonition which led him on told him that this image would, without any overt act of his, encounter him . . . and in that moment of supreme tenderness he would be transfigured. . . . Weakness and timidity and inexperience would fall from him in that magic moment. (67)

Stephen has a romantic conception of meeting an "unsubstantial" feminine image which his soul worships—as with the Virgin—and he similarly expects the encounter to be a religious, transfiguring sort of experience in which "weakness and timidity would fall from him in that magic moment." What he wants is "to meet in the real world the unsubstantial image which his soul so constantly beheld": in other words, he wants to "substantiate"—to make real and corporeal—that which is "unsubstantial" (without physical substance) in his own mind. Rather than "socialize" by subordinating and adapting his inner visions to the demands of external reality, Stephen wants instead to "substantiate" in the real world the evidence and manifestation of his own inner promptings, which is to say that, on the contrary, he wants to turn interiority into reality, to turn imagination into external actuality, to transform language into the feminine—to make the conceptual Word into material Flesh.

Soon thereafter, Stephen recalls a case of what we might now call adolescent bullying: because Stephen had admitted to some schoolfellows his admiration of the poetry of the supposedly heretical poet Byron, they had set upon him and beat him with a cane, leaving him "torn and flushed and panting . . . half blinded with tears, clenching his fists madly and sobbing" (86). But remembering that experience, Stephen now wonders "why he bore no malice now to those who had tormented him. He had not forgotten a whit of their cowardice and cruelty but the memory of it called forth no anger from him" (87). For Stephen realizes that the experience can no longer touch him or affect him in the same way because the external world seems increasingly remote and unreal to him; the only things which now matter are the "unsubstantial" visions inside his mind, the more compelling "real-ness" of interiority.

So it is a shock to Stephen when, accompanying his father to Cork, he discovers, carved into a classroom desk, "the word *Foetus* cut several times in the dark stained wood"—for "It shocked him to find in the outer world a trace of what he had deemed till then a brutish and individual malady of his own mind. His recent monstrous reveries came thronging into his memory" (95). "The letters cut in the stained wood of the desk stared upon him, mocking his bodily weakness and futile enthusiasms and making him loathe himself for his own mad and filthy orgies" (96–97): this is the mind of a devout Catholic boy's sexual guilt, for we can assume that Stephen has been experiencing wet dreams and engaging in masturbation sessions, which he had previously imagined to be peculiarities of his own depraved mind. Now the carved word "Foetus" shocks him into the realization that his internal depravity may be shared by others, and that traces of it can thus be found in the outer world, too. As a result, every experience of the external, actual/factual world now seems to him increasingly to speak to, and be directed at, his own internal guilt (as Hamlet says, "How all occasions do inform against me;" 4.4.35). So that the words of Father Arnall's hellfire sermon—like the carved word "Foetus"—now serve to speak directly to his own depravity and internal state: "Every word of it was for him. Against his sin, foul and secret, the whole wrath of God was aimed" (123); "Every word for him! It was true" (134); "That was his hell. God had allowed him to see the hell reserved for his sins: stinking, bestial, malignant, a hell of lecherous goatish fiends. For him! For him!" (149). It is clear that, at this point, the relationship between interiority and exteriority has shifted drastically for Stephen: rather than trying to "socialize"—that is, to adapt himself to the external world, increasingly Stephen seems solipsistically to imagine that the relationship should be reversed; that the real world exists only to validate the internal experience or vision (even if it is his sexual guilt).

Soon after the Jesuit director of Belvedere College has talked to Stephen and has asked him whether he has a vocation, a calling to the priesthood (from *voco, vocare*: literally, a calling), tempting him to join the Jesuit order, we find Stephen now pacing back and forth:

> From the door of Byron's publichouse to the gate of Clontarf Chapel, from the gate of Clontarf Chapel to the door of Byron's publichouse and then back again to the chapel and then back again to the publichouse he had paced slowly at first, planting his steps scrupulously in the spaces of the patchwork of the footpath, then timing their fall to the fall of verses. (178)

Significantly, Stephen finds himself pacing back and forth between a chapel and a pub, mirroring symbolically the choice he is trying to make, that between the priesthood and ordinary life (the "public" house). But note also that the tavern is called Byron's publichouse— another symbolic correspondence for Stephen, whose calling will be artistic and poetic, and who will choose to go to the university instead of the seminary. Interestingly and importantly, most places depicted in Joyce's writings were actual places in Dublin (Clontarf Chapel is on the Clontarf Road, near the bridge to the "Bull," or North Bull Island)—reflecting the extreme naturalism of Joyce's writings, in which the streets of Dublin are reproduced with an almost photographic precision. Yet such realistic naturalism seems to exist only to reflect Stephen's inner reality, to reflect the choice to be made between the priesthood and the artistic/poetic vocation. Joyce's writings are, curiously, at once extremely naturalistically accurate and symbolically resonant. The text seems to reinforce Stephen's belief that not only can the artist shape or even invent reality ("forge in the smithy of my soul the uncreated conscience of my race"), but that the outer world serves only to reflect and validate one's own inner promptings. In the "Proteus" episode of *Ulysses*, Stephen will look at the tangible, visible, external reality of Sandymount Strand as "Signatures of all things I am here to read" (*Ulysses* 3.2): that is to say, the real world exists as a set of ordered signs to be decoded by the mind. Byron's publichouse and Clontarf Chapel may be real places in Stephen's experience of the world, but that almost seems incidental; for Joyce's purposes, rather, they serve more significantly (and symbolically) as external validations and meaningful signposts for the drama of Stephen's interiority.

No wonder that, when he now hears some schoolfellows who are swimming in the ocean call his name, even the external fact of his name (recall that "Names" were one way he had earlier tried to ground his sense of an external identity) now becomes a symbol for his own inner promptings:

Now, as never before, his strange name seemed to him a prophecy. . . . Now, at the name of the fabulous artificer, he seemed to hear the noise of dim waves and to see a winged form flying above the waves and slowly climbing the air. What did it mean? Was it a quaint device opening a page of some medieval book of prophecies and symbols, a hawk-like man flying above the sea, a prophecy of the end he had been born to serve and had been following through the mists of childhood and boyhood, a symbol of the artist forging anew in his workshop out of the sluggish matter of the earth a new soaring impalpable imperishable being? (183)

Discovering that his vocation is to be an artistic one, Stephen aspires—like Daedalus creating magical wings made of wax and string ("the sluggish matter of the earth")—as artist to create something equally magical, a "new soaring impalpable imperishable being" out of the materials of everyday life.

At this point, Stephen experiences an epiphanic encounter with the birdlike girl on the strand; this is a climactic, important, resonant, and multifaceted moment that has drawn the attention of a great deal of good Joycean scholarship (and I will only address those aspects of this encounter that directly apply to my current topic):

A girl stood before him in midstream, alone and still, gazing out to sea. She seemed like one whom magic had changed into the likeness of a strange and beautiful seabird. Her long slender bare legs were delicate as a crane's and pure save where an emerald trail of seaweed had fashioned itself as a sign upon the flesh. Her thighs, fuller and softhued as ivory, were bared almost to the hips where the white fringes of her drawers were like featherings of soft white down. Her slateblue skirts were kilted boldly about her waist and dovetailed behind her. Her bosom was as a bird's soft and slight, slight and soft as the breast of some darkplumaged dove. But her long fair hair was girlish: and girlish, and touched with the wonder of mortal beauty, her face. (185–86)

First of all, note how materially specific, physically nuanced, and un-usually detailed is the description of this girl on the beach ("long slen-der bare legs," "thighs, fuller and softhued" and so on)—as if Stephen were for once conscious of the specific, individual nature and differ-ence of an actual female Other. But in fact he does not care at all about her actual reality: for while the description of the external facts is very physically and materially specific, this female Other is also imbued with the symbolic details that speak to Stephen Dedalus's interiority: birdlike creature (flying, freedom, artistic independence, Daedalus the artificer, Icarus and Satan as prideful fallers from the sky, and so on); cool purity and ivory as markers of gendered otherness; blue and white dress, like the Blessed Virgin Mary; and so on. The specific details of an external reality thus only serve the promptings of Stephen's interiority: Stephen objectifies and aestheticizes the actual female Other by turning her into an artistic symbol for his newly discovered artistic vocation. She is very much, in his mind, that "unsubstantial image" he has been seeking. Recall: "He wanted to meet in the real world the unsubstantial image which his soul so constantly beheld. He did not know where to seek it or how: but a premonition which led him on told him that this image would, without any overt act of his, encounter him. . . . and in that moment of supreme tenderness he would be transfigured" (67). And Stephen seems very much transfigured, for it is a religious, transcendent moment for him: here is the symbolic idol in his new artistic faith, almost a symbol for art itself but certainly the muse and religious icon (like the Blessed Virgin Mary) whom he is going to follow as "a priest of eternal imagination" (240) and a devotee in the Sodality of the Blessed Birdlike Female:

> Her image had passed into his soul for ever and no word had broken the holy silence of his ecstasy. Her eyes had called him and his soul had leaped at the call. To live, to err, to fall, to triumph, to recreate life out of life! A wild angel had appeared to him, the angel of mortal youth and beauty, an envoy from the fair courts of life, to throw open before him in an instant of ecstasy the gates of all the ways of error and glory. On and on and on and on! (186)

This "wild angel" is no longer a real woman in a real-world setting. Her actual person and individual difference do not matter (and Stephen certainly has no intention of running up and asking her for a date), for she exists in Stephen's mind (as does the "real world") only to validate his internal vision and reality.

This moment parallels the earlier, masculinist aestheticizations and objectifications (in *Dubliners*) of Mangan's sister by the young narrator of "Araby"; and of Gretta Conroy by Gabriel Conroy in the short story "The Dead" (as a painting titled "Distant Music"). And it prefigures the objectification of Gerty MacDowell by Leopold Bloom in the "Nausicaa" episode of *Ulysses*, another climactic moment (literally so) also taking place on a strand in which again a male character gets erotically aroused by a girl on a beach—and masturbates himself to orgasm. "Nausicaa" is thus, in a sense, a parody of and commentary on this scene in chapter IV of *A Portrait*: for Stephen's excitement at the discovery of the bird-girl seems indeed a sort of aesthetic orgasm, a form of mental masturbation—in which the external Other and the "real world" seem not really to exist for Stephen, and in which his artistic vocation and potential creativity are theorized by Stephen as a purely autoerotic experience. (In the "Scylla and Charybdis" episode of *Ulysses*, Buck Mulligan will mock Stephen's aesthetic by naming it and parodying it as a drama about masturbation: *"Everyman His Own Wife or A Honeymoon in the Hand (a national immorality in three orgasms)"* (*Ulysses* 9.1171–74).

At this point, Stephen Dedalus's solipsism seems pretty complete, a solipsistic resistance to the socialization necessary for "coming of age." The young lady he had been attracted to for years, Emma Cleary, no longer matters—for the gendered Other exists only for the purposes of inspiration: in chapter V he composes a villanelle for her ("To E___ C____") which he has no intention of actually sending her. Rather, he fantasizes that she is flirtatious and promiscuous while admitting to himself that it might all just be in his mind (219, 234–36, 239–41). By the end of the book, when Stephen triumphantly announces his ambition "to forge in the smithy of my soul the uncreated conscience of my race" (276), it is hard not to read such forging in the smithy of one's soul as the triumph of the soul's internal vision, the triumph of interiority over external reality. Rather than "learning Intimacy versus Isolation" as a young adult—which is the sixth stage in Erik Erikson's classic "Eight Stages of Development"—Stephen conversely chooses "isolation" over "intimacy." [3] Far from having been "socialized," as in a traditional bildungsroman, the hero of Joyce's novel has, instead, domesticated external reality to his own purposes, and refashioned/ forged it to conform to his own inner promptings. (In that sense, it is hard not to read the novel, as a number of Joyce scholars have, as an ironic antibildungsroman—and perhaps by extension to read modernist interiority as a rejection of realist naturalism and of the belief in a solid world "out there.") Developmentally speaking, this is a type of arrested development—for, in the socialization of an adolescent to the adult world and to one's external environment, language typically is a tool by which to learn to connect to others (and thus to overcome the self's narcissism). With Stephen, it is the other way around: the Other only exists as a means to connect with language; with the self; and, in Stephen's case, with the self's growing mastery over its own interior language.

Notes

1. Well-known examples of the bildungsroman include Johann Wilhelm von Goethe's *Wilhelm Meisters Lehrjahre* (1795–96), Charles Dickens's *Great Expectations* (1861), Gustave Flaubert's *L'Education sentimentale* (1869), and Stendhal's *Le Rouge et le noir* (1830).

2. The Child Development Institute defines "socialization" as "a learning-teaching process that, when successful, results in the human organism's moving from its infant state of helpless but total egocentricity to its ideal adult state of sensible conformity coupled with independent creativity."

3. In studying the developmental tasks involved in the social and emotional development of children and teenagers continuing into adulthood, psychiatrist Erik Erikson first elaborated his now-classic "Eight Stages of Development" in 1956:

   1. Basic Trust vs. Basic Mistrust
   2. Autonomy vs. Shame and Doubt
   3. Initiative vs. Guilt
   4. Industry vs. Inferiority

5. Identity vs. Role Confusion

6. Intimacy vs. Isolation

7. Generativity vs. Stagnation

8. Ego Integrity vs. Despair

Works Cited

Anderson, Chester G., ed. A Portrait of the Artist as a Young Man: *Text, Criticism, and Notes*. New York: Viking, 1968.

Bloom, Harold, ed. *James Joyce's* A Portrait of the Artist as a Young Man. New York: Chelsea House, 1988.

Booth, Wayne. "The Problem of Distance in *A Portrait.*" *The Rhetoric of Fiction*. Chicago: U of Chicago P, 1961. 323–36. (also reprinted in Anderson and in Wollaeger)

Brady, Philip, and James F. Carens. *Critical Essays on James Joyce's* A Portrait of the Artist as a Young Man. New York: Hall, 1998.

Buttigieg, Joseph A. A Portrait of the Artist *in Different Perspective*. Athens: Ohio UP, 1987.

Carens, James F. A Portrait of the Artist as a Young Man. *A Companion to Joyce Studies*. Eds. Zack Bowen and James F Carens. Westport, CT: Greenwood, 1984. 255–359.

Castle, Gregory. *Reading the Modernist Bildungsroman*. Gainesville: UP of Florida, 2006.

_____. "Coming of Age in the Age of Empire." *James Joyce Quarterly* 40.4 (2003): 665–90.

Cheng, Vincent J. *Joyce, Race, and Empire*. Cambridge: Cambridge UP, 1995.

_____. "Nationalism, Celticism, and Cosmopolitanism in *A Portrait.*" Kershner 389–412.

Child Development Institute, LLC. "Eight Stages of Social-Emotional Development—Erik Erikson." *Child Development Institute*, Web. 24 Jan. 2012.

Connolly, Thomas, ed. *Joyce's* Portrait: *Criticisms and Critiques*. New York: Appleton, 1962.

Eide, Marian. "The Woman of the Ballyhoura Hills: James Joyce and the Politics of Creativity." *Twentieth-Century Literature* 44.4 (Winter 1998): 377–93. (also reprinted in Wollaeger and in Riquelme)

Ellmann, Maud. "Polytropic Man: Paternity, Identity, and Naming in the *Odyssey* and *A Portrait of the Artist as a Young Man.*" *James Joyce: New Perspectives*. Ed. Colin MacCabe. Bloomington: Indiana UP, 1983. 73–104.

Froula, Christine. *Modernism's Body: Sex, Culture, and Joyce*. New York: Columbia UP, 1996.

Gottfried, Roy. *Joyce's Comic Portrait*. Gainesville: UP of Florida, 2000.

Henke, Suzette. "Stephen Dedalus and Women: A Portrait of the Artist as a Young Misogynist." *Women in Joyce*. Eds. Suzette Henke and Elaine Unkeless. Urbana: U of Illinois P, 1982. 82–107.

Joyce, James. *A Portrait of the Artist as a Young Man.* Ed. Seamus Deane. New York: Penguin, 1993.

_____. *Dubliners.* Ed. Terence Brown. New York: Penguin, 1993.

_____. *Stephen Hero.* Ed. John J. Slocum and Herbert Cahoon. Norfolk, CT: New Directions, 1959.

_____. *Ulysses.* Eds. Hans Walter Gabler et al. New York: Vintage, 1986.

Kenner, Hugh. *Dublin's Joyce.* Bloomington: Indiana UP, 1956.

_____. "The *Portrait* in Perspective." *James Joyce: Two Decades of Criticism.* Ed. Seon Givens. New York: Vanguard, 1948. 132–74. (also reprinted in Anderson and in Wollaeger)

Kershner, R. Brandon, ed. A Portrait of the Artist as a Young Man*: Case Studies in Contemporary Criticism.* Boston: Bedford/St. Martin's, 2006.

Nolan, Emer. *James Joyce and Nationalism.* London: Routledge, 1995.

Riquelme, John Paul, ed. *A Portrait of the Artist as a Young Man: A Norton Critical Edition.* New York: Norton, 2007.

Scholes, Robert, and Richard M. Kain, eds. *The Workshop of Daedalus: James Joyce and the Raw Materials for* A Portrait of the Artist as a Young Man. Evanston, IL: Northwestern UP, 1965.

Schutte, William, ed. *Twentieth-Century Interpretations of* A Portrait of the Artist as a Young Man. Englewood Cliffs, NJ: Prentice-Hall, 1968.

Staley, Thomas F., and Bernard Benstock, eds. *Approaches to Joyce's* Portrait*: Ten Essays.* Pittsburgh: U of Pittsburgh P, 1976.

Thornton, Weldon. *The Antimodernism of Joyce's* A Portrait of the Artist as a Young Man. Syracuse, NY: Syracuse UP, 1994.

Wollaeger, Mark A., ed. *James Joyce's* A Portrait of the Artist as a Young Man*: A Casebook.* Oxford, Eng.: Oxford UP, 2003.

"Missing Everybody": Language and Identity in *The Catcher in the Rye*

Annette Wannamaker

When Jonathan Yardley of *The Washington Post* decided to reread *The Catcher in the Rye* on the fiftieth anniversary of its initial publication to see how well the book was holding up, he described rereading the novel as "almost literally a painful experience: The combination of Salinger's execrable prose and Caulfield's jejune narcissism produced effects comparable to mainlining castor oil." In his newspaper column, Yardley questioned why anyone still reads a novel "about a spoiled rich kid kicked out of a fancy prep school," why anyone would care about a protagonist who is so self-centered, and why any self-respecting English teacher would "require students to read a book as badly written as this one?" (Yardley C01). Many students assigned to read the novel in high school and college English classes enthusiastically echo Yardley's complaints.

For example, some students taking the university course I teach in adolescent literature characterize Holden as "whiny" and the prose as "unreadable." Some students say they struggle to plow through Holden's repetitive ramblings, and quite a few others strongly dislike Holden as a character, saying things like, "he just needs to get over himself" and "no wonder he doesn't have any friends." However, equally as many students are deeply moved by the novel and vigorously defend both Holden and J. D. Salinger as voices speaking directly to young people about the identity crises they undergo as part of coming of age. Quite a few students are empathetic toward Holden's struggles with depression, understand his contempt of phonies, and are touched by his close and loving relationship with his younger sister.

The fact that my students feel so strongly about the novel—either negatively or positively—and often passionately criticize or defend it in lively classroom discussions that sometimes turn into heated debates tells me that there is something going on in the pages of this book that is more significant than simply the whiny, self-indulgent ramblings of a "spoiled rich kid kicked out of a fancy prep school." What is it about Holden Caulfield's character and narrative voice that provokes such strong emotional reactions from readers? Why does the novel frustrate some readers while thoroughly engaging others? After teaching the novel for several years, I think the key to beginning to understand its polarizing effect on readers lies in working to understand what the novel is saying about the relationship between language and identity. Holden's repetitious ramblings reflect the ways in which language is an imperfect communication tool that continuously fails us. In other words, the novel is purposely frustrating to read, and our experience of reading it mirrors Holden's struggles to use language to make sense of his world and himself.

Holden, like many people (both young and old), wants to understand and to communicate, to make meaningful connections with the people in his life, and to love and be loved, but he does not know how to go about developing relationships. The novel is filled with examples of one failure to communicate after another: uncompleted phone calls, awkward conversations, misunderstandings that are the result of someone thinking one thing but saying another or someone hearing one thing and understanding another. Throughout the novel, Holden struggles with language and with other forms of representation. Like many of us, he wants desperately to find ways to communicate, but he is constantly frustrated by the tools available for him to use: words never quite express what we feel, and other forms of expression like art, theater, cinema, and music attempt to represent the human condition but always seem to fall short, always feel, to use Holden's term, "phony." Carefully examining Holden's struggles to communicate and the ways these struggles frustrate both characters and readers is a way to understand why this novel can be simultaneously disconcerting to read and also, for many young readers, profoundly moving. Such a reading can also illuminate the ways in which an important aspect of coming of age is coming to terms with the limits of expression.

At the start of the novel Holden has not come to terms with the limits of expression, and it is questionable whether he has by the story's end, either. Indeed, literary critics have debated for decades whether Holden ever comes of age or whether he even learns anything at all during the course of the novel. For example, in his essay "Holden Caulfield's Legacy," David Castronovo questions whether Holden or readers of the novel grow or learn anything of value. He writes that *The Catcher in the Rye* "isn't a story about development. Holden Caulfield has no unfolding destiny, no mission . . . Holden is a drifter whose life story is a muddle, a series of pathetic, comic, poignant incidents that are altogether unlike the destiny-building moments of . . . earlier books" (181). Castronovo asks us to consider that, "once you have had your fill of Holden denouncing anything and everything, you naturally wonder what it all amounts to. Does Salinger deliver any real insight, any recognition?" (182). Or, as his little sister Phoebe puts it near the end of the novel when she is frustrated by Holden's diatribes, "You don't like *any*thing that's happening. . . . You don't like any schools. You don't like a million things. You *don't*" (169; emphasis original). Holden's gloomy perspective and his repetitive complaints can make it seem as though he has not changed from the beginning of the story. On the other hand, Aidan Chambers writes that by the end of the novel Holden does change. He is beginning to come to grips with the very important understanding that "no man is an island. You can only be yourself, you can't become yourself, in an active relationship of care and attention given to and received from others. And not as the big person among immature children, but as an equal among others whose lives are as messy and as in need of help as you recognize yours to be" (276). These differences of opinion may result from the fact that, in many ways, *The Catcher in the Rye* brings the very concept of the coming-of-age novel into question; it rejects the idea that such a narrative is even possible. Can someone ever really come of age, ever fully know herself or himself? And, if such a journey were possible to complete, what words might fully express it? How does one communicate something so abstract and subjective as self-discovery?

When Holden lets us know at the novel's beginning that he's not going to give us any of that David Copperfield "crap," he (and author J. D. Salinger) is rejecting the traditional coming-of-age narrative structure as being hollow and phony, as being an inadequate form for expressing any sort of larger truth about oneself. For instance, he says, "the first thing you'll probably want to know is where I was born, and what my lousy childhood was like, and how my parents were occupied and all before they had me" (1). In this way he lets us know, from the very first sentence, that he is not going to tell a chronological story or fulfill readers' expectations of what a typical coming-of-age story ought to be (or, at least those coming-of-age novels in print before *The Catcher in the Rye* was published). An even more significant change to the usual structure of coming-of-age narratives is Salinger's choice to tell the story just after the events being described have happened to Holden. A more conventional coming-of-age story is most often told in the past tense from the first-person perspective of an adult who is looking back on his or her childhood. Such an adult narrator has perspective and is able to reflect thoughtfully on mistakes he made as a young person, able to discern which decisions and events turned out to be life changing (Wyile 186). In an essay titled "Expanding the View of First-Person Narration," Andrea Schwenke Wyile explains that narration in young adult novels often differs from the narration in novels written for an adult audience: "Young adult literature is preoccupied with self-development. The narrator in first-person young adult literature is not always cognizant of this development to the extent adult narrators have taught us (adult readers) to expect. In much adult literature, older, wiser narrators reflect back on their past and narrate the events that have brought them to their present vantage point" (186). In other words, the adult narrator is discussing her youth and has the benefit of hindsight, but the adolescent narrator is telling us her story in the moment, as she is experiencing it, which means she may not yet be aware of the ways in which she has grown. This style of narration, however, does not necessarily mean that a young adult narrator like Holden has not developed as a character. Instead, it means that we need to read young adult novels like *The Catcher in the Rye* differently, with different expectations than those we might have for a novel written for adults by an adult narrator.

Although most of *The Catcher in the Rye* is not told in the present tense, as is the case with many contemporary young adult novels, it is clear that Holden is still very close to the events that lead to his hospitalization, that he has not had time to reflect on the events in the story, and that his reactions are still raw and unfiltered. An adult narrator might be able to understand, from a more distant perspective, which past events were most important to his development; such a narrator could also explain to the reader how these events helped him to develop into the person he is now. Holden, however—as is the case with many of the protagonists in young adult novels that have been written since the publication of *The Catcher in the Rye*—has no such distance from the events he is narrating. When it comes to self-knowledge, Holden, as a narrator and a character, is both acutely aware and painfully unaware: He is able to observe minute details about the world around him, but he is not able to understand himself, his relationships, or his own motivations. Furthermore, because we as readers are not being guided through this coming-of-age narrative by a wise, adult Holden who has learned from his mistakes and has grown into a self-reflective, mature adult, we are in the position of having to decipher and discover the larger meanings of the events in the novel on our own.

Understanding Holden's development is especially difficult because, not only does Holden lack an emotional distance from the events he is narrating, he also is unable to adequately express his thoughts, frustrations, and desires using language. Maria Nikolajeva explains that novels that attempt to express the inner workings of the mind often reveal the ways in which "language does not always have adequate means to express vague, inarticulate thoughts and emotion" (173). Language is,

---

after all, an imperfect system of communication because words do not have exact meanings. If one person uses the word "tree," she could be thinking of a maple or a Christmas tree or a palm. The person listening to her or reading the word "tree" might be thinking of an elm or an oak. Abstract terms like "love," "freedom," and "soul" are even more difficult to pin down because they mean so many different things to different people. Homonyms also create slippages in meaning, because "to," "two," and "too" all sound the same but mean different things. Furthermore, language is always evolving: new words emerge every day and the meanings of old words change with time and context.

We all experience frustrations with language as an imperfect form of expression in our daily attempts to communicate. We have all had moments when we have had a misunderstanding with a family member or friend because we meant one thing but said another or because our words were interpreted differently than we intended. Most of us have also had moments when we have tried to write a note to someone or write a paper but we just cannot find the right words to express what we mean. Finally, there are some things that are just too complex, too abstract, or too tied to emotion to express using words.

The Catcher in the Rye chronicles Holden's many attempts to find new forms of expression that will work for him, and his identity crisis is very much connected to his frustrations with the failures of language. For Holden, the phoniness of language use—the way he and people around him say one thing but mean another—reflects the phoniness of his world. Holden agonizes over every white lie and every social nicety that is required to live in polite society: "I'm always saying 'Glad to've met you' to somebody I'm not at *all* glad I met. If you want to stay alive, you have to say that stuff, though" (87). The phoniness required to interact with other human beings, because saying exactly what we think and feel would hurt others, is maddening to Holden because it feels inauthentic; it feels as if every time he does not express precisely what he thinks, he is lying, misrepresenting himself and being a "Phony." On a deeper level, these feelings of frustration may also reflect the complex relationships between identity formation and language that are the subjects of much psychoanalytic theory. In psychoanalytic terms, there is a gap between "the Real" and "the Symbolic," which plays itself out in our everyday lives in our inability to use words, images, or symbols to convey what we truly feel, think, or desire. These terms, originally coined by the philosopher Jacques Lacan, are useful tools for understanding the ways in which language and identity formation are intertwined. Dino Franco Felluga includes clear definitions of both "the Real" and "the Symbolic" in his online "Introductory Guide to Critical Theory." He explains that "the Real" is

> the state of nature from which we have been forever severed by our entrance into language. Only as neo-natal children were we close to this state of nature, a state in which there is nothing but need. A baby needs and seeks to satisfy those needs with no sense for any separation between itself and the external world or the world of others. . . . As far as humans are concerned, however, 'the real is impossible,' as Lacan was fond of saying. It is impossible in so far as we cannot express it in language. (Felluga).

Lacan argued that human beings are always longing to return to and are always searching for "the Real," a feeling of authenticity or of wholeness with the world, a feeling of contentment we imagine we had as infants and lost as we moved into consciousness of the world around us. This longing is a feeling that can never be fully explained using language and, indeed, many people get quite frustrated trying to describe it using the tools of language, art, or other forms of expression. Furthermore, the longing focuses on a state that probably never really existed and, even if it did, cannot be re-entered. We can never go back to being infants, and logically we know this, though we subconsciously long to feel that imagined state of wholeness and connection with the world again.

"The Symbolic," on the other hand, is the sense of self, relationships with others, and understanding of the world that we are able to construct using language and other symbols. Felluga writes that, "once a child enters into language and accepts the rules and dictates of society, it is able to deal with others" (Felluga). In other words, language pulls us away from "the Real" (natural, whole, pre-linguistic) world we live in as infants, but this process is necessary because we must use language in order to function as a member of society, in order to communicate with others—even if language is imperfect and lacking. According to these theories, then, we always feel that something we can never quite explain is missing, that we are never able to fully express ourselves or to completely connect with other people, that we have lost touch with some natural or authentic part of ourselves. Furthermore, we are continuously frustrated with our inability to use signs, symbols, and language to fully express ourselves or our longing for "the Real."

These concepts offer us one way to think about Holden's frustrations with phoniness, with art, music, and writing, and with other human beings. Holden longs for "the Real" and is constantly frustrated by "the Symbolic." He is searching everywhere for "the Real"—in his relationships, his schooling, his experiences, and his consumption of the arts. "The Real," however, is impossible to achieve, and he either does not consciously know this or simply does not want to accept it. Ironically, throughout the entire novel, he is trying to find "the Real" by using "the Symbolic" (words, symbols, art). This is why he is continuously frustrated by the imperfections of language and the ways that it fails to adequately express anything but the phoniness of his own identity and what he perceives as the phoniness of other characters and the world around him.

Scholars and students often debate whether Holden is surrounded by phonies or whether he is phony himself. However, when we apply the theories of language and identity discussed above to a reading of the novel, it becomes clear that we are *all* phonies, but through no fault of our own. We all need language and other means of representation like music, film, and art in order to express ourselves and to communicate. Even though these tools are frustratingly imperfect and fail to express anything authentic, these are the only tools of communication we have. Holden is hyper-aware of the gap between "the Real" and "the Symbolic"—of the inability of words and symbols to convey any sort of truth that feels authentic—and he sees this gap everywhere around him, which he expresses using the word "phony."

The first sentence of the novel, which rejects existing coming-of-age narrative structures, is also one of many unsuccessful attempts by Holden to break free from the constraints of language. He begins by saying,

> If you really want to hear about it, the first thing you'll probably want to know is where I was born, and what my lousy childhood was like, and how my parents were occupied and all before they had me, and all that David Copperfield kind of crap, but I don't feel like going into it, if you want to know the truth. (1)

The last clause, "if you want to know the truth," could be read as one of the many bits of colloquial language in the novel or could be read literally, as in, the truth cannot be known or discovered using "all that David Copperfield kind of crap." Charles Dickens's work *David Copperfield* is one of the most famous coming-of-age novels and is considered to be a bildungsroman, or a story about the development of a protagonist from birth to adulthood. Holden rejects this literary form in the very first sentence of his narrative, calling it "crap." If we want to know Holden's truth, he will not be able to convey it to us using existing literary forms or existing tools of expression. He is battling with language—both the ways in which it fails to represent the truth and the ways in which it works to shape our identities, even before we are born. The language we use, after all, pre-exists us and, as we learn to use it, we are being shaped by the words, meanings, grammatical structures, and narrative traditions that make up our systems of communication.

As the novel progresses, Holden struggles with one form of expression after another, calling them all "phony": he says, "if there's one thing I hate, it's the movies. Don't even mention them to me" (2); he does not understand why his schoolmates care about football games and other sports (2–3); he has nothing but contempt for a speech given by a school alumnus (16–17); he aborts numerous potential conversations and phone calls before they can take place; he goes to see a band, which he calls "putrid" (69); he describes another musician as "putting all these dumb, show-offy ripples in the high notes, and a lot of other very tricky stuff that gives me a pain in the ass" (84); he calls for a prostitute when he is feeling lonely but then is unable to have sex with her or even hold a conversation with her (90–98); he tries to pray before bed but says, "I couldn't pray worth a damn" (100); he takes Sally to see an afternoon theater performance but complains about how much he hates actors because "they never act like people. They just think they do" (117); and he says that he hates school because "all you do is study long enough to be smart enough to buy a goddam Cadillac some day, and you have to keep making believe you give a damn if the football team loses" (131). Almost every attempt by anyone he encounters to make sense of the human condition or to express themselves through movies, sports, oration, conversation, music, sex, prayer, theater, or education feels hollow and meaningless to him because none of them approach "the Real;" none of them fulfill his longing for something authentic. Some critics and students have called Holden a hypocrite because, for example, he says he hates the movies but continues to watch them anyway; he says he hates books but continues to read them anyhow. Viewed through the lens of psychoanalytic theories about identity and language, though, his conflicted relationship with various forms of expression makes sense as a sort of fruitless and frustrating quest for meaning.

Holden restlessly and relentlessly moves from place to place, from person to person and from random thought to random thought looking for something that feels true to him. On a few occasions, he considers moving away from the city and living out in nature, as if removing himself from civilization will give him the peace he seeks. On a casual date with Sally, Holden proposes they run away together:

> What we could do is, tomorrow morning we could drive up to Massachu-setts and Vermont, and all around there, see. It's beautiful as hell up there. . . . We'll stay in these cabin camps and stuff like that until the dough runs out, I could get a job somewhere and we could live somewhere with a brook and all and, later on, we could get married or something. I could chop all our own wood in the wintertime and all. (132)

Sally responds to Holden's wild musings saying, "You can't just *do* something like that" and "we'd starve to death" (132), effectively squashing his incoherent daydreams. Significantly, while Holden uses a lot of words to express his longing for "the Real," he is not really saying much of anything. Phrases like "stuff like that," "a job some-where," "we could live somewhere" and "get married or something" all illustrate that he only has vague ideas about living in the wilderness, and that he is longing for something he is not able to express in words.

The final portions of the novel demonstrate, in fairly literal ways, Holden's longing for "the Real": He idealizes his little sister and his dead younger brother, and he fantasizes about catching children before they fall off the edge of a cliff. He wants to protect childhood from the corrupting forces of the world, perhaps because he longs to return to his own childhood. Holden, significantly, misremembers the lyrics of Robert Burns's poem "Coming through the Rye." His little sister knows the difference and reminds him that the lyric is "if a body meet a body coming through the rye," not "if a body catch a body." Holden's misreading is significant because it forms the title of the novel and also his dream of "the Real." Chambers writes that, "Holden's Freud-ian slip—'catch' for 'meet'—is revealing. What he 'really wants' is to live in a Never-Never-Land peopled only by 'innocent' children, except for himself, the only 'big person,' who would be their guard-ian, their 'catcher'—in other words, their keeper and savior" (274).

The word "catch" implies an unequal relationship, a relationship in which Holden has information and power the children in his fantasy do not possess. The word "meet," on the other hand, implies more of an encounter between equals, an encounter with possibilities for misunderstandings and misinterpretations. The children in Holden's fantasy are less fellow human beings and more a symbol: he imagines keeping adulthood and loss of innocence forever in abeyance as he catches the children and prevents them, and more importantly, himself, from tumbling over the edge of the cliff into adulthood. The impossibility of this fantasy becomes clear to Holden the following day.

When, in the last few pages of the novel Holden sees the phrase "fuck you" written on several different walls in the city, he comes face-to-face with the limits of expression and with his inability to ever be "the catcher in the rye," a protector of children and of innocence who has returned to the bliss of "the Real" and who can protect others from having to leave it. The first place he sees "fuck you" is on a wall at his sister's school: "I thought how the other kids would see it, and how they'd wonder what the hell it meant, and then some dirty kid would tell them—all cockeyed, naturally—what it meant, and how they'd all *think* about it and maybe even *worry* about it for a couple of days" (201). He rubs the phrase off the wall in an attempt to protect the children. He imagines a bum snuck into the school to write the phrase, and it never occurs to him that one of the supposedly innocent children at the school might have been the one who wrote it. Then, just a page later, Holden sees a second "fuck you" on another wall at the school: "I tried to rub it off with my hand again, but this one was *scratched* on, with a knife or something. It wouldn't come off. It's hopeless, anyway. If you had a million years to do it in, you couldn't rub out even *half* the 'Fuck you' signs in the world. It's impossible" (202). Finally, Holden goes to the museum, where two boys ask him to help them find the room with mummies in it. The boys are frightened by the tomb and leave, but Holden stays by himself in the tomb, happy to be alone:

It was nice and peaceful. Then, all of a sudden, you'd never guess what I saw on the wall. Another 'Fuck you.' It was written with a red crayon or something, right under the glass part of the wall, under the stones.

That's the whole trouble. You can't ever find a place that's nice and peaceful, because there isn't any. You may think there is, but once you get there, when you're not looking, somebody'll sneak up and write 'Fuck you' right under your nose (204).

This last "fuck you" scrawled next to a tomb is a sign for Holden that he is never going to escape the confines of language and is never going to access "the Real." He realizes this when he says, "I think, even, if I ever die, and they stick me in a cemetery, and I have a tombstone and all, it'll say 'Holden Caulfield' on it, and then what year I was born and what year I died, and then right under that it'll say 'Fuck you.' I'm positive" (204). Holden cannot escape "the Symbolic" and finally comes face-to-face with the limits of expression and with the ways in which language shapes our identity and culture at the same time as it limits them. In other words, Holden's perceptions are shaped by words and symbols that existed long before he did and that will be around long after he is gone. Language, art, music, and other forms of expression are always going to feel "phony" because these are larger systems over which we, as individuals, have little influence. Holden, therefore, learns at the end of the novel that there are just some things we cannot put into words, and that these are the things, ironically, that may be the most meaningful to us.

While quite a few critics and students point to the scene when Holden is watching the children on the carousel as an epiphany of sorts, I am less sure it represents Holden having actually found a true moment of happiness, or "the Real," than his finally coming to terms with the limits of language. He says, very simply, "I felt so happy all of a sudden, the way old Phoebe kept going around and around. I was damn near bawling, I felt so happy, if you want to know the truth" (213). It's one of the few places in the novel where Holden is at a loss for words, where he doesn't ramble on and on in order to say very little. If there is any epiphany, it is Holden's accepting the limitations of language and the fact that he can only imagine "the Real," but can never return to it. He knows he cannot return to his own infancy by getting onto the carousel with Phoebe, he knows he cannot catch her as she falls off the cliff into adulthood, he knows that his love for her is a feeling that would feel "phony" if he tried to put it into words, and, most significantly, he is accepting these limitations rather than fruitlessly fighting against them.

In her book *Disturbing the Universe: Power and Repression in Adolescent Literature,* Roberta Seelinger Trites distinguishes between the expectations readers have for modern coming-of-age narratives and the different expectations they should have for postmodern coming-of-age narratives. While the modernists expected a character to have some sort of epiphany, to "find himself" and to come to know himself as an individual, postmodern narratives "self-consciously explore the individual's power in relation to the institutions that comprise her or his existence" (18). In other words, Holden's journey is less about making some great discovery about who he is as a person or about "finding himself" than it is about figuring out the social systems (like language) that shape his identity, his world, and his place in relation to these social systems. Trites writes that "in the adolescent novel, protagonists must learn about the social forces that have made them what they are" (3) and that these novels "tend to interrogate social constructions, foregrounding the relationship between the society and the individual rather than focusing on Self and self-discovery" (20). If this is the case for *The Catcher in the Rye*, then it makes sense to think about Holden's progress less as a coming-of-age story and more as a story of coming to terms: Holden learns that he must participate in society—even though it is imperfect—instead of imagining an idealized retreat from it.

The last enigmatic line of the novel, "Don't ever tell anybody anything. If you do, you start missing everybody" (214) hints at a small, yet important, change in Holden. The word "miss" can be read in different ways: Has Holden, "the catcher in the rye," started to miss everybody running past him off the edge of the cliff? Is he missing the people in his life, both the dead and the living? And why would writing or speaking, telling people things, lead to "missing everybody"? Because Holden is narrating this line in present tense without the benefit of hindsight, we do not know if it marks a turning point or a moment of discovery for him. It does, however, show that he understands that there is a connection between language and identity, and that talking about "the Real" misses the point.

Works Cited

Castronovo, David. "Holden Caulfield's Legacy." *New England Review* 22.2 (Spring 2001): 180–86.

Chambers, Aidan. "Finding the Form: Toward a Poetics of Youth Literature." *Lion and the Unicorn* 34.3 (2010): 267–83.

Felluga, Dino. "Modules on Psychoanalysis." *Introductory Guide to Critical Theory.* Purdue University, 1 Jan. 2011.Web. 27 July 2011.

Nikolajeva, Maria. "Imprints of the Mind: The Depiction of Consciousness in Children's Fiction." *Children's Literature Association Quarterly* 26.4 (2001): 173–87.

Salinger, J. D. *The Catcher in the Rye.* Boston: Little, 1951.

Trites, Roberta Seelinger. *Disturbing the Universe: Power and Repression in Adolescent Literature.* Iowa City: U of Iowa P, 2000.

Wyile, Andrea Schwenke. "Expanding the View of First-Person Narration." *Children's Literature in Education* 30.3 (1999): 185–202.

Yardley, Jonathan. "J. D. Salinger's Holden Caulfield, Aging Gracelessly." *Washington Post* 19 Oct. 2004, C01.

Coming of Age in Bronzeville: Gwendolyn Brooks's *Annie Allen*_____

Jane Hedley

Annie Allen, published in 1949, was the first book by an African American writer to win the Pulitzer Prize. There were critics who thought that its author, Gwendolyn Brooks, had paid too high a price for this accolade from mainstream America. "*Annie Allen* . . . seems to have been written for whites," says Don L. Lee in his preface to Brooks's 1972 memoir, *Report from Part One*; the poems in this volume demonstrate her ability to use "their language" and "their groundrules" but are too involved with their own literariness to "communicate with the masses of black people" (19). But among poets and critics who are women, the book has received a more enthusiastic reception, especially for its long and difficult central poem, "The Anniad." Both Nikki Giovanni and Elizabeth Alexander were inspired to think of themselves as potential poets because of what this poem showed them could be done with language and its focus on an African American girl's coming of age. [1]

Annie Allen is the protagonist of the entire volume, which is divided into three sections. In "Notes from the Childhood and the Girlhood," she is growing up in the 1930s in the Chicago neighborhood known as Bronzeville, where Brooks grew up. Not much happens to Annie in these poems; in "the birth in a narrow room," the omniscient voice of the poet predicts that by the time she reaches adolescence she will be thinking, "How pinchy is my room! how can I breathe! / I am not anything and I have got / Not anything, or anything to do!" (*Blacks* 83) She is a restless and dreamy girl, impatiently waiting for something or someone to rescue her life from insignificance. The form in which rescue presents itself to her imagination is romantic and matrimonial—a version of "Someday my prince will come." The book's middle section, "The Anniad," is a narrative poem in forty-three stanzas in which Annie meets her prince, marries him, and suffers the death of all her romantic illusions.

In both "Notes from the Childhood and the Girlhood" and "The Anniad," the poet's perspective on her protagonist is omniscient and detached. But in "Appendix to the Anniad: leaves from a loose-leaf war diary," Annie herself or someone very like her is speaking. This is also true of "The Womanhood," a more miscellaneous group of poems that includes a sonnet sequence, a handful of Bronzeville character sketches, and several poems of social commentary in free verse. In "The Womanhood" Annie's perspective is no longer distinct from Brooks's; like the poet, she is a mature woman whose girlish dreams have been set aside. In "the children of the poor," the sonnet sequence that begins this section of the volume, she has children of her own and is soberly wondering how to love them wisely. "What shall I give my children? who are poor, / Who are adjudged the leastwise of the land" (*Blacks* 116). She has more questions than answers, but at least she has taken the measure of what she and they are facing.

Explaining the genesis of "The Anniad" to George Stavros, the editor of *Contemporary Literature* magazine, in 1969, Brooks claimed to have named it after Homer's epic of the Trojan War: "I thought of the *Iliad* and said, I'll call this 'The Anniad'" (*RPO* 158). She may also have been thinking of Vergil's *Aeneid*, a Latin epic named for the founder of Rome. Is "The Anniad," then, an epic? According to Abrams and Harpham's *Glossary of Literary Terms,* an epic is "a long verse narrative on a serious subject, told in a formal and elevated style, and centered on a heroic or quasi-divine figure on whose actions depends the fate of a tribe, a nation, or . . . the human race" (Abrams and Harpham 97). Brooks's poem is long enough to qualify as an "epyllion," or "little epic"; its seven-line stanza is similar to the "rime royal" stanza Shakespeare used for his "little epic," "The Rape of Lucrece." But the coming of age of an ordinary girl from Bronzeville is not a promising subject for epic treatment, since it is hard to see how anything much depends on Annie's actions—except of course her own (un)happiness.

Is "The Anniad," then, a mock-epic, its generic elevation "purposely mismatched" with "a commonplace or trivial subject matter"

(Abrams and Harpham 36–37)? The purpose of such a mismatch could either be to mock the self-importance of a poem's protagonists or to call the heroic pretensions of the genre itself into question. In "The Rape of the Lock," his mock-heroic masterpiece, Alexander Pope is doing both. By parodying the style and conventions of epic to stage a quarrel between eighteenth-century beaux and belles over the theft of a lock of hair, Pope suggests they are giving a trivial matter far too much importance; at the same time, he calls attention to how thoroughly out of place the heroism of an Achilles or an Aeneas would be among the hyper-civilized aristocrats of his own day. In "The Anniad," Brooks's agenda is akin to Pope's. "Well, the girl's name was Annie," she says to Stavros, "and it was my little pompous pleasure to raise her to a height that she probably did not have." What Brooks is mocking in "The Anniad" is not her protagonist, however, but the romantic notions that have equipped her so badly for adult life in the real world. *Vis-à-vis* the genre of epic, Brooks is challenging the priorities of a poetic tradition that up until now has taken no interest in lives like Annie Allen's. She is, in effect, saying to Stavros, "Well, no one else was going to write an epic about this girl, but her story mattered to me, so I had to do it myself."

Annie's story mattered to Brooks because it could have been her own. In *Report from Part One*, a memoir of her childhood and early married life, she describes herself as having been a sweet, shy, dreamy girl well into her twenties. Like Annie, she dreamed of being swept off her feet by a dashing and handsome man who would adore her; Henry Blakely, the man she met and married at twenty-one, had a dimple in his chin like Annie's "man of tan." The "lowly room" to which "tan man" brings Annie as his bride, and which she contrives to "make a chapel of," is obviously modeled on the dreary one-room apartment Brooks recalls from the early years of her own marriage (*RPO* 59). Men from Bronzeville fought overseas in World War II; Henry Blakely was not, but could have been, among them. Had he returned from combat, like Annie's husband, a hollow shell of a man with no appetite for resuming their life together, Brooks too might thus have found herself, in her mid-twenties, "almost thoroughly / Derelict and dim and done" ("The Anniad," stanza 43; *Blacks* 109). She was resourceful and fortunate enough not to share the outcomes of Annie's life, although she had similar life circumstances.

In "Notes from the Childhood and the Girlhood," Annie's mother tries in vain to teach her how lucky she is to have a healthy body and a decent home. Annie is meanwhile trying "to teach her mother / There was somewhat of something other" ("Maxie Allen," *Blacks* 84). With no clear idea of what that "something" is—"whether . . . fleet love stopping at her foot / And giving her its never-root / To put into her pocket-book," or "just a deep and human look"—she only knows that she hasn't experienced it yet (84). And so she tunes out her mother's scolding and proudly waits for someone who will satisfy the requirements of her imagination:

> Whom I raise my shades before
> Must be gist and lacquer.
> With melted opals for my milk,
> Pearl-leaf for my cracker. ("the ballad of late Annie,"
> *Blacks* 90)

With the sheer beauty of this stanza's language Brooks conveys that romantic notions like these are necessary to the survival of Annie's imagination—of her very soul, perhaps. Tragically, however, they will take her to a worse place than if she had done without them.

The opening stanza of "The Anniad" uses a number of "epic" gestures to set Annie's story in motion:

> Think of sweet and chocolate,
> Left to folly or to fate,
> Whom the higher gods forgot,
> Whom the lower gods berate;

Physical and underfed

Fancying on the featherbed

What was never and is not. (*Blacks* 99)

Like the heroes and gods of Homer's *Iliad*, swift-footed Achilles and laughter-loving Aphrodite, our heroine gets an epithet, "sweet and chocolate," that will belong to her throughout the poem. As it turns out, her "fate" will be closely tied to the "chocolate" color of her skin. In *Report from Part One* Brooks explains that when she was in high school, "a dark-complexioned girl just didn't have a chance if there was light-skinned competition" (172): Annie's husband will lose his appetite for "chocolate" and find himself a lighter-skinned mistress. "The higher gods" are the ones who watch over, and sometimes intervene in, the lives of epic heroes, like Athena helping the Greeks to win the Trojan War; predictably enough, they will not be taking an interest in Annie's story. The "lower gods" might be authority figures like her mother, scolding her for dreaming of "something other" when she could be doing something useful. Alternatively, "the lower gods" are channeling public attitudes in the society at large: a tendency to blame poor people for their poverty was fairly widespread in 1949, though the stereotype of the welfare mother was not yet in use. Annie is "physical" in the sense that she has begun to have sexual desires and feelings, and she is "underfed" in a metaphoric or spiritual sense.

The adventures she is about to have would be easy to summarize, and yet a storyline as such is not easy to find in "The Anniad." External events are not what the poem cares about; what is happening inside Annie's psyche or soul is what makes her story worth telling. Its crucial events and turning points are often recounted metaphorically, in language that both heightens and defamiliarizes them. Oxymoron—the pairing of descriptive terms that seem to disagree with each other or pull in opposite directions—is a key stylistic device. Stanza 3, which depicts Annie waiting for something momentous to happen to her, is a case in point:

Think of ripe and rompabout,
All her harvest buttoned in,
All her ornaments untried;
Waiting for the paladin
Prosperous and ocean-eyed
Who shall rub her secrets out
And behold the hinted bride. (*Blacks* 99)

"Ripe and rompabout," a nonce (i.e., one-time) epithet for our heroine, conveys that she is ready for sexual experience but still has the boisterous energy of a child ("rompabout" being "romp[s] about" transformed into an adjective): she is being pulled in both directions. She still dresses demurely, even though her body is "ripe" for "harvest," because she is saving herself for a worthy lover; "ornaments untried" are the features and gestures that will make her attractive to him. The poem has instructed us to "think of" these things in order to stress the human importance and complexity of the point of transition Annie has reached. She is a not-yet-but-almost woman whose readiness for romantic love is mental as well as physical and includes desires she is keeping secret even from herself.

Sexual courtship presents itself to Annie's imagination as an exciting adventure. "Paladin," the poem's word for the knight in shining armor who will bring her this adventure, recalls the heroes of Christian epic poems like the *Song of Roland* and, in English, the knights of King Arthur.[2] Her paladin will be "prosperous and ocean-eyed," a man of the world who can widen her horizons. The next stanza describes him oxymoronically as "Paradisiacal and sad / With a dimple in his chin / And the mountains in the mind": he will be adorable yet awesome, heaven-sent yet down-to-earth. "Ruralist and rather bad," he will be ruggedly and unapologetically masculine; "Cosmopolitan and kind," he will also, however, be sophisticated and chivalrous. Such epithets as these turn a cliché into a miracle, "the paladin / Which no woman ever had" but every woman dreams of (stanza 4, *Blacks* 99-100).

In Spenser's *Faerie Queene* the warrior maiden Britomart, having met the man she is destined to marry, dreams of herself as a handmaid (in the temple of Isis) whose white robe suddenly and surprisingly turns red. Annie, like Spenser's heroine, is a "thaumaturgic lass"—one who believes in miracles or has a miracle-working imagination. In stanza 5, while she waits for her own life's miracle to happen, she communes with her looking-glass in a stanza that recalls a key scene from "The Rape of the Lock":

> Think of thaumaturgic lass
> Looking in her looking-glass
> At the unembroidered brown;
> Printing bastard roses there;
> Then emotionally aware
> Of the black and boisterous hair,
> Taming all that anger down. (*Blacks* 100)

Think not only of Annie but also of Pope's eighteenth-century heroine, seated at her dressing table in an important scene from "The Rape of the Lock." Annie is channeling the frustration she feels in waiting for the man of her dreams to materialize into cosmetic rituals that reflect contemporary beauty stereotypes: brightening her skin and straightening her hair. When her paladin arrives, she must be ready.

The stanza that brings him into her life is an especially good example of how the poem's key moments are both elevated and complicated by its highly metaphoric language:

> And a man of tan engages
> For the springtime of her pride
> Eats the green by easy stages,
> Nibbles at the root beneath

With intimidating teeth.

But no ravishment enrages.

No dominion is defied. (stanza 6, *Blacks* 100)

In his interview with Brooks, George Stavros uses this stanza to illustrate how much "more cryptic, more compressed" "The Anniad" is than the poems in her first published volume, *A Street in Bronzeville* (*RPO* 159): cryptic in that it speaks in metaphors, "compressed" in that the human subjects and objects of most of its verbs have been elided to produce a series of "headless" sentences (it is the "man of tan" who "eats . . . [and] . . . nibbles," but it is Annie who is not enraged and does not defy his dominion). But as Brooks points out to Stavros in response, a plainer statement would have needed *fewer* words: "Yes . . . the young man is courting her, and . . . really, I could have pushed what I wanted into two lines, you know; I *could* have said, well, he came and he pursued her, but she was all ready for the outcome, in fact, eagerly awaiting it" (159). The poem's account of "tan man's" courtship and Annie's capitulation is more vivid and interesting, however, than if we were told these things directly. The metaphoric image of a stag or a stallion grazing in a garden is both aurally and visually striking (when you say the words aloud your mouth has to "nibble" them); its unstated topic is sexual conquest. With its intimations of tenderness, intimacy, excitement, and danger, this metaphor conveys that Annie's sexual initiation is at once a violation and a consummation of her womanhood.

In stanzas 7 and 8, "tan man's" conquest and Annie's psychic thralldom get more fully developed, in phrases that conjure an awesomely powerful experience. "Narrow master master-calls; / and the godhead glitters now / Cavalierly on his brow" (*Blacks* 100): "tan man" wears Annie's adoration like a crown, but "cavalierly" (a word that evokes knightliness but also nonchalance). "What a hot theopathy / Roisters through her, gnaws the walls, / And consumes her where she falls / In her gilt humility" (100). "Theopathy," an emotional responsiveness to divine influence, is "hot" in this context; it "roisters" and "gnaws":

---

the experience of falling in love is powerful and all-consuming. "Tan man" is surprised by Annie's worship ("Unfamiliar, to be sure, / With celestial furniture") but flattered by it (stanza 8, *Blacks* 100–1). They get married in stanza 9, which brings Annie to the altar in a trance-like state of exaltation: "In the beam his track diffuses / Down her dusted demi-gloom / Like a nun of crimson ruses / She advances" (*Blacks* 101). Like Spenser's Britomart, Annie is a virgin whose "crimson ruses" suggest her readiness for adult sexuality.

No sooner have she and her husband, following "the path his pocket chooses," settled into "a lowly room. // Which she makes a chapel of" (stanzas 9–10, *Blacks* 101), than a war in Europe stakes a rival claim to his manhood. Stanza 12, one of the most cryptic in the poem, risks unintelligibility in order to convey the war's cataclysmic impact:

> Doomer, though, crescendo-comes
> Prophesying hecatombs.
> Surrealist and cynical.
> Garrulous and guttural.
> Spits upon the silver leaves.
> Spits upon the dainty eves
> Dear dexterity achieves. (*Blacks* 101–2)

"Hecatomb" is a word that means "enormous public sacrifice" (derived from the ancient Greek custom of sacrificing a hundred oxen to appease the gods). In the "oom" sound this word shares with "Doomer," the poem's resonant epithet for war, we can almost hear the booming of cannon rise to a crescendo in the stanza's opening lines. Before ending in 1945, World War II would claim almost two billion lives; the stanza's third and fourth lines describe the voice in which that prophecy is delivered with oxymoronic pairs of adjectives whose sound is part of their meaning. Lines 5 through 7 link back to the previous two stanzas, where "silver" is metaphoric shorthand for the imaginative alchemy that transforms a "lowly room" into a "chapel": "Tender candles ray by ray / Warm and gratify the gray. // "Silver flowers fill the eves / Of the metamorphosis" (stanzas 10–11, *Blacks* 101). Annie's imagination has silvered over her unpromising surroundings, but the war is no respecter of a new bride's "dear dexterity." And thus whereas stanzas 10 through 12 are full of metaphoric circumlocution, the language of stanza 13 is brutally direct. (Its headless predicates all have "Doomer" as their implied subject, as do all the predicates, adjectival or verbal, in stanza 12).

> Names him. Tames him. Takes him off,
> Throws to columns row on row.
> Where he makes the rifles cough,
> Stutter. Where the reveille
> Is staccato majesty.
> Then to marches. Then to know
> The hunched hells across the sea. (stanza 13, *Blacks* 102)

First to boot camp, then into the trenches: "tan man's" doom is speedily pronounced. The poem does not go overseas with him but remains at home with Annie—who cannot and will not face the possibility that the war has taken him away for good: "But idea and body too / Clamor 'Skirmishes can do. / Then he will come back to you'" (stanza 14, *Blacks* 102).

Come back he does, but the returning soldier is not the man she married. Combat-fatigued, with the "eerie stutter" of gunfire still in his ears (stanza 15, *Blacks* 102), he cannot adjust to civilian life. "Hometown hums with stoppages": it is hard to find work (stanza 18, *Blacks* 103). The society's pervasive racism—"this white and greater chess" (103)—is a more elusive enemy than the one he faced on the battlefield. His marriage and his wife's self-abnegating worship no longer stir him; he is addicted to the sense of danger, of ultimatum, that so recently attended his every move and moment. The woman he needs to rekindle his manhood must be everything his wife is not, a "maple banshee" whose sexuality ("a gorgeous and gold shriek") is loud and obvious: Oh those violent vinaigrettes. / Oh bad honey that can hone / Oilily the bluntest stone! (stanza 22).

These metaphors are in a register of "good things to eat" that recalls both the poem's main epithet for darker-skinned Annie, "sweet and chocolate," and the scene of her seduction in stanza 6 ("Eats the green by easy stages / Nibbles at the root beneath"). The "cavalier" seducer of the "hinted bride" can only be aroused now by a woman who is all condiment—"bad honey," "violent vinaigrette."

In the lines "Oh mad bacchanalian lass / That his random passion has!" (stanza 22, *Blacks* 104), "bacchanalian lass" is a mock-heroic epithet for barfly that references the drunken orgies of Bacchus's followers in ancient Greece. The passion such a woman arouses is "random" in the sense of there being no intimacy involved, no strings attached.

With "tan man" lost to her, Annie casts around for ways to fill her empty days and recover a sense of purpose—or at least, of possibility. The metaphors the poem uses to carry this process forward, beginning in stanza 23, are of walking the city streets faster and faster, and then (as panic mounts) of dancing and spinning herself to a standstill. In stanza 23, a lonely woman becomes "acquainted with the night" (this stanza's language is reminiscent of a sonnet of Robert Frost's that Brooks had undoubtedly read). In 24 through 27 she "seeks for solaces" season by season, crunching through the "crusted" snow in winter, passing a city fountain in "the green and fluting spring," feeling her body's loneliness acutely in the sultry heat of summer, finding at last among fallen leaves on autumn sidewalks an objective correlative for her inner desolation: "This November her true town: / All's a falling falling down" (stanza 27, *Blacks* 105). After taking her through a full round of the seasons, the poem then surveys a broad spectrum of possible diversions and commitments, in stanzas 28 through 34. If it is hard to imagine one woman doing all these things, it may make better sense to think of Brooks's heroine as standing in for many women similarly situated—i.e., similarly stranded by marital unhappiness.

The poem helps us to do this by proliferating headless sentences that imply but do not specify Annie as the doer of the activities they predicate. First she reaches out to other people: "Spins and stretches out to friends. / . . . . / Cries 'I am philanthropist'"—a word that literally means, "lover of all mankind" (stanza 28, *Blacks* 106). Then she turns to books ("Twists to Plato, Aeschylus . . ."), but stanza 30's survey of classical authors is just a list of names; this is the wrong direction for Annie to be looking for the love and companionship she craves. In stanza 31 she "tests forbidden taffeta": goes dancing, looks for partners who are not her husband. The dance may be literal, but it is also metaphoric: Annie has been spinning and flirting and twisting ever since stanza 28. She "shivers" and "pirouettes" ever faster, but in stanza 32 "the culprit magics fade," the music stops, and she has to face the emptiness inside her. "Shorn and taciturn she stands," having run out of ways to pretend to be happy or lucky or blessed (*Blacks* 107). In stanza 33 she hears an inner voice telling her to "incline to children-dear": she should gather them to her like a bridal bouquet that can be "hoarded" to charm away loneliness. "Hoard it, for a planned surprise / When the desert terrifies" (*Blacks* 107)—but in stanza 34 "the desert" becomes a monster whose "countercharm" is too strong; with its "great and gritty arms" it reaches out to enfold her in a terrifying embrace. Annie has been deserted, not only by her husband but also, at long last, by the girlish capacity for dreaming that turned her over "to folly or to fate" in the first place.

Stanzas 35 through 39 pick up the next stage of her "prodigal" husband's parallel story. Stanza 35 addresses him directly, using the poetic device of "apostrophe" to deliver the message his ruined body has for him: the party's over.

> Hence from scenic bacchanal,
> Preshrunk and droll prodigal!
> Smallness that you had to spend,

Spent. Wench, whiskey and tail-end
Of your overseas disease
Rot and rout you by degrees. (*Blacks* 107)

It is time to go home to his wife, this same voice tells him in stanza 36; she will take him back for the time he has left, which will not be long. His "overseas disease" could be syphilis, which many soldiers brought back from Europe, or it could be tuberculosis. Annie takes him back out of pity for a man she once loved and who is the father of her children. No one but she will miss him when he dies: his children (the "bouncy sprouts" of stanza 38) have learned to do without a father who scarcely ever played with or cared for them; his mistress will easily find another "fool" to "kick and kiss" her and pay for the drinks (stanza 39, *Blacks* 108).

Only Annie, his erstwhile "devotee," will think of him as she passes the chair he always sat in, or the tavern where he spent his evenings, or when, in the silence of their apartment, she is startled by the telephone's ring (stanza 40, *Blacks* 109). Outwardly stiff and numb ("[She who] is starch or who is stone"), she holds herself together by going through the motions of everyday life: "Washes coffee-cups and hair, / Sweeps, determines what to wear" (109). Meanwhile, however,

In the indignant dark there ride
Roughnesses and spiny things
On infallible hundred heels.
And a bodiless bee stings.
Cyclone concentration reels.
Harried sods dilate, divide,
Suck her sorrowfully inside. (stanza 41, *Blacks* 109)

This inner landscape has the terrifying strangeness of a scene from a horror movie, all the more so in that it does not give us a complete or stable image. The "spiny things," the "bodiless bee," are feelings of anguish and remorse that Annie can no longer keep at bay. Her despair is a grave that opens up beneath her feet, an earthquake that threatens to bury her alive.

After this climax the poem comes swiftly to a close. We can suppose that "tan man" is dead or dying; either way, Annie's life is as good as over:

> Think of tweaked and twenty-four.
> Fuchsias gone or gripped or gray,
> All haycolored that was green.
> Soft aesthetic looted, lean. (stanza 42, *Blacks* 109)

The woman we are invited to "think of" here has come of age, but her life is all behind her. She is no longer a "sweet and chocolate" morsel for a paladin; "all [is] hay-colored that was green" when he first came courting her in stanza 6. "Soft aesthetic" is Brooks's way of summing up and dismissing the whole false basis of Annie's adult life thus far, her Cinderella fairy-tale notion that she was somehow meant to find true love and live happily ever after. The poem is ready to set this scenario aside, but she is not quite ready to do so. In the final stanza she is alone and "derelict" in her shabby one-room apartment, "Hugging old and Sunday sun. / Kissing in her kitchenette / The minuets of memory." No longer able to dream of a rosy future, she takes refuge from the bleakness of the present in nostalgia for the youth and innocence she has lost. A minuet is a stately dance that was popular among the upper classes in Europe before the French Revolution; Brooks rhymes "minuet" with "kitchenette" as an encouragement to picture Annie dancing without a partner to music only she can hear, and which cuts her off from the society around her.

In "The Womanhood" this "soft aesthetic" gives way to a stance that is socially and politically engaged. The poems of social commentary and social protest that predominate in the volume's third section bring

---

Annie to grips with the harsh reality of ordinary life in Bronzeville circa 1949. She finds her voice and begins to claim membership in a nation within a nation, a community of people who share a common set of problems and a common destiny.

Annie Allen was written in the shadow of World War II: it begins with an elegy for Brooks's friend Ed Bland, who was killed in Germany two months before the war ended. In an "Appendix to the Anniad" subtitled "leaves from a loose-leaf war diary," three poems take us into the feelings and attitudes of the women who waited out the war years at home. Annie could be speaking in these poems, but they do not quite seem to belong to the story of her marriage that has just been told in "The Anniad." The most interesting of them, "the sonnet-ballad," marries the structure of a sonnet to the stance and tone of a popular love-lament:

> Oh mother, mother, where is happiness?
> They took my lover's tallness off to war,
> Left me lamenting.
> . . . .
> Some day the war will end, but, oh, I knew
> When he went walking grandly out that door
> That my sweet love would have to be untrue.
> . . . . Would have to court
> Coquettish death. (*Blacks* 112)

The hero's death this young woman's lover "courted" is the ultimate rival, a lady of the night whose "coquettish" wiles have proven irresistible to his young manhood. The sonnet is an elevated literary genre with a distinguished European pedigree; the ballad is a popular form with its roots in an oral tradition of collective authorship. For Don Lee this poem is an example of "using their ground rules" to beat them at their own game (*RPO* 17): Brooks has invented a hybrid form that allows an ordinary Bronzeville girl to be as eloquent as Petrarch or

Shakespeare. She uses the sonnet form again in "the children of the poor," which Lee prefers for its stronger and more specific social message (17).

World War II was a watershed experience for African American communities that sent young men into combat, because it called attention to their uniquely American predicament of second-class citizenship. These young men were fighting and dying in segregated battalions for a country that still consigned them to the lowest-paying jobs in the poorest neighborhoods. American race relations are for the most part only indirectly referenced in *Annie Allen*, but by the end of the volume a voice of social protest can be heard. Be it Annie's voice or Brooks's, its message is that racial equality and racial integration are not going to happen: it is time for black Americans to stop dreaming that particular dream.

In this voice and in its message a whole people can be said to be coming of age, by way of a profound and pervasive experience of disillusionment.

> One cannot walk this winding street with pride,
> Straight-shouldered, tranquil-eyed,
> Knowing one knows for sure the way back home.
> One wonders if one has a home. (*Blacks* 132)

This is the middle stanza of a poem that begins "One wants a Teller in a time like this," whose bottom line is that there is no "Teller-with-a-capital-T" whose reassurance can be trusted. *"Be patient, time brings all good things":* African Americans would be naïve indeed if they still believed such bromides, living as they still do in segregated neighborhoods with bleak economic prospects almost a century after the end of slavery. The final poem in the volume begins in a voice of supplication, calling on white America to "admit me to our mutual estate" (*Blacks* 139), but by the end of the poem white America's self-serving counsel of patience has provoked its speaker to turn toward her own people with a call for black solidarity that is an early harbinger of the Black Power movement of the 1960s. "Rise. / Let us combine," she says to her Bronzeville compatriots: "There are no magics or elves / Or timely godmothers to guide us. We are lost, must / Wizard a track through our own screaming weed" (*Blacks* 140).

Not only did Annie not have a fairy godmother; none of us does. That being so, our collective destiny is our own responsibility, and we will have to take it into our own hands.

Notes

1. Perhaps the best discussion of this poem to date is to be found in Hortense Spillers's essay, "Gwendolyn the Terrible: Propositions on Eleven Poems."

2. In the Christian epics of the Renaissance, coming of age begins to be a more important subject than it was in Homer's and Virgil's epics. Before they are eligible to lead their people or shape their destiny, the heroes of Christian epic typically must undergo suffering, purification, and/or enlightenment; they must find out who they really are or are destined to become. In the medieval Arthurian saga, King Arthur comes of age when he pulls the sword Excalibur from a stone; in Spenser's *Faerie Queene*, Arthur figures as a young knight who has not yet come of age but is being tested in every virtue on the way to claiming his destiny.

Works Cited

Alexander, Elizabeth. "Meditations on 'Mecca': Gwendolyn Brooks and the Responsibilities of the Black Poet." *The Black Interior: Essays*. St. Paul, MN: Graywolf, 2004. 43–58.

Abrams, M. H., and Geoffrey Galt Harpham. *A Glossary of Literary Terms*. 9th ed. Boston: Wadsworth, 2009.

Brooks, Gwendolyn. *Blacks*. Chicago: Third World, 1992.

_____. *Report from Part One*. Detroit: Broadside, 1973. Cited as *RPO*.

Giovanni, Nikki. "To Gwen Brooks from Nikki Giovanni." *Essence* 1 (Apr. 1971): 26.

Lee, Don L. "Gwendolyn Brooks: Beyond the Wordmaker—The Making of an African Poet." Brooks, *Report* 13–30.

Spillers, Hortense. "Gwendolyn the Terrible: Propositions on Eleven Poems." *A Life Distilled: Gwendolyn Brooks, Her Poetry and Fiction*. Eds. Maria K. Mootry and Gary Smith. Urbana/Chicago: U of Illinois P, 1987.

Ready or Not: Antonio Márez y Luna Is Thrown into the World of Rudolfo Anaya's *Bless Me, Ultima*_____

Phillip Serrato

> "Men will do what they must do," [Ultima] answered. . . . "The ways of men are strange, and hard to learn," I heard her say.
>
> "Will I learn them?" I asked. I felt the weight on my eyelids.
>
> "You will learn much, you will see much," I heard her faraway voice.
>
> (Anaya, *Bless Me, Ultima*)

In *Being and Time* (1927), German philosopher Martin Heidegger depicts the human subject as "thrown" into human society. With the premise that "without personal choice, with no previous knowledge" (Steiner 87) the human subject finds himself or herself cast or thrust into what Heidegger calls "Being-in-the-world," Heidegger conceptualizes human existence and experience in terms of a random, arbitrary entry into a social world that "was there before us and will be there after us" (Steiner 87). Particularly potent about the figure that Heidegger offers are its connotations of the human subject's potential traumatization. As noted, for example, by George Steiner, Heidegger's account carries an overtone of violence in its suggestion of the human subject's profound unpreparedness for Being-in-the-world (xii). Indicating as much, when Heidegger asserts that "Being-in-the-world [is the human subject's] way of Being" (174) and that it is thus that the human subject "finds itself in its thrownness" (174), he emphasizes, "The expression 'thrownness' is meant to suggest the *facticity of its being delivered over*" to and into Being-in-the-world (174). Once Heidegger describes the human subject as haplessly "delivered over" to Being-in-the-world, a sense of this subject's fundamental vulnerability, if not victimization, begins to emerge.

Curiously, in the course of discussing thrownness as the primal fact of human life, Heidegger devotes no specific attention to or concern with children or childhood. Given the consonance between his figuration of thrownness and the nature of childhood, such inattention is conspicuous to say the least. After all, to be a child is to be new to the world and forced to come to terms with the alienating, unfamiliar, baffling, and even frightening experiences, ideas, circumstances, and people that one encounters for the first time. If anything, childhood actually seems to epitomize Heidegger's idea that the human subject is "'delivered over' . . . to an actuality, to a 'there,' to a complete, enveloping presentness . . . [and] must take up this presentness . . . [and] assume it into its own existence" (Steiner 88). For this reason, thrownness could be said to pertain especially acutely to children.

While Heidegger thus overlooks childhood as the site par excellence for grasping the fundamental human conditions of thrownness and Being-in-the-world, we can find in literary representations compelling portrayals of what Mary Galbraith calls "the existential predicament of childhood in an adult-dominated world" (200). As Galbraith rightly notes, "Literature . . . has been the real pioneer in presenting the [existential] experience of individual child [selves]" (194). Among other things, we can find in various texts the specific applicability of Heidegger's conceptualization of human ontology to childhood as a dramatic if not unnerving initiation into the social world. Works ranging from Lewis Carroll's *Alice's Adventures in Wonderland* (1865) to James Joyce's *A Portrait of the Artist as a Young Man* (1916) to J. K. Rowling's *Harry Potter* books (to name just a very few) effectively depict young people confronting and negotiating thrownness in different ways and working through the disorientation, frustration, and anxiety that, as Heidegger explains, thrownness necessarily precipitates.

Rudolfo Anaya's *Bless Me, Ultima* (1972) provides a particularly intriguing dramatization of a child for whom coming of age entails the negotiation of the conditions of existence that Heidegger describes. In this classic novel, Anaya portrays a notably stressful year in the life of six-year-old Antonio Márez y Luna. Encapsulating the density of the tight timeframe that Anaya covers, Ramón Saldívar says, "In the year of narrative time, Antonio experiences in rapid succession the brutality perpetrated by man against man and man against woman, the loss of childhood innocence, the horror of evil, [and] doubts about his traditional Catholic faith" (105). By portraying a childhood challenged and haunted by an assortment of existential realities, Anaya's novel most obviously extends twentieth-century acknowledgments of children and childhood as far more complex and conflicted than traditionally recognized and allowed, for instance, by earlier romantic figurations.[1] In fact, owing to Anaya's willingness to portray a palpably stressful childhood that is not so safely divorced or even buffered from the corruption and brutality of the "adult world," *Bless Me, Ultima* exemplifies Patricia Pace's observation of "a contemporary trend in the popular imagination: the child-self . . . and childhood itself, as a beleaguered and endangered space" (233). Importantly, as *Bless Me, Ultima* depicts some of the moral, social, and ontological conflicts that child subjects must negotiate as their experience of the world broadens beyond the immediate confines of the home—which is to say, as they find themselves Being-in-the-world—it ends up enabling an important respect for children and childhood and the conditions (namely, the duress) under which children come of age. To be sure, Antonio is only six years old, which makes him seem young for a coming-of-age narrative. However, through Antonio, Anaya manages to portray coming of age as a process that is jumpstarted in early childhood. In the process, the text recovers not just the complexity, but the relatable pathos of the child's subjectivity and existential condition. By thereby disputing the traditional—and patronizing—reduction of children and childhood to a state of unadulterated, unaware, even blissful simplicity, the novel presents the child as a very human subject whose coming-of-age experience merits a more nuanced understanding as well as greater respect.

The Denial of a Pastoral Childhood

As occurs with any coming-of-age narrative, the setting of *Bless Me, Ultima* is integral to understanding and appreciating the growth that Antonio experiences. Initially, the grandeur of the rural New Mexico landscape might suggest an idyllic stage for Antonio's childhood.[2] A number of references early in the novel to Antonio's developing relationship to the awe-inspiring landscape certainly entice a reader into expecting this novel to be a Southwestern American version of Frances Hodgson Burnett's *The Secret Garden* (1911). In the opening sentences, Antonio relates,

> Ultima came to stay with us the summer I was almost seven. When she came the beauty of the llano unfolded before my eyes, and the gurgling waters of the river sang to the hum of the turning earth. The magical time of childhood stood still, and the pulse of the living earth pressed its mystery into my living blood. She took my hand, and the silent magic powers she possessed made beauty from the raw, sun-baked llano, the green river valley, and the blue bowl which was the white sun's home. My bare feet felt the throbbing earth and my body trembled with excitement. Time stood still, and it shared with me all that had been, and all that was to come. (1)

In this beautifully rendered passage Antonio twice refers to the sensation of existing outside of time. Such references, coupled with the exuberance with which the boy intimates his communion with nature, immediately suture a reader into Antonio's excitement over the possibility of living harmoniously with and within nature, utterly outside of civilization and free from the trappings of modernity. Shortly thereafter, Antonio, again in the presence of Ultima, narrates yet another alluringly transcendent moment:

> [Ultima] took my hand and I felt the power of a whirlwind sweep around me. Her eyes swept the surrounding hills and through them I saw for the first time the wild beauty of our hills and the magic of the green river. My nostrils quivered as I felt the song of the mockingbirds and the drone of the grasshoppers mingle with the pulse of the earth. The four directions of the llano met in me, and the white sun shone on my soul. The granules of

sand at my feet and the sun and sky above me seemed to dissolve into one strange, complete being. (11)

At once Antonio feels himself not only alive, but a fully live, integrated part of the grander fabric of life. Because of this and other moments in which Antonio thrillingly experiences himself as "a very important part of the llano and the river" (Anaya 37), Theresa Kanoza remarks that Antonio "comes to luxuriate in the synchronized workings of the world" (168).

Soon enough, however, it turns out that "the beginning that came with Ultima" (Anaya 1) is not solely the inauguration of some idyllic communion with nature for Antonio. What eventually predominates in Antonio's experience is the Heideggerian realization that Being-in-the-world means coming to terms with all that the world actually contains, which includes not just the inspiring beauty of nature (a delimitation which Kanoza inadvertently performs when she refers to "the world" in the quotation above), but social reality and the conflict, stress, confusion, and even danger that it entails. For this reason, Heidegger explains, "As thrown, [the human subject] has indeed been delivered over to itself and to its potentiality-for-Being, *but as Being-in-the-world*. As thrown, it has been submitted to a 'world', and exists factically with Others" (435). Antonio himself quickly realizes the impossibility of a pastoral childhood due to Being-in-the-world as an immutable fact of life when he states that "through [Ultima] I learned that my spirit shared in the spirit of all things. But the innocence which our isolation sheltered could not last forever, and the affairs of the town began to reach across our bridge and enter my life. Ultima's owl gave the warning that the time of peace on our hill was drawing to an end" (14). Especially noteworthy is Antonio's statement that "the affairs of the town began to reach across our bridge and enter my life." With a touch of worry and latent helplessness, Antonio recognizes the impossibility of a pastoral existence, which shows him to be on his way to learning and accepting both the inevitability and the ramifications of existing "factically with Others."

Thus, as much as the setting might at first point toward the possibility of a pastoral childhood, such an idea turns out to be untenable. As Kanoza points out, Antonio's childhood is indeed "set in a sacred place imbued with a spiritual presence and long inhabited by indigenous people," and it stands as "a world where the Anglo is of little consequence to its strong Chicano characters" (160). Yet geographical seclusion does not guarantee utopia. This becomes clear as soon as we consider that "Guadalupe, an isolated village that is set apart from the greater New Mexican landmass by a river which encircles it, is at once . . . insular and internally diverse" (160). With internal diversity comes interpersonal conflict, which Kanoza highlights in her description of the social backdrop for this year in the life of Antonio:

> A varied constituency . . . comprises Antonio's world. Besides the stark differences in the mores and temperaments of the peaceful farmers who are his maternal relatives and his raucous, rootless paternal uncles who ride the *llano*, Antonio finds sharp contrasts among his friends. Catholic and Protestant classmates taunt each other in the schoolyard about their conflicting beliefs of heaven and hell, while those secretly faithful to the cult of the golden carp, such as Cico, Samuel, and Jason, are contemptuous of these arcane concerns. Children of no particular religious persuasion, some of whom are eerily animal-like in appearance and endowed with preternatural strength and speed, watch the squabbles in amusement. All are terrified by the three Trementina sisters, who are legendary for practicing black magic. (162)

Surrounded by diverse people and ideologies, Antonio finds himself immersed in (or thrown into) an environment (or world) characterized by suspicion, division, resentment, and fear.

At this point, it is worth considering that Antonio's immediate environment is, microcosmically, a reflection and product of the larger world and historical moment within which he lives. To be sure, history seems to work in subtle ways in *Bless Me, Ultima*—so much so that the novel has drawn criticism from some scholars for what they perceive as an irresponsible lack of interest on the part of the author in broader socio-historical issues—yet it plays an important role both in the novel as a whole and in the experience of Antonio specifically.[3] The novel is set during World War II, and while the war itself is terribly destructive and psychically devastating, the atomic testing underway in the New Mexican desert frays nerves even more. Consequently, when Antonio begins to ask his father, "Papá, the people say *the bomb* causes the winds to blow—" (184), although the boy means to inquire literally about the potential meteorological effects of the atomic testing, there is actually a powerful symbolic truth to the concern in terms of the anxiety that is "in the air" due to the arrival of the atomic age. Antonio gleans firsthand the scary, almost apocalyptic uncertainty of the times from the distress of the people around him.

When a dust storm blows up one day, Antonio relates that the local people nervously attribute the unusual weather to "the new bomb that had been made to end the war. 'The atomic bomb,' they whispered, 'a ball of white heat beyond the imagination, beyond hell—'" (183). On another occasion, Antonio overhears his father "solemnly" reflecting on the war: "Now the people are scattered, driven like tumbleweeds by the winds of war. The war sucks everything dry, it takes the young boys overseas, and their families move to California, where there is work" (3). Later, Antonio's maternal grandfather similarly frets: "A sad thing, a tragedy. . . . This war of the Germans and the Japanese is reaching into all of us. Even into the refuge of the Valle de los Luna it reaches, we have just finished burying one of the boys of Santos Estevan. There is much evil running loose in the world—" (46–47). While the massive conflict and mass anxiety of World War II thereby impinge on Antonio's subjectivity, the stress of the times finally becomes all too real for him through the breakup of his family. First, his brothers leave home to fight in the war. Then, although they physically return, they never really return to the family. According to Antonio, "The war had changed them. Now they needed to lead their own lives" (62). Insisting to their parents, "We have to go! We have to go!" (66), Antonio's brothers eventually leave home again to pursue a new life in Santa Fe. For Antonio, this wrenching loss only amplifies his increasingly lonely and difficult experience of Being-in-the-world at this moment in history.

With the world teeming with conflict and stress and otherwise in flux on global and local levels, Antonio himself becomes increasingly distressed by the fact that Being-in-the-world places him in the position of having to adjudicate and negotiate a proliferating range of painfully indeterminate ideas, issues, and realities. Incidentally, this burden is set in motion at the boy's birth. In one of Antonio's seven dream sequences, the opposition between the families of his father and mother is revealed, with each side claiming Antonio for itself. Upon the birth of the boy, members of the Márez clan first exclaim to Antonio's father, "Gabriel . . . you have a fine son! He will make a fine vaquero!" and they insist on burying the afterbirth "in our fields . . . to assure that the baby will follow in our ways" (5). But in the same instant, the Lunas interrupt: "No! . . . He must come to El Puerto and rule over the Lunas of the valley. The blood of the Lunas is strong in him" (5–6). These rival declarations then give way to an intense scene in which "Curses and threats filled the air, pistols were drawn, and the opposing sides made ready for battle" (6). As Antonio grows up, the rival claims of the Máreces and the Lunas continue to hold sway over him, leaving him struggling to resolve the false dilemma of his identity at different points in the novel.[4]

Above all else, in the course of his coming of age Antonio finds himself wrestling with the various contradictions and breakdowns that he begins to see in his Catholic faith. In numerous instances, he finds the faith that he has been taught to be more rickety than he would like it to be. When he sees Ultima heal his uncle Lucas, he says, "I had been thinking how Ultima's medicine had cured my uncle and how the medicine of the doctors and of the priest had failed. In my mind I could not understand how the power of God could fail. But it had" (98). His incertitude becomes especially intense as he approaches his First Communion, which he hopes will (somehow) provide the answers to the various moral and philosophical questions that have increasingly troubled him (and which at one point prompt him to think, "Oh, it was hard to grow up. I hoped that in a few years the taking of the first holy communion would bring me understanding" [69]). In church one day, he mentions, "I sat on the hard, wooden pew and shivered. Man tries to know and his knowledge will kill us all. I want to know. I want to know the mysteries of God. I want to take God into my body and have Him answer my questions. Why was Narciso killed? Why does evil go unpunished? Why does he allow evil to exist?" (184). Ultimately, regarding the questions that occur to him and that his peers also pose in the rather savvy theological debates and discussions in which they engage, Antonio concedes, "Yes. There seemed to be so many pitfalls in the questions we asked" (189).

But as commonly occurs in coming-of-age narratives, it is precisely Antonio's confrontation with the daunting questions and difficult situations that arise that shows and enables his developing selfhood. For example, when he begins narrating the events leading up to the arrival of Ultima, he recounts the conversations his mother and father had about her, including their concern with having a curandera (an herbal healer) in the house. In this moment, Antonio reveals that he already understands more than his parents assume he understands. When his father asks Antonio's mother, "And the children?" Antonio reveals,

I knew why he expressed concern for me and my sisters. It was because Ultima was a curandera, a woman who knew the herbs and remedies of the ancients, a miracle-worker who could heal the sick. And I had heard that Ultima could lift the curses laid by brujas, that she could exorcise the evil the witches planted in people to make them sick. And because a curandera had this power, she was misunderstood and often suspected of practicing witchcraft herself. (4)

In this passage, readers see a certain sophistication on the part of Antonio that belies popular expectations for children. He knows what his father has in mind even though his father does not explicitly state it; he is fully aware of the controversy that surrounds Ultima and the bases for the controversy; and he understands the faulty ambivalence with which the people in the community regard curanderas such as Ultima.[5]

At the same time, Antonio proves himself to be a boy moving above and beyond the egocentrism and naïveté typically ascribed to children through his evolving capacity for understanding and empathizing with other people. In the above example of his description of the circumstances surrounding Ultima, he is attuned to his father's worry as well as to the reasons people fear curanderas. Elsewhere, reflecting on his mother's situation in life, he remarks, "As long as I could remember she always raged about the Márez family and their friends. She called the village of Las Pasturas beautiful; she had gotten used to the loneliness, but she had never accepted its people" (8). Shortly thereafter, he spends some time thinking about Jasón, and carefully concludes, "Jasón was not a bad boy, he was just Jasón. He was quiet and moody, and sometimes for no reason at all wild, loud sounds came exploding from his throat and lungs" (9). Through these observations, Antonio shows that in spite of his young age, he is fully capable of contemplating other people and arriving at insightful and empathetic understandings of them. Even more importantly, he can skeptically sift through the beliefs that circulate within the larger community and formulate his own viewpoint. All of this, it must be noted, is part of his ongoing process of sorting out and making sense of the world into which he has been thrown. Little by little he puts everything and everyone into perspective so as to ultimately figure out his own relationship to it all.

Unsurprisingly, however, Antonio's capacity to put everything and everyone into perspective is tested as the range of his movement away from home expands. Of course, in a coming-of-age narrative, such a correlation is standard stuff. At first we see how home stands as a place of familiarity and security for Antonio when he introduces it in terms of its comforting order: "The attic of our home was partitioned into two small rooms. My sisters, Deborah and Theresa, slept in one and I slept in the small cubicle by the door. The wooden steps creaked down into a small hallway that led into the kitchen. From the top of the stairs I had a vantage point into the heart of our home, my mother's kitchen" (1). While home thus functions for him as a safe and stable space, he finds that stepping away from it and out into the world literally and figuratively takes him into strange, new territory that challenges him in different ways. Going to school for the first time is one such experience. In anticipation (or dread) of the first day of school, he reveals, "My heart sank. When I thought of leaving my mother and going to school a warm, sick feeling came to my stomach" (6). When the day actually arrives, he then says, "On the first day of school I awoke with a sick feeling in my stomach. It did not hurt, it just made me feel weak. The sun did not sing as it came over the hill. Today I would take the goat path and trek into town for years and years of schooling. For the first time I would be away from the protection of my mother. I was excited and sad about it" (48).

Among other things, in this passage Antonio indicates a disruption of what had been his beautiful connection with nature: under the stress of his social reality of having to go to school, he does not experience the sun singing as it formerly did. Moreover, wracked as he is by nerves and dread, the boy experiences anxiety as an intrusion on the transcendent embodiment that he previously enjoyed. Basically, as the terms of Being-in-the-world become more real for him, the unsustainability of a pastoral existence becomes more pronounced. In response to the stress posed by the specter of going off to school and away from his home and mother, Antonio adds, "I wished that I could always be near her, but that was impossible. The war had taken my brothers away, and so the school would take me away" (30). Once he arrives at school, he faces the stark loneliness that initially greets one when one enters the larger social world: "I had come to the town," he says, "and I had come to school, and I was very lost and afraid in the nervous, excited swarm of kids" (53).

Discussing Antonio's coming of age vis-à-vis his first day of school, Robert Anderson reads the boy's movement away from home in terms of a "ritual of an agony, a death, and a resurrection" (98). In Anderson's reading, Antonio follows the descent "down the hill in a *descensus ad infernos* trajectory. Once in the valley he must cross the archetypal bridge, *the dividing line* between the 'quiet peace of the hills of the llano' and 'the turbulence of the town and its sin' . . . and venture into the underworld scenario of his initiation and eventual metamorphosis" (98–99). For Antonio, the world across the bridge and away from home is specifically replete with dangerous belief systems (in the form of Florence's atheism), violence (in the form of the murderous Tenorio), and sex (in the form of Rosie's brothel).

Perhaps the best example of both the difficulty of Being-in-the-world and the resilience that it requires of Antonio is his witnessing of the death of Lupito. When Chávez arrives at Antonio's home to inform Gabriel that Lupito has killed the sheriff, Antonio finds himself having to process the concepts of danger, death, and violence. As his father reaches for his rifle so he can go with Chávez and others to look for Lupito, Antonio remarks, "Now he too was armed. I had only seen him shoot the rifle when we slaughtered pigs in the fall. Now [he and Chávez] were going armed for a man" (15). Shortly thereafter, we see Antonio's mother and father literally try to shelter the children from danger, death, and violence. When Antonio's father tells his wife, "Keep the doors locked," Antonio narrates, "My mother went to the door and shut the latch. We never locked our doors, but tonight there was something strange and fearful in the air" (16). Despite the efforts of his parents, Antonio's curiosity is piqued by this first real encounter with the hitherto unknown reality of murder and the specter of danger. Consequently, he decides to follow his father and Chávez to gain some understanding of these unfamiliar aspects of the world. Notably, with the statement, "I slipped out the kitchen door and into the night" (16),

---

Antonio actually says a great deal. At once we see him moving beyond the order and security of the home that is specifically epitomized by the kitchen and into the disorder and literal and metaphorical darkness of the world outside. What he encounters outside the home ends up alternately shocking and terrifying him. Stumbling across Lupito, he says, "What I saw made my blood run cold" (16). Once the pursuing men discover Lupito and shine a light on him, Antonio explains that he saw "a face twisted with madness. I do not know if he saw me, or if the light cut off his vision, but I saw his bitter, contorted grin. As long as I live I will never forget those wild eyes, like the eyes of a trapped, savage animal" (16–17). That Antonio perceives Lupito as "wild," "savage," and "mad" bespeaks the extent to which the sight and condition of Lupito is outside of the realm of Antonio's experience. Wildness, savagery, and madness all signify a perceived aberration from social order and normalcy. Through this encounter with Lupito, then, a very unprepared Antonio gets a disturbingly more expansive glimpse of the world that is "out there."

As occurs when Carroll's Alice lands in Wonderland and when Joyce's Stephen Dedalus heads to boarding school, Antonio's venture into the greater outside world almost immediately prompts in him a desire to return to the safety of home. With his sense of the order, coherence, and safety of the world profoundly shaken by the sight of the breakdown and death of Lupito, the boy desperately wishes to return to the place that, for him, literally and symbolically embodies stability and comfort. Interestingly, the details of his return home underscore the traumatic nature of the evening. Antonio explains, "I turned and ran. The dark shadows of the river enveloped me as I raced for the safety of home. Branches whipped at my face and cut it, and vines and tree trunks caught at my feet and tripped me. In my headlong rush I disturbed sleeping birds and their shrill cries and slapping wings hit at my face. The horror of darkness had never been so complete as it was for me that night" (20). On one level, the sensation of being overwhelmed by darkness obviously captures the epistemological breakdown wrought within Antonio by what he has just witnessed. Basically, what he sees explodes his capacity for knowing the world and for knowing people, plunging him into the abyss of what could be called "an epistemic deficit."[6]

On another level, the narrative attention to the physical distress that Antonio suffers in the course of the episode with Lupito completes the intense subjective dimension of the scene and brings to mind Pace's discussion of the physical as well as psychic dimensions of trauma. Invoking Kai Ericson's reminder that the medical usage of trauma refers to "a blow to the tissues of the body" (Ericson qtd. in Pace 240), Pace opens up a more encompassing consideration of trauma, one that goes beyond the popular "therapeutic usage wherein trauma has come to mean a state of mind" (Pace 240). She foregrounds trauma as an experience that devastates the entirety of the self by registering on physical and psychic levels alike. To think through this idea, the work of Judith Herman provides a useful addendum. In *Trauma and Recovery* (1992), Herman delineates the interaction of the psyche and the body in times of acute distress: "The ordinary human response to danger is a complex, integrated system of reactions, encompassing both body and mind. Threat initially arouses the sympathetic nervous system, causing the person in danger to feel an adrenalin rush and go into a state of alert" (34). In a move incidentally relevant for a consideration of Antonio in traumatized terms, Herman proceeds to illustrate the imbrication of the mind and the body by quoting Abram Kardner's description of the pathology of combat neurosis: "When a person is overwhelmed by terror and helplessness, '*the whole apparatus for concerted, coordinated and purposeful activity is smashed*. The perceptions become inaccurate and pervaded with terror, the coordinative functions of judgment and discrimination fail. . . . The functions of the autonomic nervous system may also become disassociated with the rest of the organism'" (35).

As the scene with Lupito unfolds in *Bless Me, Ultima*, readers see Antonio in a hyperaroused state that resonates with the emotionally turbulent conditions described by Herman and Kardner. As Antonio becomes "frozen by [his] fear" (Anaya 20) only to turn and desperately attempt to flee what has transpired, his feeling of being overwhelmed by terror and helplessness becomes apparent. That he is tripped, scratched, and otherwise beaten and battered on his way back home—all of which is caused by the selfsame nature which had previously provided him a joyous sense of connection and vitality—implies the impossibility any longer of any return to safety and stability. Once privy to the underside of human society, there is, to his dismay, no returning to the safety and stability he associates with earlier, "innocent" states of ignorance and naïveté. Such are the nonnegotiable implications, it turns out, of coming of age.

From Pity to Respect

To say that Antonio experiences a lot in *Bless Me, Ultima* would be an understatement. At one point we even see him teeter on nihilism because of all that he has seen, heard, and endured over the year of narrative time. Near the end of the novel, the various moral, philosophical, and theological doubts and questions that have arisen within him boil over into a dream in which an assortment of fears are articulated. Describing the ending of his dream, Antonio narrates: "'What is left?' I asked in horror. Nothing, the reply rolled like silent thunder through the mist of my dream. . . . Everything I believed was destroyed. A painful wrenching in my heart made me cry aloud, 'My God, my God, why have you forsaken me!'" (233). Apparently, Antonio feels unable to believe in or hold onto anything anymore. Within this selfsame dream, however, a way of putting into perspective Antonio's verging on an existential breakdown appears. When the boy asks, "Why must I be witness to so much violence!" he hears a voice answer, "The germ of creation lies in violence" (232). As regards Antonio, we might say that the germ of his coming of age, the germ of his selfhood, lies in violent thrownness. Each new experience and situation and idea that presents itself to him jolts his consciousness into new areas. He has to figure out, among other things, how to understand Lupito, the men who shoot Lupito, Ultima, his brothers, Rosie's place, and of course his Catholic faith and God. Although the stress of thrownness compels him at one point to remark, "I knew I had to grow up and be a man, but oh it was so very hard" (55), we might bear in mind Heidegger's claim that "in anxiety there lies the possibility of a disclosure which is quite distinctive; for anxiety individualizes" (235). As summarized by John Haugeland, Heidegger's idea is that "in anxiety, a person's individuality is 'brought home' to him or her in an utterly unmistakable and undeniable way" (64) via a sharpened sense of consciousness and, by extension, an evolving, sharpening experience of selfhood vis-à-vis the self's experience of and relation to the world.

Some (if not most) scholarship on *Bless Me, Ultima* reads Antonio as having resolved by the end of the novel the various issues that arise in the course of the novel. Kanoza, for instance, says of Antonio, "In tune with the cosmic harmonies, Antonio joins together diverse and discordant beliefs, temperaments, and values, for he realizes that he can 'take the llano and the river valley, the moon and the sea, God and the golden carp—and make something new'" (168). Likewise, with the premise that "Antonio learns to accept the greater reality of life" (68), Jane Rogers posits that "Antonio has avoided annihilation on the sheer cliffs of the Wandering Rocks . . . and he has moved through the narrow strait and evaded the menace of Scylla and Charybdis as he comes to face the reality of his manhood" (68). But a consideration of the narrative arrangement in which the adult Antonio is recounting his childhood complicates the semblance of resolution which Kanoza, Rogers, and many others foreground. One might question, When is Antonio telling this and why? In answer to the first part, it appears that Antonio narrates the novel as a grown adult. As to why he indulges in this recollection at this point in his life, we might consider Pace's words on trauma-centered autobiographies: "The memoir as a testimony of traumatic event[s] returns to childhood in an effort to restore meaning to the subject, to mend the tear in the body by rehearsing the losses, mourning, and healing by which we measure our psychic life" (244). In a discussion of remembrance and mourning as a stage in the recovery process for trauma survivors, Herman similarly posits: "In the second stage of recovery, the survivor tells the story of the trauma. She tells it completely, in depth and in detail. This work of reconstruction actually transforms the traumatic memory, so that it can be integrated into the survivor's life story" (175). Along these lines, we might see Antonio as a traumatized subject who finds himself compelled to revisit his own distressing childhood. By "choosing to confront the horrors of the past" (Herman 175) and narrativizing them, he seems to be working to piece back together this one particular year so as to somehow, finally, come to terms with it.

Although the novel closes with Antonio seemingly accepting all that occurred, including the death of Ultima, a sense of incompleteness remains. After all, Antonio has narrativized his past but makes no gesture toward how this has been integrated into his present evolving self. A sense of how this past fits into the present self seems to be the next step for him to take, but as he finishes, "Ultima was really buried here. Tonight" (248), he seems unsure of how to take this step or really where to go from the finality of death, be it the concept in general or Ultima's death specifically.

Consequently, we might go so far as to say that the novel presents coming of age—and the subject formation that this involves—as a process that begins when one is young and remains ongoing. Caminero-Santangelo points toward this kind of an idea when she proposes, "Just as Antonio's development to maturity is not complete by the novel's end, so also the process of identity (re)construction is an ongoing process, rather than one that is fully accomplished at the novel's conclusion" (124). That Antonio shows signs of traumatization adds, it must be noted, an important layer to Caminero-Santangelo's proposal. Once we bear in mind Being-in-the-world and thrownness as the fundamental terms upon which subject formation in general and childhood in particular turn, it emerges that coming of age and subject formation involve the struggle to resolve the existential traumas that are part and parcel of Being-in-the-world. Interestingly, because the example of Antonio suggests that these traumas linger into adulthood, we might borrow from trauma theory and conceptualize coming of age as a lengthy movement through "a spiral . . . in which earlier issues are continually revisited on a higher level of integration" (Herman 155). In turn, Antonio can be seen as occupying a position beyond childhood but having to return to it, still working to integrate his childhood experiences into his life's story and sense of self as he advances into and through adulthood. Anaya's text thereby begins to challenge the compartmentalization of childhood and adulthood.

Working with a spiral model of coming of age and subject development that is informed by trauma theory leads us to Pace's point that "In the painful, excruciating repetitive recounting of childhood as traumatic event we find a . . . meaning of childhood performed as radical doubleness; the meaning of childhood is performed as profoundly liminal—not child and not adult—but one and both wounded and commemorated" (240). In the process, a respect for the child and for childhood is encouraged that carries the potential to counter the dismissal of the child as an "other." The radical otherness of children has been uttered by individuals in various contexts and ranging from "We do not know childhood" (Rousseau xlii) to "Given sufficient information, one can always find a way to understand an idiot, a child, a person from a so-called primitive culture, or a foreigner" (Sartre 43) to "While child specialists inform on stages of development and historians document the cultural record, we know little about the yeastiness of being young in the world" (Lundin 126). Remarks such as these end up denying the child subjectivity and respect by rendering him or her into a kind of "other." *Bless Me, Ultima* challenges this alienated status of the child by Antonio as a child with a complicated subjectivity. Granted, acknowledgement of the complicated if not traumatizing nature of childhood runs the risk of reinscribing the otherness of childhood by rendering it the object of a patronizing pity. However, Anaya's text seems to secure for the child respect over pity by validating him as a fully complicated, and thus fully human, subject. Inspiring such a reading is Anderson's suggestion that "in its articulation of fundamental human experiences, *Bless Me, Ultima* transcends ethnicity, time, and space. Rudolfo Anaya's portrayal of the initiation, which is so effectively done by means of archetypal patterns and images, proves itself to be an extraordinary exploration of mankind's deepest and most intimate thoughts and feelings" (104). It is precisely this universality—in which children share in "mankind's deepest and most intimate thoughts and feelings"—that offers to lift children from the status of "an overlooked underclass" (Griswold 54) to that of fellow subjects with whom adults share the permanent condition of subject formation and Being-in-the-world.

Notes

1. Two essay collections edited by James Holt McGavran, Jr. (*Romanticism and Children's Literature in Nineteenth-Century England* [1991] and *Literature and the Child: Romantic Continuations, Postmodern Contestations* [1999]) provide useful overviews and examinations of romantic constructions of childhood and subsequent figurations.

2. One might look to Pat Mora's picture book *The Desert Is My Mother* (1994) as an example of a text that portrays a joyously liberated childhood enabled by its setting in an untouched desert space.

3. In their respective pieces, Genaro Padilla and Marta Caminero-Santangelo take different approaches to the criticism that *Bless Me, Ultima* has received for its handling of history. While Caminero-Santangelo echoes this criticism by re-indicting the narrative's lack of an "obvious connection" to socio-historical matters (116), Padilla offers a more sympathetic and strategic reading of the ways that "Anaya's mythic concerns . . . [seem] to overwhelm the social contexts of the novel" (128). In his own essay, Horst Tonn offers the excellent postulation—upon which I build here—that "a historical dimension is structurally embedded in the narration" (65). He convincingly contends that "the lack of historical context should not be regarded as a flaw of the novel. Instead, it can be seen as an inherent limitation in the choice of narrative voice which is highly effective in re-creating an approximation of the protagonist's world. The perceptual limitations of the young boy restrict the use of historical material in the text" (65).

4. In her reading of the identity dilemma that Antonio struggles to resolve, Caminero-Santangelo invokes Gloria Anzaldúa's discussion of border identity: "The struggle of Ultima's young protagonist . . . to negotiate a dual inheritance,

the elements of which seem incompatible if not mutually exclusive, may call to mind Gloria Anzaldúa's description of the new mestiza who also negotiates apparently incompatible aspects of identity" (115). The problem with this reading, however, is that it appeals to the surface notion of split identity while disregarding the specific cultural and gender politics at stake in Anzaldúa's discussion and the more existential identity stakes involved in Antonio's situation.

5. The essay "The Representation of Curanderismo in Selected Mexican American Works" by Melissa Pabón with Dr. Héctor Pérez, as well as Matthew Alschbach's master's thesis *Misogyny, Women, and Witchcraft: The Curandera in Mexico Before and After the Conquest* (2008), provide useful introductions to the tradition of curanderismo and the different ways that curanderas have been regarded. Ambivalence toward curanderas has been so entrenched within Mexican/Chicano culture that Gloria Anzaldúa takes it to task (and rewrites it) in her picture books for children. In *Friends from the Other Side* (1993) and *Prietita and the Ghost Woman* (1995), the curandera Doña Lola serves as a wise mentor for Prietita, the young protagonist of the two stories. Another, more recent example of the undoing of this ambivalence can be found in Monica Brown's *Clara and the Curandera* (2011).

6. I borrow here the phrase "epistemic deficit" from Chris Meyers and Sara Waller's discussion of horror texts in which the source of horror is absent. In their words, "The epistemic deficit offers us a glimpse of something worse than anything we could describe . . . or depict . . . , because if it could be described or depicted then it would at least be within the limits of what we can grasp" (121). For Antonio, the dramatic horror of the incident with Lupito lies in the fact that what he witnesses is overwhelmingly outside of what he can grasp. In effect he is left radically disoriented and, therefore, in a panic.

Works Cited

Alschbach, Matthew J. *Misogyny, Women, and Witchcraft: The Curandera in Mexico before and after the Conquest*. Diss. San Diego State U, 2008.

Anaya, Rudolfo. *Bless Me, Ultima*. Berkeley, CA: Tonatiuh, 1972.

Anderson, Robert K. "Márez y Luna and the Masculine-Feminine Dialectic." *Crítica Hispánica* 6.2 (Fall 1984): 97–105.

Anzaldúa, Gloria. *Friends from the Other Side/Amigos del otro lado*. San Francisco: Children's Book, 1993.

_____. *Prietita and the Ghost Woman/Prietita y la llorona*. San Francisco: Children's Book, 1995.

Brown, Monica. *Clara and the Curandera/Clara y la curandera*. Houston: Piñata, 2011.

Caminero-Santangelo, Marta. "'Jasón's Indian': Mexican Americans and the Denial of Indigenous Ethnicity in Anaya's *Bless Me, Ultima*." *Critique* 45.2 (Winter 2004): 115–28.

Galbraith, Mary. "Hear My Cry: A Manifesto for an Emancipatory Childhood Studies Approach to Children's Literature." *Lion and the Unicorn* 25.2 (2001): 187–205.

Griswold, Jerome. *Feeling Like a Kid*. Baltimore: Johns Hopkins UP, 2006.

Haugeland, John. "Truth and Finitude: Heidegger's Transcendental Existentialism." *Heidegger, Authenticity, and Modernity: Essays in Honor of Hubert L. Dreyfus.* Vol. I. Eds. Mark Wrathall and Jeff Malpas. Cambridge, MA: MIT P, 2000. 43–78.

Heidegger, Martin. *Being and Time*. Trans. John Macquarrie and Edward Robinson. New York: Harper, 1962.

Herman, Judith. *Trauma and Recovery*. New York: Basic, 1992.

Kanoza, Theresa M. "The Golden Carp and Moby Dick: Rudolfo Anaya's Multi-Culturalism." *MELUS* 24.2 (Summer 1999): 159–71.

Lundin, Anne. Rev. of *Feeling like a Kid: Childhood and Children's Literature* by Jerome Griswold. *Lion and the Unicorn* 32.1 (Jan. 2008): 124–26.

McGavran, James Holt, ed. *Literature and the Child: Romantic Continuations, Postmodern Contestations*. Iowa City: U of Iowa P, 1999.

_____. *Romanticism and Children's Literature in Nineteenth-Century England*. Athens: U of Georgia P, 1991.

Meyers, Chris, and Sara Waller. "Disenstoried Horror: Art Horror without Narrative." *Film and Philosophy* 5 (2001): 117–26.

Mora, Pat. *The Desert Is My Mother/El desierto es mi madre*. Houston: Arte Público, 1994.

Pabón, Melissa, and Héctor Pérez. "The Representation of Curanderismo in Selected Mexican American Works." *Journal of Hispanic Higher Education* 6.3 (2007): 257–71.

Pace, Patricia. "All Our Lost Children: Trauma and Testimony in the Performance of Childhood." *Text and Performance Quarterly* 18.3 (1998): 233–47.

Padilla, Genaro. "Myth and Comparative Cultural Nationalism: The Ideological Uses of Aztlán." *Aztlán: Essays on the Chicano Homeland*. Eds. Rudolfo A. Anaya and Francisco Lomelí. Albuquerque: U of New Mexico P, 1989. 111–34.

Rogers, Jane. "The Function of the La Llorona Motif in Rudolfo Anaya's *Bless Me, Ultima*." *Latin American Literary Review* 5.10 (1977): 64–69.

Rousseau, Jean-Jacques. *Émile*. Trans. William H. Payne. Amherst, NY: Prometheus, 2003.

Saldívar, Ramón. *Chicano Narrative: The Dialectics of Difference*. Madison: U of Wisconsin P, 1990.

Sartre, Jean-Paul. *Existentialism Is a Humanism*. Trans. Carol Macomber. New Haven, CT: Yale UP, 2007.

Steiner, George. *Martin Heidegger*. Chicago: U of Chicago P, 1978.

Tonn, Horst. "*Bless Me, Ultima*: A Fictional Response to Times of Transition." *Aztlán* 18.1: 59–68.

Song for a Murdered Cousin: Violence in
*The Woman Warrior*_____

Tomo Hattori

Despite what Maxine Hong Kingston may say, violence is the central preoccupation of her memoir *The Woman Warrior* (1976). In interviews, Kingston expresses regret for allowing her novel to be titled *The Woman Warrior* and wishes it had "not had a metaphor of a warrior person who uses weapons and goes to war" (Skenazy and Martin 37, 132). Altering the title, however, would have mattered little. Within its pages, a home is attacked, women are raped, soldiers are killed, a baron is beheaded, a little girl is bullied, and a mother drowns herself in a well with her newborn infant. Entire chapters are set in mythical and historical wars. Critics cannot help but notice that *The Woman Warrior* is "permeated with images of violence against women" (Huntley 111), that it would be "almost perverse" not to see the narrator as engaged metaphorically in war (Aubrey 81), and that the opening story of the novel is set "resolutely in the context of sexual violence" (Grice 33). To Sidonie Smith, the novel's five chapters are "decidedly five confrontations with the fictions of self-representation" (151). The threat of personal violence is the constant anxiety of the young female narrator. To understand the relevance of the theme of violence in *The Woman Warrior*, one needs to unravel the emotional entanglements of the buried legacies of family violence that haunt the narrator. The narrator's realization of the scale of violence that women in her family have mastered to become full human subjects is the basis of her own experience of coming of age.

Around the time that the novel's unnamed narrator begins her menses, her mother approaches her with a shocking family secret: "In China, your father had a sister who killed herself. She jumped into the family well" (Kingston 3). In this chapter entitled "The No Name Aunt," the narrator learns that her newly discovered aunt was married in a rural village in China in 1924 in a group ceremony of seventeen couples.

Immediately afterward, the men boarded ships to the United States to work as laborers. A few years after the husband leaves, the aunt becomes pregnant. The villagers are outraged by what they assume is her adultery and arrive as a mob on the night that her baby is due to punish her. What follows is a brutal collective act of terror and intimidation. Some of them are disguised with white masks. They tear the rice from the paddies; they slaughter the livestock; they throw mud, rocks, and eggs at the house; and they smear blood on the doors and walls. The aunt's husband's family offers no resistance, but instead breaks down and starts to curse her. She goes into labor and runs outside to the pigsty where she bears her child. She then takes the newborn to the family well and jumps in, drowning them both. The mother's narration of this brutal history to her daughter, the unnamed narrator, leaves volumes unspoken: "The next morning when I went for the water, I found her and the baby plugging up the family well" (5).

The narrator, as an adolescent Chinese American girl growing up in California in the 1960s, wonders what must have really happened to her aunt, what she must have thought and felt, and what her life must have been. She thinks that her aunt must have been raped: "Women in the old China did not choose. Some man had commanded her to lie with him and be his secret evil" (6). Absorbing the details of the aunt's life, her hasty mass wedding to someone who was probably a stranger, her immediate and long-term separation from him, the narrator ponders what her experience with her husband must have been: "The night she first saw him, he had sex with her. Then he left for America" (7). The narrator compares this experience with what she imagines must have been her aunt's experience with the man who impregnates her. She imagines that the rapist was "not, after all, much different from her husband. They both gave orders: she followed" (7). The narrator is willing to believe that the man who impregnated her aunt may have even organized the raid against her (7). Ultimately, the narrator concludes that both men represent tradition and sexual violence and thus represent two different facets of the same oppressive patriarchal order.

The narrator, however, cannot bear to think of the aunt as only a brutalized, voiceless victim. She feels the need to use her imagination to invest her aunt with an identity and an inner life, calling her a woman caught by a "rare urge" who crosses boundaries "not delineated in space" (8). Describing her aunt as "my forerunner" (8), the narrator reclaims and adopts her as an alternative ancestor. In reimagining her aunt, she also recreates her in ways related to her own personality as an adolescent American teenager: "Unless I see her life branching into mine, she gives me no ancestral help" (8). She uses the story of her aunt to act out possibilities for herself as an adolescent coming of age. She recreates her aunt as a woman with sexual desire, who looks at a man "because she liked the way the hair was tucked behind his ears" or because of "the question-mark line of a long torso curving at the shoulder and straight at the hip" (8). For a moment, she even considers whether her aunt might have been "a wild woman" who kept "rollicking company" and who was "free with sex" (8). She imagines her aunt as working at her appearance in the mirror "guessing at the colors and shapes that would interest him" and seeking the gaze of men (9).

The desire that the narrator theorizes at the mirror also produces agency as the aunt combs "individuality into her bob" (9). Desire is the first step in the narrator's process of inventing her aunt as a self-conscious person capable of critical thought and independent action. In comparison to children and lovers who "have no singularity" the narrator sees her aunt as someone who uses "a secret voice" and "a separate attentiveness" (11). With a personal voice and a distinct individuality, the aunt can then also become an ethical subject who can bear responsibility for her actions. The narrator also believes that, in certain circumstances like the one in which the aunt finds herself, the very act of becoming an individual can be a radical and controversial action. Having "a private life, secret and apart" from the other villagers is what the narrator believes raises their anger and violence against her (13). In the narrator's mind, the aunt, as an ethical subject with personal agency, also becomes capable of controversial personal actions. Another act that the narrator attributes to her newly imagined aunt is that she "kept the man's name to herself" and that she did not reveal the identity of the baby's father to anyone before she died: "To save her inseminator's name she gave silent birth" (11). The narrator sees the aunt's act of giving birth to her baby in the pigsty as "a last act of responsibility" that protects the child in the same way that the aunt protects the child's father (15). In a problematic final attribution of meaning, the narrator sympathizes with the aunt's actions to the point of seeing her carrying of the baby to the well to drown her as a sign of "loving" (15).

The interpretation of the violence in this scene requires that we start at the very beginning. Critics have taken an interest in how the original teller of the tale, the narrator's mother, sets the scene before unraveling the details of the story. Her first words are: "You must not tell anyone . . . what I am about to tell you" (3). Anyone who has ever heard this statement from a parent knows that if the parent truly did not want the child to expose the secret, then she or he would not tell the child anything to start with. This is the contradiction Smith emphasizes in her analysis of the mother's dual and conflicting intentions. On the one hand, the mother does not want anyone to know about the shameful conduct and death of her husband's sister. On the other hand, the mother is dying to tell someone and her daughter is almost an adult. Smith sees the mother's ambivalence in terms of her relationship to patriarchy. The mother is defending her husband and the male social order with a voice that "enforces the authority and legitimacy of the old culture to name" and that controls "the place of women within the patrilineage" (Smith 151). At the same time, the mother wants to give her daughter some insight into how to survive in a repressive and sometimes violent male-dominated society. This part of the mother's intention is an empowering act of telling "tales of female power and authority that seem to create a space of cultural significance for the daughter" (Smith 151). Violence by women, under certain circumstances, can be seen as a means of "revealing their strength and willingness to take action" (Huntley 112). One can even take the view that the mother, for all her outward sternness, is "telling the forbidden story in a secret pact with her daughter for the pleasure of telling it" (Rabine 483). From that perspective, one can even conceive of the mother as a secret feminist who is really on her daughter's side and who seeks "her own release from silence" while giving her daughter "the means and material to break the injunction" of silence (483).

As a guide for sexual conduct, then, the mother's message is mixed. The mother's story "at once affirms and seeks to cut off" the daughter's identification with the aunt and her "unrepressed sexuality" (Smith 153). Thus, the narrator gets no clear direction from her mother about how to understand the ethics of her aunt's behavior. From the perspective of traditional Chinese morality, one can respect the No Name Aunt for at least finally obeying the implicit social injunction to commit suicide for her sexual transgression.

In this sense, the aunt appears to "capitulate before the monolithic power of the order against which she has transgressed" (Smith 155). Alternatively, the aunt's suicide might be read as an act of rebellion in the way that a suicide bomber destroys herself or himself for political cause. In jumping into the family well, the aunt not only contaminates the family's water supply, but also destroys the child as the property of the man who raped her. Moreover, by withholding the name of her lover/rapist, she destroys any chance that her husband's family may have of at least partially clearing their name or of pursuing justice or revenge. The aunt's story thus represents a dilemma in the narrator's quest for ethical feminist role models; the narrator is not sure if the aunt's suicide was an act of freedom or a concession to authority.

The ambivalence at the heart of the narrator's identification with the No Name Woman extends into her next imaginary re-creation of female power. In the chapter entitled "White Tigers," the narrator imagines that she is the legendary Chinese woman warrior Fa Mu Lan, a peasant girl who raises an army to become a "female avenger" by defeating and deposing an oppressive baron. Fa Mu Lan trains as a warrior, raises an army, has a husband, bears a child, leads soldiers into battle, and kills the baron in a satisfying fantasy of perfect revenge. Although she leads the fight for freedom and is the general of her own army, she is not able to move freely about her troops as a woman. Unlike the No Name Woman, Fa Mu Lan is happily married and can have a baby without being attacked by her community, but these are only possible because she keeps her gender identity a secret from her troops (Kingston 19). When she gets pregnant during her battle campaign, she is compelled to disguise her pregnancy by altering her armor so that she looks like "a powerful big man" (19).

King-Kok Cheung notes that as much as the narrator tries to break away from patriarchy she is caught in the "law of the same" that confuses gender conformity with equality (86). Dressing and fighting like a man does not make Fa Mu Lan the social equal of men if the men only treat her equally because they think she is a man. For Cheung, the self-empowering fantasy of Fa Mu Lan is self-defeating (87). Once she kills the baron and returns to her village and to her own gender identity, Cheung points out that "she must once more be subservient, kowtowing to her parents-in-law and resuming her *son*-bearing function" (87). While Fa Mu Lan is able to reveal her identity to the evil baron just before she kills him (Kingston 44), she has to live under a "don't ask, don't tell" policy among her own people. Indeed, this policy of suppressed speech and information connects both the historical No Name Aunt story and the mythical Fa Mu Lan tale.

I suspect that the narrator's investment in her lost aunt and in the mythical character of Fa Mu Lan emerges from the same rebellious impulse to disobey her mother's order of silence. However, if we see the mother as still defending, at least partially, the father's rule of silence, we see that her daughter has internalized the mother's habit in her elaborations of her aunt's and Fa Mu Lan's stories. In other words, both stories simultaneously encode rebellion but also deception. Anne Anlin Cheng emphasizes the similarity between the mother and the daughter. The daughter has been warned by her mother not to be like her aunt *only because she has the potential of being exactly like the aunt*" [emphasis original] (85). Likewise, in disobeying the mother's prohibition against speaking about the aunt, the narrator repeats the mother's disobedience of the father's prohibition against speaking about the aunt. After all, suggests Cheng, is not the mother the ultimate role model for the narrator and "the true Woman Warrior in the book?" (87). The narrator herself intimates from the outset that she is not entirely on her aunt's side. She knows that her aunt died to keep a secret that she, in telling her aunt's story, betrays; she knows that she is "telling on her" (Kingston 16). Because of this guilt, the narrator feels threatened by her aunt even though the aunt is dead: "I do not think she always means me well" (16). The narrator imagines her aunt as a ghost coming back up the well waiting "to pull down a substitute" (16).

What the narrator realizes is that the models of female power offered by her mother, her aunt, and her ancestral mythology are all fraught with compromise. Identifying with her aunt means partially capitulating to the very forces that seek her destruction. Identifying with her mother means mostly accepting her father's repression and censure of her aunt. Even the fantasy warrior Fa Mu Lan can fight and defeat a powerful Chinese man, but she cannot defeat the patriarchal culture that leaves nothing for her afterward except a return to gendered subservience. As an American adolescent of the 1960s, the narrator might imagine that she can be empowered by the second-wave feminism of that era. Nonetheless, she still imagines herself in the persona of her aunt working in front of the mirror to conform to the expectations of men. If the narrator's ability to think and practice feminist power is subverted or at least compromised by every available role model, the question is whether she can at least rely on her ethnic achievement as a source of ethical power.

The story of the No Name Woman and the novel in which she appears have become celebrated achievements in Asian American history and the history of Asian American women. Paul W. McBride argues that Kingston's novel "excavates the invisible" and allows "a glimpse of the personal and microhistorical truth" that does not usually appear in historical documents (96). McBride lauds Kingston's narrative as "a tribute to all women without identities who have challenged the restraints of their cultures" and "who have asserted their own personhood" (96). The narrator indicates that The No Name Woman story begins in 1924; David Leiwei Li regards this specific date for the story as a crucial marker of the significance of the No Name Woman's actions within history:

> The year 1924 was when the 1882 Chinese Exclusion Act was expanded to exclude all Asians from entry as immigrants, even Chinese alien wives of U.S. citizens. Can we afford to neglect the historical contingency from which Kingston stages her narrative incident, an incident about marriage and estrangement, deviation and discipline that occurred under the shadow of legislative racism against Asian Americans? (199)

According to Li, the No Name Woman's actions can be interpreted not only as a rebellion against restrictive Chinese morals and traditions, but also as a reaction to American legislative racism. Within that possibility, the aunt's suicide may attest to both the transnational reach of American racial oppression and to the transnational reach of the moral energies of protest, critique, and redemption. This is an ideal interpretation, but within the novel itself, the internal contradictions in the narrator's relationship to her aunt force a psychic meltdown before the novel is over, destroying any simple understanding and assimilation of her as a border-crossing feminist hero.

In the last chapter of the novel, entitled "A Song for a Barbarian Reed Pipe," the narrator enacts her own form of violence. She verbally and physically abuses a Chinese classmate in the school bathroom. This is her last tantrum before her final harmonious reconciliation with her mother's power and voice. The narrator is in the sixth grade and her victim is a girl who is one year older than she is, who has been in her class since first grade (Kingston 172–73). The narrator describes her victim as "the quiet girl" (172). She assaults her verbally with taunts and insults and then assaults her physically by pinching her cheeks, pulling her hair, and grabbing her shoulders (176–78). The narrator openly describes the motives for her attack as hatred:

> I hated the younger sister, the quiet one. I hated her when she was the last chosen for her team and I, the last chosen for my team. I hated her for her China doll hair cut. I hated her at music time for the wheezes that came out of her plastic flute. (173)

One might wish to overlook the narrator's words, actions, and motives as part of a harmless culture of school bullying, but some critics use stronger and more consequential language. King-Kok Cheung describes the narrator as a "tormentor" who engages in "savagery" (88, 89). Anne Anlin Cheng sees the event as "a painful and protracted scene of torture" (73). My point is that the narrator's hatred is the product of a long pattern of violence.

At the beginning of this last chapter, the narrator mentions that her mother cut her at birth as "the first thing my mother did when she saw me" (164). The narrator expresses deep anxieties about her ability to talk. The mother, a trained midwife, sliced the narrator's frenum, the fold of tissue underneath the daughter's tongue. While the daughter displays anxiety about her mother's intentions, asking "Why did you do that to me, Mother?" (164), the mother explains that she did it to facilitate the motion of the daughter's tongue so that she can articulate language effectively in later life (164). The narrator confesses that she is both "proud" of and also "terrified" by her mother's "powerful act" (164). Her attack against the quiet girl can be understood as a delayed defensive reaction to what the narrator misunderstands as a primal attack by her mother against her capacity for speech at infancy. The mother's action is well-intentioned but necessarily conducted without the narrator's consent and is an invasive physical act involving cutting and bleeding that causes the daughter considerable recurrent anxiety. The trauma that the narrator absorbs from infancy becomes the violent intentions against the quiet girl: "You're going to talk. . . . I am going to make you talk, sissy-girl" (175).

The narrator's attack against the quiet Chinese girl is also motivated by three interconnected cultural features of the way the narrator has come to think about herself as a racially Chinese girl growing up in the United States. Part of the anxiety of adapting to a new country for immigrants who do not speak the host country's language is the fear that one will not be able to communicate in the country's dominant language. Cheng believes that the trauma that the narrator is working out on the quiet girl comes from that aspect of the immigrant experience (86, 88). The specific consequence for the narrator is that she has come to hate her Chinese ethnicity and to wish that she was racially white and what she calls "American-normal" (Kingston 87). Being nonetheless Chinese American, she thus comes to hate herself. Cheung sees the quiet girl as the narrator's "ethnic double" who "represents a phase in the narrator's life when her racial self-hatred is most acute and her acceptance of white norms ostensibly complete" (90). Attacking the quiet girl is also part of the narrator's effort to defeat "her own fears of insubstantiality and dumbness" and her "own failure to take a voice" (Smith 169). The quiet girl is the scapegoat for the narrator's insecurities and, in a more general context, shows that "the torture of the other is self-torture" (Kennedy and Morse 130). As a dynamic of violence that emerges from the experience of race, one can either emphasize the register of the narrator's "virulent contempt at being Chinese" (Cheung 89) or see the torture as the way in which the narrator "associates with 'Americanness'" (Cheng 75). Either way, the violence the narrator delivers to the quiet girl is visible as racial trauma that results in self-hatred and rage.

Smith's analysis of the bathroom scene begins with the observation that "the bathroom is that most private of female spaces—only for girls, only for certain activities" (168). Because the bathroom is related to the elimination of matter from the body, it ultimately becomes associated with female pollution and shame (168). The last time a watery enclosure is turned into a private female space of pollution and shame is the family well in China that the No Name Aunt defiles at the beginning of the novel. The bathroom scene can be regarded as a symbolic recurrence of the opening violence of the novel. We should recall that at the end of the first chapter, the narrator calls the drowned aunt a "spite suicide" and that she haunts the narrator and "waits silently by the water to pull down a substitute" (16). The threat that the quiet girl represents to the narrator occurs in the same symbolic environment as the one in which the No Name Woman dealt death to her newborn daughter. The stage of life at which the aunt's newborn was killed is the same stage of life when the narrator's mother slices the narrator's tongue. Both the aunt and the mother are women who perform violent physical actions against their own newborn daughters. Additionally the mother, even into the narrator's present life, continues to protect those who complied with the aunt's extermination. Not only can the narrator's mother wield power and violence against the daughter, she is also capable of erasing the aunt. The narrator has to confront the unromantic fact that women warriors are women who kill. In reality, neither the aunt nor the mother are completely reassuring presences in her life. The narrator's most primal fear is that, growing up in a family of lethal and potentially lethal mothers, she might end up like her drowned Chinese cousin.

The language that the narrator uses to describe the quiet girl emphasizes her infantile physical qualities. Despite being a year older than the narrator, the girl is "baby soft" (176) with tiny, white "baby teeth" (178). Thinking that the quiet girl is quiet because she does not know how to use language, the narrator thinks that she is less than human and more "like an animal" (179) or "a plant" (180). Pinching the girl's cheek, she doubly denies its human quality by calling it "not dough, but meat" (176). In every regard, the narrator is not able to concede that the girl is a fully formed human being. Her skin is "like squid out of which the glassy blades of bones had been pulled" (176) and her ears are "like white cutworms curled underneath her hair" (177). The only reason she stops pinching the quiet girl's check is because she worries that the skin is so soft that it might come away in her hands (181).

The narrator never knew the sex of the baby that the aunt in China drowned but infers that "it was probably a girl" (15). The substitute that the drowned aunt waits by the water to pull down might not necessarily be a substitute for herself, but a substitute for her daughter. The quiet girl may be the drowned baby's double in the same way that the quiet girl serves as the narrator's double. If that is the case, the drowned baby is the negative state that the narrator might achieve if she does not hurry up and learn to talk. From the narrator's perspective, that threat must be eliminated at all costs. As much as the narrator detests being Chinese and as much as she wishes she were a white American, the underlying anxiety beneath these cultural anxieties is that the narrator does not know if she will be counted as human at all. Her cousin has already been wiped out of existence and buried from the family record by the very person whose duty is to protect her. The power of the women in the narrator's family might not be, in her deepest fears, because they are mothers but because they are antimothers. Coming of age for the narrator means confronting the idea that the tactic that women in her family have devised for defeating oppressive institutions of motherhood is to destroy or to be capable of destroying their own offspring. The narrator comes of age through the realization that the female power that she has discovered and idealized deeply threatens her own self. The narrator has to accept the fact that she cherishes her aunt because she was powerful enough to kill her own daughter, the narrator's cousin, and that her mother inspires her because she is powerful enough to kill her.

The idea that "torture of the other is self-torture" and that violence, whether discreet or open, always returns to its perpetrator, is a disturbing idea in a country whose freedom is based on war. One can take a conventional view, as James R. Aubrey does, that the violence in the book is justified "because the warrior women in the book bring about social changes that lead to harmony" and that its "warlike means" are used to secure "peaceable ends" (81). Aubrey excuses the violence in the novel as simply a metaphor for social conflict and asserts that the woman warrior is really at heart "a peacemaker" (81). If so, then the quiet girl can be rationalized as a noncombatant victim of a regrettable but perhaps unavoidable instance of collateral damage. Seeing the quiet girl as the return of the drowned cousin, however, offers another starting point for the redemptive theme of the novel.

Laura Kang has noted the striking near-absence of proper names in the text of the novel (34). Nowhere in the text does the narrator explicitly state that she is identical to the novel's author Maxine Hong Kingston. The mother is called "Brave Orchid" in portions of the novel in distinction to her younger sister who is called "Moon Orchid," but these are not their actual names. The aunt, as the No Name Woman, is the emblematic example of this narrative style. But none of these erasures imply that they do not have names. They have names; the reader just does not learn what they are. In distinction, the No Name Aunt's daughter is the only female subject in the text whom one might reasonably conjecture never had a name assigned to her to start with. She does not suffer from erasure so much as from discursive non-creation. In that regard, we can see her as the absolute instance of namelessness in this novel and the absolute example of the failure of human recognition on the part of others. If the aunt comes of age because she can kill her own daughter as a conscious act of personhood, then the narrator comes of age because she recognizes her mortal kinship with the killed daughter, her cousin.

The narrator herself overlooks the possibility that the aunt's baby's life could branch into hers. Perhaps that is why the baby has to branch into the narrator's life. The aunt does not appear to have taken into consideration the possibility that her daughter's life is not hers to take. The narrator repeats the aunt's treatment of her in also failing to consider her as a discrete human entity. The specific and unique existence of life in the baby's life is also neglected in criticism. Carrying the baby to the well may indeed show "loving," as the narrator wishes it did (15), but love could also have been practiced by leaving the newborn in the pigsty and going to the well alone. If the project of feminist and historicist interpretation, including the narrator's own, has been to interpret the aunt's behavior as a set of conscious personal and political actions, the vast portion of those causes could well have been served solely by the aunt's suicide. The well would still be defiled, the baby's father's identity would still be lost, and while the aunt would not have the satisfaction of destroying lover/rapist's human property, her own suicide would still function as social protest. If one wishes to see the aunt's suicide and other actions in her final moments as deliberate, conscious choices, then one will ultimately have to evaluate her responsibility for her infanticide.

Growing up in a family of warriors may not be an empowering experience if some of them are insane. Much of the narrator's anxiety, when it is not concerned with voice and agency, is concerned with her own mental stability and the stability of the people around her. Anne Cheng offers what is perhaps the most harrowing implication of the narrator's last, but perhaps not final, regression into violence:

> Surely what is most disarming about the bathroom incident is that the aggression is being performed by someone repeating her own trauma in the form of persecution. This bathroom trauma thus offers the profound and disturbing suggestion that the denigrated body comes to voice, and the pleasure of that voice, only by assuming the voice of authority. (75)

As long as the infliction of pain and death to others is considered an acceptable cost in the pursuit of our own psychic wholeness and freedom, we can never entirely escape the possibility that one day we may be an acceptable cost to others.

If what Cheng suggests is true, that to come to voice and pleasure one must assume the voice of authority, and if what Kingston's novel suggests is true, that to come to authority one must use or be ready to use violence, then we are left with a novel that teaches a profoundly unnerving lesson about American maturity. If being an American means inheriting the national traditions and practices of authority, and if the future maintenance of that authority requires the continuation of violence, then an American is a person who needs to know that violence is the hallmark of American coming of age. The relevance of *The Woman Warrior* to its current and next generation of readers is that it insists upon the psychic return of even the smallest and most utterly alienated victims of violence. The ethical achievement of this American novel is its conviction that no one ever gets left behind. For this reason, among many others elaborated by a generation of readers and critics, *The Woman Warrior* is a novel that continues to provide a dynamic stage for the reinvention of new American people.

Works Cited

Aubrey, James R. "Women Warriors and Military Students." Lim 80–86.

Cheng, Anne Anlin. *The Melancholy of Race: Psychoanalysis, Assimilation, and Hidden Grief.* New York: Oxford UP, 2001.

Cheung, King-Kok. *Articulate Silences: Hisaye Yamamoto, Maxine Hong Kingston, Joy Kogawa.* Ithaca, NY: Cornell UP, 1993.

Grice, Helena. *Maxine Hong Kingston.* New York: Manchester UP, 2006.

Huntley, E. D. *Maxine Hong Kingston: A Critical Companion.* Westport, CT: Greenwood, 2001.

Kang, Laura Hyun Yi. *Compositional Subjects: Enfiguring Asian/American Women.* Durham: Duke UP, 2002.

Kennedy, Colleen, and Deborah Morse. "A Dialogue with(in) Tradition: Two Perspectives on *The Woman Warrior.*" Lim 121–30.

Kingston, Maxine Hong. *The Woman Warrior: Memoirs of a Girlhood among Ghosts.* New York: Vintage, 1989.

Li, David Leiwei. "Re-presenting *The Woman Warrior*: An Essay of Interpretive History." *Critical Essays on Maxine Hong Kingston.* Ed. Laura E. Skandera-Trombley. New York: G.K. Hall, 1998. 182–203.

Lim, Shirley Geok-lin, ed. *Approaches to Teaching Kingston's* The Woman Warrior. New York: MLA, 1991.

McBride, Paul W. "*The Woman Warrior* in the History Classroom." Lim 93–100.

Rabine, Leslie W. "No Lost Paradise: Social Gender and Symbolic Gender in the Writings of Maxine Hong Kingston." *Signs* 12.3 (1987): 471–92.

Skenazy, Paul, and Tera Martin, eds. *Conversations with Maxine Hong Kingston.* Jackson: UP of Mississippi, 1998.

Smith, Sidonie. *A Poetics of Women's Autobiography: Marginality and the Fictions of Self-Representation.* Bloomington: Indiana UP, 1987.

School Stories: Education, Coming of Age, and the American Indian Literary Tradition_____

Amelia V. Katanski

In her autobiographical essay "Impressions of an Indian Childhood," first published in the *Atlantic Monthly* in 1900, the Yankton Dakota author and activist Zitkala-Ša identified her decision to leave home to attend an Indian boarding school as a major turning point in her young life. Swayed by the persuasive words of white missionaries who came to her village along the Missouri River in eastern Dakota Territory, Zitkala-Ša worked hard to convince her mother that boarding school would be the right choice for her. As she explains:

> [My friend] Judéwin had told me of the great tree [in the East] where grew red, red apples; and how we could reach out our hands and pick all the red apples we could eat. I had never seen apple trees. I had never tasted more than a dozen red apples in my life; and when I heard of the orchards of the East, I was eager to roam among them. The missionaries smiled into my eyes and patted my head. I wondered how mother could say such hard words against him [sic.].
>
> "Mother, ask them if little girls may have all the red apples they want when they go East," I whispered aloud, in my excitement.
>
> The interpreter heard me, and answered "Yes, little girl, the nice red apples are for those who pick them; and you will have a ride on the iron horse if you go with these good people."
>
> I had never seen a train and he knew it.
>
> "Mother, I am going East! I like big red apples, and I want to ride on the iron horse! Mother, say yes!" I pleaded. (41–42)

In this passage, the adult Zitkala-Ša revisits the moment she fell to the temptation to leave her family and Dakota community to attend a school that promised adventure, knowledge, and an exotic life of plenty (all the apples you want!). Zitkala-Ša's mother was right to be suspicious of the intent of the school recruiters. While they promised apples and fun, their schools were institutions designed to advance the US federal government's Indian assimilation policy—a policy that grew from the devaluation of American Indian cultures the white educators considered to be savage or inferior. In the words of Richard Pratt, the founder of the prototypical Carlisle Indian Industrial School, Indian boarding schools were designed to "kill the Indian to save the Man," that is, to attempt to suppress and eliminate knowledge of and connections to tribal cultures, languages, and religions in young American Indian people (Prucha 260). As a Dakota girl who spoke only her tribal language and had been educated properly according to her community's customs and traditions, Zitkala-Ša was targeted by the educators to attend a school whose primary goal was what is recognized today as cultural genocide. Narratives of education had been a distinct genre of American Indian life stories in the oral tradition for centuries (Brumble 22–23), but stories of education took on even greater significance for young American Indian people with the advent of these Indian boarding schools in the late nineteenth century. By writing about their experiences at school, American Indian authors recounted the hardships they faced there, asserted continued connection to their Native and tribal cultures, and actively constructed complex identities, drawing from both the educations they received from their home communities and their experiences at school. This essay will focus on American Indian narratives of education as moments of coming of age, looking specifically at the boarding-school-era autobiographical essays of Zitkala-Ša and the early twenty-first-century young adult novel *The Absolutely True Diary of a Part-Time Indian*, by Sherman Alexie.

The above excerpt from Zitkala-Ša's autobiographical essays is particularly illustrative of the complexity of American Indian educational narratives because of the way she tells the story of how she was convinced to go to boarding school. She clearly frames her experience as a narrative of temptation, in which the missionaries entice her with visions of apple trees to leave her community, go East, and attend their school. This apple imagery alludes to the biblical story of the Garden of Eden, in which Eve is tempted by Satan (in the form of a snake) to eat from the tree of the knowledge of good and evil, in violation of God's prohibition against eating that tree's fruit. In the biblical story, once Adam and Eve succumb to this temptation and eat the fruit, they gain knowledge but lose access to paradise, as God dismisses them from the garden, sentencing them and all of humanity to a life of struggle and toil. Significantly, in her rewriting of the Eden myth, Zitkala-Ša casts the Christian missionaries in the role of Satan. They are the ones who lure her away from her Edenic life among her fellow Dakota with the temptation of knowledge. Thus, her narrative aligns the educators with evil, despite their claims to Christian authority. Rather than providing salvation through assimilation, her story suggests, attending Indian boarding school was a fall from grace that would lead to a life of struggle and challenge for Zitkala-Ša and her Dakota community. But by using biblical allegory to indict the assimilative project of the boarding schools, Zitkala-Ša demonstrates that she was a successful student who learned about the Bible and gained proficiency in the English language.

It is the very knowledge she acquired through her time at school that enables her to write this autobiographical narrative in English, critiquing the school experience, naming its assimilative policies as evil, and publishing that critique in the *Atlantic Monthly*, a respected journal that reached a national audience. Furthermore, Zitkala-Ša's narrative demonstrates not only her mastery of her lessons at school, but also her ability to make the English language her own. Her reference to red apples alludes to popular interpretations of biblical cosmology and also uses what linguist William Leap refers to as "boarding school English" (162). "Apple" was a term used by boarding school students to refer to someone who was "red" on the outside but "white" on the inside—that is, someone who was phenotypically American Indian but who had internalized European American culture and values. To accept the fruit of knowledge from the missionaries put one at risk of *becoming* an "apple," or losing one's identity as an American Indian, and

Zitkala-Ša's narrative both identifies that danger and connects itself to other narratives written by American Indian writers that also make use of boarding-school English. Through this process, these writers make English an American Indian language, in a move that directly reverses the assimilative goals of the schools (Katanski 217; see also Child and Lomawaima).

Many, many American Indian writers from the late nineteenth century onward have focused on the impact of Indian boarding schools on their coming of age. Zitkala-Ša's writings show how students' literary responses to their educational experiences are complex and demonstrate their creativity in forming identities that maintain a close connection to tribal culture even as they add elements of European American cultural practices to their literary repertoires. Contemporary American Indian students do not face a concerted government effort to alienate them from their cultures and communities, but the reality of their school experiences may challenge that connection and make it difficult to maintain. Sherman Alexie's young adult novel, *The Absolutely True Diary of a Part-Time Indian* (2007) demonstrates how school is still a site where American Indian youth encounter assimilative pressures. The protagonist, Junior, challenges and maintains his identity as Indian in contradistinction to those pressures, making use of humor and artistic expression to chart his own course.

Historical Background

Coming-of-age stories often focus on the ways that growing up challenges young people to rework their identities and situate themselves within their communities. The concept of coming of age is a particularly difficult and complex issue in American Indian communities. From the beginning of contact between Europeans and indigenous communities in what is now the United States, European colonizers frequently sought to portray American Indian people as childlike, as needing to "grow up" and "advance" in order to be considered civilized or "adult" like Europeans and European Americans. This ethnocentric, Eurocentric approach to American Indian cultures acted as a false justification for taking land and resources from Native communities. Historian David Adams notes that in the early years of the United States the most important policy issue "could be reduced to this fact: Indians possessed the land, and whites wanted the land. . . . A major priority was the creation of a mechanism and rationale for divesting Indians of their real estate. The matter was an especially delicate one, for although the divestiture of Indian land was essential to the extension of American ideals, that divestiture must also be ultimately justified by those same ideals" (5).

By the nineteenth century, social evolutionary theory had developed as a "scientific" way to justify the appropriation of Indian land. Social evolutionists believed that human societies function much as biological organisms throughout evolutionary history: having begun as simple structures, they grow increasingly complex over time. Some social evolutionists, such as Lewis Henry Morgan, the "father" of anthropology, believed that some human cultures had gotten stuck in early evolutionary stages, while other cultures had moved forward (Morgan 39–40). These early social scientists used their own European American culture as the standard for what a "civilized" society must be, and then judged and evaluated other cultures based on how similar to or different from European American culture they were. Based on social scientists' theories and classifications, American Indian cultures were assessed as "savage," "barbaric," and as falling short of the ideals of civilization. In particular, these indigenous communities fell short because they lacked literacy in English, Christianity, and an appreciation for the private ownership of property (Katanski 29–33). Since, according to the social evolutionary scale, these "less developed" cultures were viewed as incapable of owning their own land or taking care of themselves, the US government justified its practice of seizing control over their territories and resources. This system of beliefs translated into a series of policies that placed the US government in the role of the paternalistic father figure that treated Indian communities as "wards" and attempted to transform Indian people through assimilation. Throughout the nineteenth, twentieth, and twenty-first centuries, coming of age for American Indian people has meant reckoning with their relationship to this historical struggle. Coming into one's individual role as an American Indian adult has also necessitated a rejection of this racist understanding of Native communities as childlike and the assertion of Indian nations' status as sovereign entities.

The curriculum of Indian boarding schools was designed to achieve the US government's paternalistic, assimilative goals. Students were taken from their families and communities and placed in schools for years at a time without the option to return home. While Zitkala-Ša chose to attend boarding school, most other children did not face a choice. They were forcibly taken from their families, or their communities were, in essence, blackmailed with the threat of loss of treaty payments and access to food if they did not send their children to the schools (Pratt 220). School administrators brought together students from many different tribes, stripped them of their customary clothing, forbade them from speaking their native languages or practicing their native religions, and disciplined them harshly. Students spent half of their day in the classroom and the other half in "industrial" training, learning farming, trades, or domestic work. Over twenty-five federally run, off-reservation boarding schools enrolled a very significant percentage of American Indian people through the 1930s at least (and longer, in some locations). A similar curriculum was also put into place in a number of on-reservation boarding schools, and the result was that entire generations of American Indian people spent time in educational institutions that devalued—and in fact actively worked to undermine— their tribal cultures, languages, religions, economies, and sovereignty.

Boarding school education had a direct impact on the production of American Indian literature. The schools' drive to eliminate American Indian cultures and traditions meant that they sought to suppress and restrict Indian people's self-representation and literary expression as Indians. As an 1868 US military report noted:

By educating the children of these tribes in the English languages these differences [between the tribes and the white settlers who lived near them] would have disappeared, and civilization would have followed at once. Nothing then would have been left but the antipathy of race, and that too is always softened in the beams of a higher civilization. . . . Through sameness of language is produced sameness of sentiment and thought . . . (Prucha 198)

Furthermore, according to the report, teaching all American Indians how to communicate in English would weaken tribal ties and "blot out the boundary lines which divide them into distinct nations" (198). Learning to speak, read, and write English, then, was supposed to immediately assimilate American Indian students and change their very thought patterns. These changed thought patterns would invalidate and dismantle tribes as nations. Explicitly connected to English language education in the schools was, therefore, the educators' belief in their control over how (and if) their students textually represented themselves as Indian people. The controlling pedagogy of the anti-tribal schools was to monitor and restrict representations of Indianness so that students would affirm the schools' assimilative project and embrace a sense of tribal culture as inferior and "savage."

While federal American Indian policy officially moved away from assimilation by the late 1920s, and Native communities slowly gained more control over the education of their children, Indian education in the United States remains problematic. A 1991 report indicated "that students in BIA schools on average achieved far below non-Native students and generally did not receive high-quality education" (Reyhner and Eder 308–9), and the 1990 Indian Nations At Risk Task Force (assembled by the Secretary of Education) noted that many Native students—at tribe-run, private, *and* public schools—testified that their schools had "'an unfriendly school climate that fails to promote appropriate academic, social, cultural, and spiritual development among many Native students.' Schools also had a Eurocentric curriculum, low teacher expectations, 'a lack of native educators as role models,' and 'overt and subtle racism'" (Reyhner and Eder 314).

Despite this continued failure of educational institutions to work in their best interests, the work of Zitkala-Ša, Sherman Alexie, and other American Indian writers demonstrates that American Indian writers have been able to take control of the English language and put it to their own purposes, making English an "Indian" language and telling stories about the full complexity of their school experiences and about their ability to select what and how they would adopt and adapt from their boarding school educations and their experiences in contemporary tribal and public schools. These writers have sought to tell their own stories of coming of age—of developing into adults with complex relationships to their tribal cultures, American Indian culture as a whole, and, more broadly, to the United States—and their educational experiences have played a vital role in such narratives.

Zitkala-Ša's American Indian Stories

Zitkala-Ša's autobiographical essays, first published in the *Atlantic Monthly* in 1900 and later collected in *American Indian Stories* in 1921, focus directly upon the impact of educational experiences on the development of her writing and her identity. Zitkala-Ša begins her series of autobiographical essays with a discussion of her first educational experience—learning the knowledge and skills required to be an accomplished participant in Dakota society. By asserting that she received a Dakota education, Zitkala-Ša countered the notion that Indian children were "blank slates" when they arrived at boarding school (Adams 52). Her Dakota education did not take place in a classroom, Zitkala-Ša explained, but instead was based on observation, active participation, and creative play.

Zitkala-Ša's mother, Táte I Yóhin Win, acts as her primary teacher and articulates a Dakota philosophy of education that stresses independent learning and perseverance. For example, in learning the art of beadwork, Zitkala-Ša must design her own patterns, and she must finish whatever she starts. She notes that "the quietness of [my mother's] oversight made me feel strongly responsible and dependent upon my own judgment. She treated me as a dignified individual as long as I was on my good behavior; and how humiliated I was when some boldness of mine drew forth a rebuke from her" (20). Zitkala-Ša learns that even when she makes mistakes (such as when she attempts to make coffee for a visiting elder, demonstrating the Dakota value of hospitality, but serves a cup of "worse than muddy warm water") her mother "treated my best judgment, poor as it was, with the utmost respect. It was not till long years afterward that I learned how ridiculous a thing I had done" (29). As long as she tries to live by the values of the community and to put the knowledge she is learning to use, she is supported and affirmed as a student. This educational philosophy helps her to develop a strong sense of identity as a Dakota woman and as a creative individual.

Zitkala-Ša's sense of self is undermined when she succumbs to the temptation of the missionaries and goes East to attend boarding school at White's Manual Institute in Indiana. The language she uses to describe her initial days at school reveals how alien is the new environment in which she finds herself. She writes, for example, of being "taken along an upward incline of wooden boxes, which I learned afterward to call a stairway" (50–51). When she cries as she thinks of her mother, she is cautioned by an older student to "wait until you are alone in the night" (50). This strange world demands its own vocabulary and a particular performance of self from the students, and Zitkala-Ša must master these to survive.

Developing the ability to speak and understand English was the most important survival skill the students could possess. Zitkala-Ša demonstrates the importance of language acquisition to students' abilities to protect themselves from the harsh corporal punishment at boarding school when she relates a story about the time she and her friends Thowin and Judéwin play in the snow against the dorm matron's orders. When they are summoned to receive punishment from the matron, Judéwin, who speaks a little English, warns them to " 'wait until [the matron] stops [talking loudly]. Then, after a tiny pause, say 'no'" (57). The girls practice the one word at their disposal over and over, but when Thowin goes before the matron, she is, unfortunately, asked "'Are you going to obey my word the next time?'" (58). When Thowin responds with the only English word she knows, she is beaten with "blows [meant] to smart" (58) and shrieks in pain. Being "deaf to the English language" clearly put students at risk and threatened their ability to survive (57).

For Zitkala-Ša, mastering the English language became not only a survival strategy, but also a means of resistance to the schools' assimilative agenda. She writes, "As soon as I comprehended a part of what was said and done, a mischievous spirit of revenge possessed me" (59). Her first recorded act of resistance is explicitly linked to her newfound competency in English, which provides the means for her to wage a linguistic rebellion against the boarding-school ideology. When she was punished for breaking a rule "which seemed to me very needlessly binding," she is put on kitchen duty and ordered to mash turnips (59). Taking the words of her disciplinarian literally— "The order was 'Mash these turnips,' and mash them I would!"—she attacks the turnips with such violence that she crushes the bowl that holds them, and they fall out the bottom when a matron attempts to bring them to the table (60). She is mildly sorry for ruining the jar, but ecstatic about her success at turning the lessons—and the words—of the educators back on themselves. She concludes, "As I sat eating my dinner and no turnips were served, I whooped in my heart for having once asserted the rebellion within me" (61). Learning English did not, then, lead to Zitkala-Ša's assimilation into European American society and force her to lose a sense of herself as American Indian. Instead, acquiring fluency in the English language armed her with a weapon to resist the indoctrinating ideology of the boarding schools and to use her voice to criticize the educational system and its structures of discipline and control.

Zitkala-Ša sought to use her voice in the interests of other American Indian people. After graduating from White's Manual Institute and attending Earlham College, she briefly became a teacher at the Carlisle Indian School, under headmaster Richard Pratt. Realizing that she could not dismantle this educational system from the inside, she soon left her teaching position to become a writer and activist. In the final words of her essay "An Indian Teacher among Indians," which describes her frustrating time at Carlisle, Zitkala-Ša launches a devastating attack against the boarding schools' educational program:

> Examining the neatly figured pages, and gazing upon the Indian girls and boys bending over their books, the white visitors walked out of the school-house well satisfied: they were educating the children of the red man! . . . In this fashion many have passed idly through the Indian Schools during the last decade afterward to boast of their charity to the North American Indian. But few there are who have paused to question whether real life or long-lasting death lies beneath this semblance of civilization. (98–99)

The adult Zitkala-Ša, the writer, possesses insight into the working of the schools that the self-satisfied white visitors do not. She has experienced the violence of Richard Pratt's desire to "kill the Indian to save the Man," but has managed to survive and has constituted a Dakota Indian identity for herself through the creative use of language. By telling powerful stories of the Indian boarding school experience, Zitkala-Ša avoids the "long-lasting death" of the school curriculum so as to chart her own path as an advocate for Indian people.

Sherman Alexie's *The Absolutely True Diary of a Part-Time Indian*

More than one century after Zitkala-Ša used her mastery of English to critique the educational institutions that attempted to eradicate Indian identity, Sherman Alexie published his novel for young adults, *The Absolutely True Diary of a Part-Time Indian*. Alexie's protagonist, Arnold Spirit (known to all as "Junior"), is a fourteen-year-old Spokane boy who starts his freshman year of high school as the novel begins. Junior tells the story of this painful year of growth, adjustment, and loss with openness, lots of humor, and a combination of first person narrative and cartoons, which he identifies as a universal language. "So I draw because I want to talk to the world," Junior explains. "And I want the world to pay attention to me. . . . I think the world is a series of broken dams and floods, and my cartoons are tiny little lifeboats" (6). His artistry is what allows him to reach beyond himself, to connect with others across difference. We do not meet the adult Junior in this novel, but because the novel is presented as excerpts from Junior's diary we do come to understand him as the author of his own developing identity.

On his first day of school at the reservation high school, Junior has a life-changing experience when he opens his geometry textbook to find his mother's name written in it and realizes that the textbook must, therefore, be at least thirty years old. "And let me tell you," Junior says, "that old, old, old, *decrepit* geometry book hit my heart with the force of a nuclear bomb. My hopes and dreams floated up in a mushroom cloud. And what do you do when the world has declared nuclear war on you?" (31, emphasis original). The answer to Junior's question is depicted in a cartoon. We see him throw his textbook into the face of his teacher, Mr. P, whose name is an allusion to Carlisle's Richard Pratt. Later, Mr. P tells Junior:

> I have to forgive you. It's the only thing that keeps me from smacking you with an ugly stick. When I first started teaching here, that's what we did to the rowdy ones, you know? We beat them. That's how we were taught to teach you. We were supposed to kill the Indian to save the child. . . . We were supposed to make you give up being Indian. Your songs and stories and language and dancing. Everything. We weren't trying to kill Indian people. We were trying to kill Indian culture. (35)

Mr. P goes on to apologize to Junior for the way he treated all of the Indian students he had hurt. And he insists:

> "You have to leave this reservation. . . . You were right to throw that book at me. I deserved to get smashed in the face for what I've done to Indians. Every white person on this rez should get smashed in the face. But, let me tell you this. All the Indians should get smashed in the face, too. . . . All these kids have given up," he said. "All your friends. All the bullies. And their mothers and fathers have given up, too. And their grandparents gave up and their grandparents before them. And me and every other teacher here. We're all defeated." (42)

The remorseful Mr. P again urges Junior to go to school off the reservation, insisting that "You're going to find more and more hope the farther and farther you walk away from this sad, sad, sad reservation" (43).

The encounter between Junior and Mr. P sets in motion the complex struggles with identity, education, and the quest for a better life that Junior deals with throughout the novel. He chooses to attend high school off the reservation, in the nearby town of Reardan, where the only other Indian is the school mascot. And in making this choice for a more hopeful life for himself, he sets himself apart from his Spokane community, including his best friend, Rowdy, who sees Junior's departure as a betrayal of their friendship and connection. In an interview, Alexie explained this complicated dynamic by saying, "We all know the Indians were colonized by the Europeans . . . but every colonized Indian has been colonized by the Indian reaction to colonization" (Konigsberg). In other words, Junior must struggle against not only the educational aftermath of the Indian boarding schools—non-Native teachers who do not respect American Indian cultures and instead work to undermine them—but also the "long-lasting death" Zitkala-Ša saw in the school curriculum's impact on Indian students who internalized the racism of the educators until they came to believe that being Indian meant being hopeless and without a future.

Junior's status as a "part-time Indian" reflects this complexity. His choice to attend school off the reservation has affected his identity in unexpected ways. He notes that he is not considered fully Indian by many on the reservation because "some Indians think you have to act white to make your life better. Some Indians think you *become* white if you try to make your life better, if you become successful" (131, emphasis original). At the same time, Junior is unquestionably, stereotypically Indian to the white students at his off-reservation school in Reardan, who call him "Chief" and tell him racist jokes. When told a joke that is "the most racist thing I'd ever heard in my life," Junior punches the student who told the joke, and decides that this was maybe "the most important moment of my life. Maybe I was telling the world that I was no longer a human target" (65). His choice to fight back against the identity categories that others use to target and belittle him begins a process by which he develops a more expansive, hopeful sense of self—maintaining his connection to his family and community while moving outside the boundaries of the reservation and staking a claim to his membership in multiple "tribes." While being considered a "part-time" Indian is most often a source of pain for Junior, it may also be, he discovers, a source of possibility.

As Junior explains to Gordy, a nerdy white boy in his class, "The people at home, . . . a lot of them call me an apple" (131–32). When he explains the meaning of the term "apple" to Gordy, Gordy replies that "life is a constant struggle between being an individual and being a member of the community" (132). When Junior presses Gordy for an explanation of this statement, Gordy explains that back in the early days of human existence, communities depended upon one another and needed trust in order to survive. "So, back in the day, weird people threatened the strength of the tribe. If you weren't good for making food, shelter, or babies, then you were tossed out on your own. . . . Weird people still get banished" (132). Acknowledging that both he and Gordy are "weird" in their own ways, Junior notes that together, these outcasts make "a tribe of two" (132). Later in the novel, when he visits the graves of the many important people in his life who have died over the course of the year (including his grandmother, his sister, and his father's best friend), Junior begins to cry for those he has lost, but also to cry "because I was going to have a better life out in the white world. I realized that I might be a lonely Indian boy, but I was not alone in my loneliness. There were millions of other Americans who had left their birthplaces in search of a dream. I realized that, sure, I was a Spokane Indian. I belonged to that tribe. But I also belonged to the tribe of American immigrants. And to the tribe of basketball players. And to the tribe of bookworms" (217). Junior continues with a litany of the many affiliations, major and minor, that constitute his multiple tribes. This ability to affiliate across racial and ethnic boundaries is his survival skill, and he developed that skill through his educational choices.

While affiliation with multiple tribes might seem to be a diminishment of his Spokane identity, a kind of assimilation, Junior eventually learns that the opposite is true. At the end of the school year, Junior reconnects with Rowdy. In an emotional moment, Rowdy tells Junior that leaving the reservation for school made him nomadic, like "old-time Indians" (229). While, as Rowdy explains, most Indians are no longer nomadic, Junior is "an old-time nomad. . . . You're going to keep moving all over the world in search of food and water and grazing land. That's pretty cool" (230). Junior's choice to leave, then, becomes understood as a choice that enhances, rather than diminishes, his connection to his Indianness. He becomes more "old-time" than those who appear to embrace Spokane culture closely by staying within the reservation boundaries. Though his decision will never be easy or simple, and he hopes not only that his family will forgive him, but also that he can forgive himself for making the decision to leave, the novel ends with this moment of reintegration, as Junior and Rowdy play basketball without keeping score—finding joy in the paradoxical arrangement of playing both with and against one another at the same time. This appreciation of movement and resistance to rigid identity constructions runs counter to the rigid notions of assimilation boarding school educators attempted to impose on their Indian students. As Junior has come to understand, flexibility in the face of change is the key to both personal and cultural survival.

Conclusion

Zitkala-Ša and Alexie both represent school as a potentially devastating site where American Indian students have been forced to address complex questions of identity. In the works of both, Indian students demonstrate that they can be active agents who resolve these identity questions through their spirited, generative narrative creativity. It is, in fact, the ability to narrate these experiences that enables both Zitkala-Ša's and Junior's survival. Reading these two texts alongside one another, we can see how educational narratives have created literary forms and tropes that constitute the American Indian literary tradition. When Junior says he is called an apple, he is making use of the boarding school English that Zitkala-Ša helped to develop, reinventing English as an Indian language. Likewise, when Alexie names his teacher Mr. P, he is alluding to the boarding school experience, calling to mind the historical context that shapes Junior's contemporary environment. Both writers also tell stories of educational rebellion—a literary form repeated in many memoirs and stories by American Indian authors. These texts point toward a repertoire of shared representational forms, connecting intertextually to form a significant part of the discourse of American Indian literature. In doing so, they affirm the continued presence of Native communities and engage in rhetorical sovereignty, or the right and ability of a people to determine the mode and language of their own public discourse (Lyons 449–50). By telling their stories, these students engage in both personal and community self-determination, coming of age triumphantly.

Works Cited

Adams, David Wallace. *Education for Extinction: American Indians and the Boarding School Experience, 1875–1928*. Lawrence: UP Kansas, 1995.

Alexie, Sherman. *The Absolutely True Diary of a Part-Time Indian*. New York: Little, 2007.

Brumble, H. David. *American Indian Autobiography*. Berkeley: U of California P, 1988.

Child, Brenda J. *Boarding School Seasons*. Lincoln: U of Nebraska P, 1998.

Katanski, Amelia V. *Learning to Write "Indian": The Boarding School Experience and American Indian Literature*. Norman: U of Oklahoma P, 2005.

Konigsberg, Eric. "In His Own Literary World, A Native Son Without Borders." *New York Times*. 20 Oct. 2009. Web. 19 Sept. 2011.

Leap, William L. *American Indian English*. Salt Lake City: U of Utah P, 1993.

Lomawaima, K. Tsianina. *They Called It Prairie Light: The Story of Chilocco Indian School*. Lincoln: U Nebraska P, 1994.

Lyons, Scott Richard. "Rhetorical Sovereignty: What Do American Indians Want from Writing?" *College Composition and Communication* 51.3 (Feb. 2000): 447–68.

Morgan, Lewis Henry. *Ancient Society*. 1877. Tucson: U of Arizona P, 1985.

Pratt, Richard H. *Battlefield and Classroom: Four Decades with the American Indian*. Norman: U of Oklahoma P, 2003.

Prucha, Frances P. *Americanizing the American Indians: Writings by the "Friends of the Indian" 1880–1900*. Cambridge: Harvard UP, 1973.

Reyhner, Jon, and Jeanne Eder. *American Indian Education: A History*. Norman: U of Oklahoma P, 2004.

Zitkala-Ša. *American Indian Stories*. 1921. Lincoln: U of Nebraska P, 1985.

RESOURCES

Additional Works on Coming of Age_____

Drama
The Glass Menagerie by Tennessee Williams, 1944
A Taste of Honey by Shelagh Delaney, 1958
Six Degrees of Separation by John Guare, 1990
The Cryptogram by David Mamet, 1995
How I Learned to Drive by Paula Vogel, 1997

Graphic Novels
Mind Riot: Coming of Age in Comix edited by Karen D. Hirsch, 1997
One Hundred Demons by Lynda Barry, 2002
The Complete Persepolis by Marjane Satrapi, 2007
Stuck in the Middle: 17 Comics from an Unpleasant Age edited by Ariel Schrag, 2007
Black Hole by Charles Burns, 1995–2005

Long Fiction
The History of Tom Jones, a Foundling by Henry Fielding, 1749
David Copperfield by Charles Dickens, 1849–50
Ragged Dick; or, Street Life in New York with the Boot Blacks by Horatio Alger, 1867–68
Kim by Rudyard Kipling, 1900–1
Sons and Lovers by D. H. Lawrence, 1913
Bread Givers by Anzia Yezierska, 1925
Their Eyes Were Watching God by Zora Neale Hurston, 1937
Siddhartha by Hermann Hesse, 1951
To Kill a Mockingbird by Harper Lee, 1960
A Clockwork Orange by Anthony Burgess, 1962
The Bluest Eye by Toni Morrison, 1970
The House on Mango Street by Sandra Cisneros, 1984
The Whale Rider by Witi Ihimaera, 1987
This Boy's Life by Tobias Wolff, 1989
The *Harry Potter* series by J. K. Rowling, 1997–2007

Poetry
"To the Virgins, to Make Much of Time" by Robert Herrick, 1648
"Ode on a Distant Prospect of Eton College" by Thomas Gray, 1747
"Spring and Fall" by Gerard Manley Hopkins, 1880

"If" by Rudyard Kipling, 1895

"When I Was One-and Twenty" by A. E. Housman, 1896

"[in Just-]" by e. e. cummings, 1920

"Theme for English B" by Langston Hughes, 1949

"On Being Twenty-six" by Philip Larkin, 1949

"Adolescence: I–IV" by Rita Dove, 1989

Out of the Dust by Karen Hesse, 1999

17: A Novel in Prose Poems by Liz Rosenberg, 2002

Red Hot Salsa: Bilingual Poems on Being Young and Latino in the United States edited by Lori Marie Carlson, 2005

The Realm of Possibility by David Levithan, 2006

Short Fiction

"Araby" by James Joyce, 1914

Winesburg, Ohio by Sherwood Anderson, 1919

"Barn Burning" by William Faulkner, 1939

"I Stand Here Ironing" by Tillie Olsen, 1960

"A & P" by John Updike, 1961

"Where Are You Going, Where Have You Been" by Joyce Carol Oates, 1966

Lives of Girls and Women by Alice Munro, 1971

Rites of Passage: Stories about Growing Up by Black Writers from around the World edited by Tonya Bolden, 1994

An Island Like You: Stories of the Barrio by Judith Ortiz Cofer, 1996

Leaving Home: Stories edited by Hazel Rochman and Darlene Z. McCampbell, 1998

Baseball in April and Other Stories by Gary Soto, 2000

Athletic Shorts: Six Short Stories by Chris Crutcher, 2002

Writes of Passage: Coming-of-Age Stories and Memoirs from the Hudson Review edited by Paula Deitz, 2008

Bibliography

Abel, Elizabeth, Marianne Hirsch, and Elizabeth Langland. *The Voyage In: Fictions of Female Development*. Hanover, NH: UP of New England, 1983.

Aronson, Marc. *Exploding the Myths: The Truth About Teenagers and Reading*. Lanham, MD: Scarecrow, 2001.

Austin, Joe, and Michael Nevin Willard, eds. *Generations of Youth: Youth Cultures and History in Twentieth-Century America*. New York: New York UP, 1998.

Baxter, Kent. *The Modern Age: Turn-of-the-Century American Culture and the Invention of Adolescence*. Tuscaloosa: U of Alabama P, 2008.

Bremner, Robert H., ed. *Children and Youth in America, A Documentary History*. 3 vols. Cambridge, MA: Harvard UP, 1970–74.

Buckley, Jerome Hamilton. *Season of Youth: The Bildungsroman from Dickens to Golding*. Cambridge: Harvard UP, 1974.

Burt, Stephen. *The Forms of Youth: Twentieth-Century Poetry and Adolescence*. New York: Columbia UP, 2007.

Cart, Michael. *From Romance to Realism: Fifty Years of Growth and Change in Young Adult Literature*. New York: HarperCollins, 1996.

Castle, Gregory. *Reading the Modernist Bildungsroman*. Gainesville: UP of Florida, 2006.

Dalsimer, Katherine. *Female Adolescence: Psychoanalytic Reflections on Works of Literature*. New Haven: Yale UP, 1986.

DeMarr, Mary Jean, and Jane S. Bakerman. *The Adolescent in the American Novel Since 1960*. New York: Ungar, 1986.

Esman, Aaron H. *Adolescence and Culture*. New York: Columbia UP, 1990.

Fuderer, Laura Sue. *The Female Bildungsroman in English: An Annotated Bibliography of Criticism*. New York: MLA, 1991.

Garber, Marjorie. *Coming of Age in Shakespeare*. New York: Methuen, 1981.

Gillis, John R. *Youth and History: Tradition and Change in European Age Relations, 1770–Present*. New York: Academic, 1974.

Griswold, Jerome. *Audacious Kids: Coming of Age in America's Classic Children's Books*. Oxford, Eng.: Oxford UP, 1992.

Hall, Stuart, and Tony Jefferson, eds. *Resistance through Rituals: Youth Subcultures in Post-War Britain*. New York: Routledge, 1990.

Hardin, James N., ed. *Reflection and Action: Essays on the Bildungsroman*. Columbia: U of South Carolina P, 1991.

Hedley, Jane. *I Made You to Find Me: The Coming of Age of the Woman Poet and the Politics of Poetic Address*. Columbus: The Ohio State UP, 2009.

Hine, Thomas. *The Rise and Fall of the American Teenager*. New York: Avon, 1999.

Inness, Sherrie A., ed. *Delinquents and Debutantes: Twentieth-Century American Girls' Cultures*. New York: New York UP, 1998.

_____. *Nancy Drew and Company: Culture, Gender, and Girls' Series*. Bowling Green: Popular, 1997.

Jacobson, Marcia. *Being a Boy Again: Autobiography and the American Boy Book*. Tuscaloosa: U of Alabama P, 1994.

Japtok, Martin Michael. *Growing Up Ethnic: Nationalism and the Bildungsroman in African American and Jewish American Fiction*. Iowa City: U of Iowa P, 2005.

Katanski, Amelia. *Learning to Write "Indian": The Boarding School Experience and American Indian Literature*. Norman: U of Oklahoma P, 2005.

Kett, Joseph F. *Rites of Passage: Adolescence in America, 1790 to the Present*. New York: Basic, 1977.

Labovitz, Esther Kleinbord. *The Myth of the Heroine: The Female Bildungsroman in the Twentieth Century: Dorothy Richardson, Simone de Beauvoir, Doris Lessing, Christa Wolf*. New York: Peter Lang, 1987.

Latrobe, Kathy H., and Judy Drury. *Critical Approaches to Young Adult Literature*. New York: Neal-Schuman, 2009.

LeSeur, Geta. *Ten Is The Age of Darkness: The Black Bildungsroman*. Columbia: U of Missouri P, 1995.

Macleod, David I. *The Age of the Child: Children in America, 1890–1920*. New York: Twayne, 1998.

_____. *Building Character in the American Boy: The Boy Scouts, YMCA, and Their Forerunners, 1870–1920*. Madison: U of Wisconsin P, 1983.

Millard, Kenneth. *Coming of Age in Contemporary American Fiction*. Edinburgh: Edinburgh UP, 2007.

Mintz, Steven. *Huck's Raft: A History of American Childhood*. Cambridge: Belknap, 2004.

Nash, Ilana. *American Sweethearts: Teenage Girls in Twentieth-Century Popular Culture*. Bloomington: Indiana UP, 2006.

Neubauer, John. *The Fin-de-Siècle Culture of Adolescence*. New Haven: Yale UP, 1992.

Popkin, Debra, ed. *Francophone Women Coming of Age: Memoirs of Childhood and Adolescence from France, Africa, Quebec, and the Caribbean*. Newcastle: Cambridge Scholars, 2007.

Rishoi, Christy. *From Girl to Woman: American Woman's Coming-of-Age Narratives*. Albany: State U of New York P, 2003.

Savage, Jon. *Teenage: The Creation of Youth Culture*. New York: Viking, 2007.

Spacks, Patricia Meyer. *The Adolescent Idea: Myths of Youth and the Adult Imagination*. New York: Basic, 1981.

Springhall, John. *Coming of Age: Adolescence in Britain, 1860–1960*. Dublin: Gill, 1986.

Critical Insights

Summerfield, Giovanna, and Lisa Downward. *New Perspectives on the European Bildungsroman.* New York: Continuum, 2010.

Trites, Roberta Seelinger. *Disturbing the Universe: Power and Repression in Adolescent Literature.* Iowa City: U of Iowa P, 2000.

Vallone, Lynne. *Disciplines of Virtue: Girls' Culture in the Eighteenth and Nineteenth Centuries.* New Haven: Yale UP, 1995.

Wannamaker, Annette, ed. *Mediated Boyhoods: Boys, Teens, and Young Men in Popular Media and Culture.* New York: Lang, 2011.

White, Barbara A. *Growing up Female: Adolescent Girlhood in American Fiction.* Westport, CT: Greenwood, 1985.

Witham, W. Tasker. *The Adolescent in the American Novel, 1920–1960.* New York: Ungar, 1964.

Academic Journals with Articles Relevant to Coming of Age

Children's Literature
Children's Literature Association Quarterly
English Journal
Journal of Adolescent and Adult Literacy
Journal of the History of Childhood and Youth
Lion and the Unicorn

CRITICAL
INSIGHTS

About the Editor

Kent Baxter is associate professor of English at California State University Northridge, where he teaches twentieth-century American literature and culture, children's and young adult literature, and age studies. He received his PhD from the University of Southern California in 1998. His book *The Modern Age: Turn-of-the-Century American Culture and the Invention of Adolescence* (U of Alabama P, 2008) examines both theoretical and fictional discourses that focus on the developmental stage of adolescence, arguing that the common construction of the impulsive, conflicted, and rebellious adolescent found its origin and most vigorous articulation in the United States in the early decades of the twentieth century and that it was inspired by broader cultural anxieties that characterized American society at that time. He is also the author of a number of scholarly articles on literature about adolescence and the construction of adolescence in Western society. His recent research has focused on how and why eighteen has become the age when individuals are accepted by US society as "official" adults.

Contributors_____

Kent Baxter is associate professor of English at California State University, Northridge, where he teaches twentieth-century American literature and culture, children's and young adult literature, and age studies. He is the author of *The Modern Age: Turn-of-the-Century American Culture and the Invention of Adolescence* (2008) and a number of articles discussing adolescence and its construction in Western society. His recent research has focused on how and why eighteen has become the age when individuals become "official" adults in US society.

Vincent J. Cheng is Shirley Sutton Thomas Professor of English at the University of Utah. He is the author of several books including *Inauthentic: The Anxiety over Culture and Identity* (2004); *Joyce, Race, and Empire* (1995); and *"Le Cid": A Translation in Rhymed Couplets* (1987). The recipient of numerous scholarly awards and fellowships, Cheng has recently worked on a study of amnesia and forgetting in modern literature.

Gregory Eiselein is professor of English and Coffman University Distinguished Teaching Scholar at Kansas State University. The author of *Literature and Humanitarian Reform in the Civil War Era* (1996) and numerous articles on American literature and culture, he is also the editor of the Norton Critical Edition of *Little Women* (2003); *Emma Lazarus: Selected Poems and Other Writings* (2002); and *Adah Isaacs Menken:* Infelicia *and Other Writings* (2002). His recent research has focused on authors such as Louisa May Alcott and William James, as well as the intersections among nineteenth-century literary texts, cultures, and emotions in the United States.

Tomo Hattori is assistant professor of Asian American and Pacific Islander literary and cultural studies at California State University, Northridge. His teaching specializations include Asian American literature and culture, American literature and culture, and critical theory. His work has appeared in anthologies such as *Representations: Doing Asian American Rhetoric* (2008), and journals including *differences: A Journal of Feminist Cultural Studies* and *NOVEL: A Forum on Fiction*. His recent research interests have included Asian American children's literature and adolescent culture.

Jane Hedley is K. Laurence Stapleton Professor of English at Bryn Mawr College, where she teaches Renaissance literature and poetry from all historical periods. She has published *Power in Verse* (1988), a study of English lyric poetry from Thomas Wyatt to John Donne; *In the Frame: Women's Ekphrastic Poetry from Marianne Moore to Susan Wheeler* (2009); and *"I Made You to Find Me": The Coming of Age of the Woman Poet and the Politics of Poetic Address* (2009).

Heather James is associate professor of English and comparative literature at the University of Southern California. She is the editor of the *Norton Anthology of World Literature* and author of *Shakespeare's Troy: Drama, Politics, and the Translation of Empire* (1997), as well as many articles on aspects of classical transmission and early modern poetry and drama.

Amelia Katanski is associate professor of English at Kalamazoo College, where she teaches American Indian, world indigenous, and multi-ethnic American literatures. She is the author of *Learning to Write "Indian": The Boarding School Experience and American Indian Literature* (2005); "Writing the Living Law: American Indian Literature as Legal Narrative" (2008); and several articles on contemporary American Indian authors. Her recent research has explored the complex relationships between American Indian nations' creative and literary productions and US and tribal customary law, as well as the relationship among food sovereignty, tribal sovereignty, and storytelling in Great Lakes American Indian communities.

Michelle Martin holds the Augusta Baker Endowed Chair in Childhood Literacy at the University of South Carolina. Her publications include *Brown Gold: Milestones of African-American Children's Picture Books, 1845–2002* and *Sexual Pedagogies: Sex Education in Britain, Australia, and America, 1879–2000*, which she coedited with Claudia Nelson. She has published articles in the periodicals *The Lion and the Unicorn, Children's Literature Association Quarterly, Sankofa: A Journal of African Children's and Young Adult Literature*, and *Obsidian III*. Her recent work has centered on a book-length critical examination of Arna Bontemps's and Langston Hughes's writings for young people from the 1920s to the 1960s.

Richard Matlak is the director of the Center for Interdisciplinary and Special Studies and professor of English at the College of the Holy Cross. He has published numerous articles and authored two psychobiographical studies: *The Poetry of Relationship: The Wordsworths and Coleridge, 1797–1800* (1997) and *Deep Distresses: William Wordsworth—John Wordsworth—Sir George Beaumont, 1800–1809* (2003). He has edited *Approaches to Teaching Coleridge's Poetry and Prose* (1991) and coedited the anthology *British Literature: 1780–1830* (1996). He is presently working on a screenplay and a two-volume edition of Wordsworth's poetry.

Steven Mintz is a leading authority on the history of children and the family and has authored or edited thirteen books, including *Huck's Raft: A History of American Childhood* (2004) and *Domestic Revolutions: A Social History of American Family Life* (1989). The director of the Teaching Center at Columbia University's Graduate School of Arts & Sciences and a professor of history, he is also the president of the Society for the History of Children and Youth, past president of H-Net: Humanities and Social Sciences Online, and past chair of the Council on Contemporary Families.

Anne K. Phillips is associate professor and associate department head in the English department at Kansas State University. She specializes in nineteenth- and twentieth-century American children's literature. Her teaching focuses on the family sagas of Laura Ingalls Wilder and Mildred Taylor, illustration in children's and adolescent literature, and film adaptations of children's and adolescent literature. With Gregory Eiselein, she has coedited *The Louisa May Alcott Encyclopedia* (2001) and the Norton Critical Edition of *Little Women* (2004). She also coedited an Alcott-themed issue of the periodical *Children's Literature*.

Phillip Serrato is associate professor of English and comparative literature at San Diego State University and a faculty member of the National Center for the Study of Children's Literature. His academic interests include race, gender, and sexuality in children's and adolescent literature, particularly in Chicano and Chicana children's and adolescent literature. His publications discuss Francisco Jiménez's *The Circuit*, Robert Rodriguez's *Spy Kids* films, and the children's television program *Dragon Tales*. His recent work has focused on masculinity in Chicano and Chicana literature, film, and performance, as well as the emergence and development of Chicano and Chicana children's literature.

William G. Thalmann is professor of classics and comparative literature at the University of Southern California and has also taught at Yale and at Hobart and William Smith Colleges. His publications include *Conventions of Form and Thought in Early Greek Epic Poetry* (1984), *The* Odyssey*: An Epic of Return* (1992), and *The Swineherd and the Bow: Representations of Class in the* Odyssey (1998), as well as articles on Greek epic poetry, ancient conceptions of conflict, and Greek and Roman drama.

Roberta Seelinger Trites is a professor of English at Illinois State University. Her books include *Waking Sleeping Beauty: Feminist Voices in Children's Novels* (1997); *Disturbing the Universe: Power and Repression in Adolescent Literature* (2000); and *Twain, Alcott, and the Birth of the American Reform Novel* (2007). She has served as president of the Children's Literature Association and editor of the *Children's Literature Association Quarterly*. Her essays have appeared in various book collections and periodicals such as *Children's Literature*, *African American Review*, and *Canadian Children's Literature*.

Annette Wannamaker teaches children's and adolescent literature at Eastern Michigan University, where she serves as coordinator of the undergraduate and graduate programs in children's literature. She is the author of *Boys in Children's Literature and Popular Culture: Masculinity, Abjection, and the Fictional Child* (2008) and the editor of *Mediated Boyhoods: Boys, Teens, and Young Men in Popular Culture and Media* (2011). Her recent work has included a discussion of Tarzan in popular culture.

Rachelle D. Washington is assistant professor of language and literacy education at Clemson University. Her academic focus is on sociocultural aspects of children's literature, immigrant constructions in children's literature, and using children's literature to teach social justice.

Beth Wightman is associate professor of English at California State University, Northridge. Her research and teaching interests include twentieth-century British literature, Irish literature, and postcolonial literatures.

Index